Bilingual Children's Language and Literacy Development

Child Language and Child Development: Multilingual-Multicultural Perspectives

Children are brought up in diverse yet specific cultural environments; they are engaged from birth in socially meaningful and appropriate activities; their development is affected by an array of social forces. This book series is a response to the need for a comprehensive and interdisciplinary documentation of up-to-date research on child language and child development from a multilingual and multicultural perspective. Publications from the series will cover language development of bilingual and multilingual children, acquisition of languages other than English, cultural variations in child rearing practices, cognitive development of children in multicultural environments, speech and language disorders in bilingual children and children speaking languages other than English, and education and healthcare for children speaking non-standard or non-native varieties of English. The series will be of particular interests to linguists, psychologists, speech and language therapists, and teachers, as well as to other practitioners and professionals working with children of multilingual and multicultural backgrounds.

Other Books in the Series

Culture-Specific Language Styles: The Development of Oral Narrative and Literacy
Masahiko Minami
Language and Literacy in Bilingual Children
D. Kimbrough Oller and Rebecca E. Eilers (eds)
Phonological Development in Specific Contexts: Studies of Chinese- Speaking Children
Zhu Hua

Other Books of Interest

The Care and Education of a Deaf Child: A Book for Parents
Pamela Knight and Ruth Swanwick
The Care and Education of Young Bilinguals: An Introduction to Professionals
Colin Baker
Child-Rearing in Ethnic Minorities
J.S. Dosanjh and Paul A.S. Ghuman
Cross-linguistic Influence in Third Language Acquisition
J. Cenoz, B. Hufeisen and U. Jessner (eds)
Dyslexia: A Parents' and Teachers' Guide
Trevor Payne and Elizabeth Turner
Foundations of Bilingual Education and Bilingualism
Colin Baker
Encyclopedia of Bilingualism and Bilingual Education
Colin Baker and Sylvia Prys Jones

Please contact us for the latest book information:
Multilingual Matters , Frankfurt Lodge, Clevedon Hall,
Victoria Road, Clevedon, BS21 7HH, England
http://www.multilingual-matters.com

CHILD LANGUAGE AND CHILD DEVELOPMENT 4
Series Editor: Li Wei, University of Newcastle

Bilingual Children's Language and Literacy Development

Edited by
Roger Barnard and Ted Glynn

MULTILINGUAL MATTERS LTD
Clevedon • Buffalo • Toronto • Sydney

Library of Congress Cataloging in Publication Data
Bilingual Children's Language and Literacy Development: New Zealand Case Studies
Edited by Roger Barnard and Ted Glynn. 1st edn.
1. Bilingualism in children–New Zealand.2. Education, Primary–New Zealand.
3. Language and education–New Zealand. I. Barnard, Roger. II. Glynn, T. (Ted)
P115.2.B553 2003
306.44'6'0830993–dc22 2003017734

British Library Cataloguing in Publication Data
A catalogue entry for this book is available from the British Library.

ISBN 1-85359- 712-0 (hbk)
ISBN 1-85359- 711-2 (pbk)

Multilingual Matters Ltd
UK: Frankfurt Lodge, Clevedon Hall, Victoria Road, Clevedon BS21 7HH.
USA: UTP, 2250 Military Road, Tonawanda, NY 14150, USA.
Canada: UTP, 5201 Dufferin Street, North York, Ontario M3H 5T8, Canada.
Australia: Footprint Books, PO Box 418, Church Point, NSW 2103, Australia.

Typeset by Wordworks Ltd.
Printed and bound in Great Britain by the Cromwell Press Ltd.

Contents

Notes on the Contributors

Saili Aukuso is a teacher in the *O le Taiala* bilingual unit at Finlayson Park School in South Auckland. She grew up fluent in Samoan literacy and trained as a primary teacher in Samoa, where she taught for six years before moving to New Zealand. She retrained at Christchurch College of Education, and went on to gain a B.Ed at Auckland College of Education and a Postgraduate Diploma in TESL (Teaching English as a Second language) at Victoria University of Wellington. From 1994 to 1997 she worked with the Principal to establish and teach Wellington's first Samoan bilingual unit at Strathmore Park School. In 1998 she moved to Finlayson Park School to teach in *O le Taiala.*

Gary Barkhuizen is a Senior Lecturer in the Department of Applied Language Studies and Linguistics at the University of Auckland, where he teaches courses in language teaching and sociolinguistics. His research interests lie at the interface of language education and social context. He is particularly interested in listening to people's language stories. Before moving to New Zealand he was involved in teacher education at Rhodes University in South Africa, and before that he taught high school ESL for a number of years. He completed his doctorate at Columbia University in New York.

Roger Barnard is Chairman of the Department of General and Applied Linguistics at the University of Waikato, where he teaches postgraduate programmes in Second Language Teaching and Applied Linguistics. Before settling in New Zealand in 1995, he worked in a wide range of second language education projects in Europe and the Middle East, focusing mainly on children's language acquisition, the professional development of language teachers, and curriculum design, implementation and evaluation. His current research interests lie in immigrant and international students in primary and secondary schools and in tertiary institutions, viewed from a sociocultural perspective.

Mere Berryman is of Māori descent and is affiliated to Ngāi Tūhoe, a tribe from the Bay of Plenty, New Zealand. She had many years of primary teaching experience, in both English and bilingual settings, before beginning work in the field of special education, bilingual education and educational research. Mere manages the Ministry of Education's *Poutama Pounamu* Education Research and Development Centre, which seeks to improve the quality of education for Māori students who have learning and behavioural needs. The research group endeavours to work collaboratively in ways that are appropriate to Māori aspirations and are respectful of the diverse ethnic and cultural composition of New Zealand.

Yael Biederman is a teacher at a school for the deaf, and she recently completed a PhD in Education at the University of California at Berkeley. For her Masters degree, Yael investigated the use of Reading Recovery with deaf students. She is a collaborator on the Berkeley Sign Language Acquisition Project and is a co-developer of the Berkeley Transcription System, an internationally-used morphological-level system for transcribing sign language. In 2001, Yael was awarded a Fulbright Fellowship to New Zealand in order to collect data for her doctoral thesis: an ethnography of a bilingual–bicultural classroom that examines deaf students' English literacy development in a signing environment.

Lesley Elia is Associate Principal at Finlayson Park School. She is responsible for the overall supervision and support to the bilingual programmes, and has many other duties related to literacy and curriculum across the school. Lesley has spent most of her career in multicultural schools, the last 16 years at Finlayson Park. She has played a major role in establishing Samoan bilingual education and in ensuring that the philosophy and policies of *O le Taiala* are reflected in the everyday pedagogy of the school.

Ted Glynn is Foundation Professor of Teacher Education at the University of Waikato and a Fellow of the Royal Society of New Zealand. He has a wide background in applied behaviour analysis, inclusive education, and bicultural and bilingual education. He helped to pioneer the *Pause Prompt Praise* reading tutoring procedures, and the Māori language version, *Tatari Tautoko Tauawhi.* He is a member of the New Zealand Universities Consortium that produced *Resource Teachers: Learning and Behaviour* (RTLB) – part of the New Zealand Government's Special Education 2000 policy initiative. Like Mere, Ted is a member of the *Poutama Pounamu* Education Research Centre.

Penny Haworth is a senior lecturer in the Department of Arts and Language Education at Massey University's College of Education, where she teaches courses in ESOL (English as a second or other language) and intercultural teaching at undergraduate and postgraduate level. Penny first taught in primary schools, and has also taught ESOL in a variety of contexts. Her special interests include English for specific and for academic purposes. Penny is familiar with both case study and collaborative action research methodologies. In 1997, her Masters thesis won the New Zealand Association in Research in Education's Rae Munro Award. She is currently pursuing her doctoral study, investigating classrooms with small numbers of NESB (non-English-speaking background) students.

Nora Ioapo is Senior Teacher at *O le Taiala* at Finlayson Park School. She trained as a teacher in Samoa, and taught there for seven years before moving to New Zealand in 1970. She retrained for New Zealand registration at Auckland College of Education. In 1994, Nora took up her first teaching position in New Zealand at Finlayson Park School. She has been a strong force in the development of the bilingual unit, and in the development of the *Ulimasao* teacher support network.

John McCaffery is a senior lecturer at the Auckland College of Education, where he works in the Centre for Language and Languages. He is closely involved in Pacific Islands Education, The National Diploma of TESOL and *Te Uepu Māori*. He has a long-term involvement with all aspects of language, literacy and cultural diversity both at the research and the community level, with a special interest in bilingual education in early childhood and primary education. John has served as the Chairman of the New Zealand Education Institute's Māori Education Committee, as a member of the Māori Language Syllabus Committee, as a biliteracy consultant in Samoa and Kiribati, and as a peer reviewer on language and literacy policy and practices in the Cook Islands and Tonga. He has assisted schools and community partnerships to develop bilingual and immersion education programmes for Māori, Pacific, European and Asian languages.

Rachel Locker McKee is Senior Lecturer in Deaf Studies in the School of Linguistics and Applied Language Studies at Victoria University of Wellington. Her professional experience as a sign language interpreter led to her involvement in the establishment of training courses for interpreters and for grassroots deaf people as teachers of New Zealand Sign Language (NZSL). Her research interests have included the culture of the deaf community, linguistic analysis of NZSL, and interpreting. Language and cultural identity issues that characterise members of the deaf community and their childhood experiences prompted her recently to study deaf children's access to learning in mainstream classrooms from a sociocultural perspective. Rachel recently published *People of the Eye: Stories from the Deaf World*, an anthology of deaf people's oral histories translated from NZSL.

Shirley Maihi, QSM, has been a school principal for 19 years, 15 of these at Finlayson Park School in Manukau City. She has created a coherent vision of culturally appropriate education, giving rise to Finlayson Park's reputation as a national leader in bilingual and multicultural schooling. She believes that a bilingual programme is best achieved by recruiting and training high quality staff, and by establishing active and empowering partnerships with parents and the wider community.

Roger Peddie is Honorary Research Fellow (and former Associate Professor) in Cultural and Policy Studies in Education at the University of Auckland. He began his career as a secondary school teacher of English, French and Latin, before moving to the Secondary Teachers' College where he trained language teachers. At the University of Auckland, for his PhD, he investigated foreign language learning through error analysis. Between 1987 and 1999 he conducted a longitudinal comparative study of languages policy development and implementation in New Zealand and in Victoria, Australia. Roger has published widely on language policy issues and, more recently, on assessment. He has been principal evaluator for a number of Ministry of Education programmes and projects, including the Second Languages Learning Project, and Assessment for Better Learning – both of which were focused mainly on primary schools.

Nikhat Shameem leads the Language Teacher Education Programme at the UNITEC Institute of Technology in Auckland. Her PhD thesis was in language maintenance and language shift amongst teenage immigrants, with a focus on assessment of reported language ability. Nikhat has worked in Fiji, in New Zealand and in Western Samoa, and her current research interests focus on the educational implications of multilingualism.

Donna Starks is a senior lecturer in the Department of Applied Language Studies and Linguistics at the University of Auckland. Her research interests focus on the maintenance of minority languages. Current projects include collaborating in editing a volume on the *Languages of New Zealand* and a large-scale research project that assesses the status and role of the Pasifika languages of Manukau City in South Auckland.

Patisepa (Pati) Tuafuti was born and educated in Western Samoa before she migrated to New Zealand in 1976. She graduated from Auckland College of Education in 1979 with a New Zealand teaching diploma and from 1980 to 1993 taught mainly in primary schools in South Auckland. Pati holds a postgraduate Dip. TESSOL and a Dip. Special Education from Auckland College of Education (ACE). Pati gained her Higher and Advanced Diploma of Teaching, and later an MA (Applied Linguistics) from the University of Waikato in 1997. She has since worked as a Pacific Island Education advisor, as a Samoan facilitator for a Ministry of Education project, and as director of a Samoan language contract in Auckland. Pati is a senior lecturer at the Auckland College of Education where she is the Co-ordinator of the Graduate Diploma of Pasifika bilingual education. She also teaches in the Pacific Islands Early Childhood Diploma of Teaching.

Elaine Vine is a senior lecturer in the School of Linguistics and Applied Language Studies at Victoria University of Wellington. Her background is in primary school mainstream and ESOL teaching, and her research interests are in classroom discourse and language across the curriculum. She currently teaches discourse analysis, sociocultural theories of language teaching and learning, and ESOL teacher education.

Introduction

ROGER BARNARD

The connection between children's language and their cognitive and cultural development is so close as to be indivisible. In an educational context, Agar (1994) has coined the word 'languaculture' to indicate that language and learning cannot be considered separately. From a socio-cultural perspective, which is the one that is drawn upon by most of the contributors to this volume, language is the cultural tool by which common knowledge is sought and mutual understanding is reached.

> Language is designed for doing something much more interesting than transmitting information accurately from one brain to another: it allows the mental resources of individuals to combine in a collective, communicative intelligence which enables people to make better sense of the world and to devise practical ways of dealing with it. (Mercer, 2000: 6)

Sociocultural theory is based on Vygotsky's (1978: 57) view that, while innate biological factors play an important part in human development, any learning of cognitive and cultural concepts is primarily stimulated by, and realised through, the *interactive* use of cultural tools, chief among which is language. There is, in this view, an inextricable causal relationship between cognitive and cultural development and interpersonal language.

This book presents and discusses recent case study research that has been conducted in a number of primary school contexts in New Zealand, with a view to sharing our experiences with teachers, researchers and all others interested in cross-linguistic and cross-cultural education.

Teachers in primary schools build upon the social and cognitive foundations laid by parents and other caregivers to initiate their students into the formal discourses of learning. Equally – perhaps more – importantly, teachers guide children to make sense of the cultural and behavioural norms expected by the wider society. In New Zealand, as in many places elsewhere, primary school children are encouraged to begin to make their own choices about what and how they learn, and the standards of achievement to which they themselves aspire. At the same time, they are expected to collaborate with, and respect, all the other members of the learning community. Teaching is often conducted through informal dialogue between teacher and students; in this way, the teacher may create collective zones of proximal development (Vygotsky, 1978) in which the children are guided to move from their existing level of development towards their potential level. Rather than receiving direct instruction, their learning is scaffolded (Bruner, 1983) by the teacher; thereafter, they are often expected to work fairly independently on individual or group projects, and they are commonly asked to assess their own work, and sometimes that of their peers. Periodically, they are asked to complete criteria-referenced self-evaluations of the progress they have made over a term, and formulate and discuss objectives for future achievement – in terms of appropriate classroom behaviour, task performance and academic development. These common classroom practices for the co-construction of knowledge are based upon values and beliefs about learner-centred education and autonomy, often implicit, which derive from the culture into which the teachers themselves have long been socialised.

Difficulties arise when those values and beliefs are not shared, or even understood, by students and parents whose cultural and linguistic background may differ markedly from those held by the school and its teachers. The difficulties are compounded when teachers themselves are not aware of the possible disparity between their beliefs and those held by the families of their students. There is a need, therefore, for a close dialogue among all members of a multicultural school community to ensure that common understanding is achieved and that all parties collaborate in the educational venture. A broader zone of proximal development – within which common understanding can be co-constructed – should then extend beyond the classroom to embrace the wider school community. In this way, not only are the students themselves empowered, but also their families and (through the educational process being made more effective) the schools and teachers too. In the case studies presented in this book, it may be observed that, where such mutual understanding is co-constructed, the educational benefits are manifold; conversely, where it is lacking, the cultural, linguistic and cognitive development of the children concerned may well be severely hindered.

New Zealand has – rather more recently than the USA, Britain, Australia and Canada – awoken to the complex linguistic and cultural diversity in its midst. As Roger Peddie points out in Chapter 1, the country is far from being the monolinguistic community that many people (even some New Zealanders) may imagine. Peddie thus sets the broad linguistic and cultural context for all the case studies that follow. He presents and discusses statistics that show national and educational demographic trends, and introduces some of the key current issues concerning languages in New Zealand. He goes on to explain the background to the need for, but absence of, a national languages policy, and then considers the (limited) extent of second language learning in New Zealand schools, and outlines a recent project to introduce second language learning in primary schools. He presents the findings of an evaluation of this project, and suggests a number of key elements that should be included in a future national strategy of language teaching in primary education.

The next two chapters present case studies that focus on aspects of the education of Māori children. In Chapter 2, Ted Glynn and Mere Berryman examine the operation of a literacy partnership with parents and extended family of 7–9 year old learners in a school that operated in both English and *te reo Māori* (the indigenous language of New Zealand). They do so by means of a collaborative narrative in which a home–school liaison worker reflects on how she succeeded in involving the parents in the partnership project. As a result, reading and writing outcomes for their children (whether they were in Māori- or English-medium classes) were improved over and above outcomes for students participating in the regular school programme. Glynn and Berryman conclude that this project was conducted in ways that represent the cultural preferences, practices and aspirations of Māori people. Collaborative storytelling ensured that the research methodology and the way in which the research group worked was understandable within a Māori world-view, while maintaining the integrity of the people, their knowledge and their culture.

In Chapter 3, Berryman and Glynn look at another aspect of the home–school literacy partnership – the tutoring interaction between two mother–son pairs from one of the schools involved. The sociocultural metaphor that underlies their investigation is the Māori term *ako* – the unified cooperation and reciprocal relationship of learner and teacher in a single enterprise. This is related to the firm assumption in Māori culture that the older person has the clear obligation to help the younger person or child, but that both partners come to a learning task with existing skills and knowledge. In the case study that they report, the authors provide evidence to show that the parents were able to provide effective tutoring in reading skills, despite the fact that they were less proficient in te reo Māori than were their children . The scheme also provided both parents and children with the confidence to learn Māori and to use the language in settings outside the home and school. Berryman and Glynn also point to the important social and cultural learning that was taking place through partnership – not only that between parent and child, but also partnership among the home–school tutors and the home–school liaison worker described in the previous chapter.

In Chapter 4, John McCaffery, Pati Tuafuti and their associates develop some of the points introduced by Roger Peddie regarding the context of Pasifika languages in New Zealand. They point to the need for empowerment models to be applied, not only to bilingual education programmes in schools, but also among those who carry out research into such programmes. The authors then present a case study of a dual-medium, dual-literacy unit in a primary school in Auckland – the region with the largest population of Pacific Island people in the world. The Samoan/English programme, *O le Taiala* ('the world of the navigator'), has been in operation in the school long enough for an entire cohort to pass through its stages of design, implementation, development and evaluation. After reviewing quantitative and qualitative data that indicate the success of many aspects of the programme, the authors point to some of the issues that still need to be researched, and conclude with comments from some of the students of the bilingual programme.

Each of the next three chapters considers a different facet of the experience in English-medium mainstream classrooms of students from diverse language backgrounds.

In Chapter 5, Elaine Vine presents Fa'afetai, a five-year old Samoan boy, six weeks after his arrival in school. She begins by outlining the assumptions made about such children in the national curriculum documents, and points to the lack of relevant training opportunities for mainstream teachers in New Zealand's primary schools. To explore the actual learning opportunities available to Fa'afetai in his new mainstream classroom, more than nine hours of interactional data were collected over three days, by means of audio and video recording, live observation, and follow-up interviews. The resulting data were collaboratively transcribed and analysed by the researchers. The class teacher could not speak or understand Samoan and initially Fa'afetai could speak no English – he was the only non-English speaker in the room. Despite this apparent communication barrier, the study showed that the teacher nevertheless subtly and effectively scaffolded the boy's entry into the languaculture of the classroom, his participation in learning activities, and his valorisation as a member of the community of learning.

Penny Haworth in Chapter 6 studies several young students from diverse language backgrounds and their two teachers in a mainstream classroom. After surveying local and international research into the area, she comments that most of these studies have looked at either the children's interactions or the teachers' reactions, while her own case study seeks to look at both. She then describes and discusses the interplay of teachers and learners in classroom interaction zones, in directed teaching sessions, and in independent learning situations. This is followed by a discussion of the teachers' experience of, and perceptions about, teaching learners from diverse language backgrounds, and their (lack of) confidence in their ability to deal with them effectively. This ethnographic study provides sharp insights into the context of bilingual learners in mainstream classes, and – among other things – highlights the complex challenges classroom teachers constantly face in meeting the many needs of their learners.

In Chapter 7, Roger Barnard considers the case of an eleven-year old Korean boy, 'Jack'. Like Fa'afetai, Jack was a minimal user of English on entry to the school, just three days after his family immigrated to New Zealand – and he remained at this stage for the rest of the school year. The focus of analysis is Jack's use of private speech (Vygotsky, 1978), and Barnard reviews the theoretical assumptions behind this notion, and empirical studies carried out in this area, which identify the range of functions that private speech serves for learners in bilingual contexts. Barnard then illustrates and interprets transcripts of Jack's private speech over a period of several months. The extracts reveal Jack's intense efforts to come to terms with the languaculture of the classroom, and the tremendous frustration he at times felt. The chapter then discusses the implications for pedagogy and research that arise from this case study.

Chapter 8, by Rachel Locker McKee and Yael Biederman, discusses how educational contexts are constructed for deaf children whose first language is New Zealand Sign Language. As the authors point out, since most deaf children are raised in families who hear and speak, the children face the challenge of acquiring a primary language, forming relationships, and learning to understand the world in a communicative environment that is largely inaccessible. Two settings are examined to identify elements that might be truly learning contexts for deaf children. The first setting is a bilingual class at a Deaf Education Centre, and the second is a mainstream classroom in a school that (atypically) regards deaf children as bilingual. By presenting and discussing a number of classroom transcripts, the authors point to how zones of proximal development are created in the deaf classroom, but not in the mainstream setting, and discuss some implications of 'inclusive' policies in mainstream schools.

In Chapter 9, Nikhat Shameem considers the social and individual importance of maintaining community languages. She points to the difficulties faced by immigrant communities in maintaining their language and culture. The problems are especially acute in countries such as New

Zealand, where there is no national language policy that might provide official support for their endeavours. Shameem begins by reporting the nature of community language teaching in New Zealand and the challenges faced by minority language groups in this regard. She then explains how she sought to discover, by means of a survey, the perceptions of community leaders and teachers in Auckland as to the desirability and need for teacher education in community languages. She also solicited views as to what might be included in such a programme, and how best it might be delivered. Based on this survey data, Shameem has designed a programme specifically aimed at enhancing the competence of community language teachers.

Donna Starks and Gary Barkhuizen in Chapter 10 make the point that the absence of a languages policy has not prevented a great number of language planning activities from taking place in New Zealand. One such activity is the gathering of data in order to establish the range of languages spoken in schools, the needs of their students, and the awareness of language issues of all members of a school community. The authors report on their use of school students as data gatherers on a range of such language issues. Responding to a short self-report questionnaire, almost a thousand Auckland students reported their awareness of their own and other languages, their opinions about the use of languages and the language(s) they would like to speak, and their attitudes towards languages policy. Based on the valuable data that emerged, the authors firmly conclude that students deserve to be active participants, and not merely respondents, in the language planning process.

In the final chapter, 'Responding to language diversity: A way forward for New Zealand education', Ted Glynn draws together threads from the previous chapters that are of concern for future planning and development. Reviewing the main points of each of the chapters, Glynn points to the need for more effective school and community partnerships, for more inclusive pedagogies and bilingual competence, and for a more focused and integrated languages policy.

We hope that readers will be able to relate the stories we tell in this book to their own particular situations. New Zealand is a small nation, and geographically remote from others. Nevertheless, we believe that our experiences as teachers and researchers intimately involved in bilingual children's language and development are not dissimilar to those faced by many educators across the increasingly multilingual and multicultural world. We do not seek, as Neil Mercer has written, merely to transmit information from one to another (Mercer, 2000), but rather to provide a stimulus that will enable our readers to co-construct with us some sense of the (educational) world, and perhaps to consider and share practical ways of dealing with the challenges it poses.

References

Agar, M. (1994) *Language Shock: Understanding the Culture of Conversation*. New York: Quill, William Morrow.

Bruner, J.S. (1983) *Child's Talk: Learning to Use Language*. New York: Norton.

Mercer, N. (2000) *Words and Minds: How We Use Language to Think Together*. London and New York: Routledge.

Vygotsky, L.S. (1978) *Mind in Society: The Development of Higher Psychological Processes*. Cambridge, MA: Harvard University Press.

Chapter 1

Languages in New Zealand: Population, Politics and Policy

ROGER PEDDIE

Introduction

In the last months of 2002, a major public debate about immigration erupted in the media and in the Parliament of New Zealand. Sparked by minority party leader Winston Peters, the debate centred on the sharply-increased numbers of Asian migrants who had settled in New Zealand in recent years (see later in the chapter). While strong feelings were expressed, and various 'statistics' were presented, the issues revolve around two main areas. First, there are concerns about cultural differences in a country where a common rhetoric holds that 'real New Zealanders' are white/Anglo English-speaking peoples, with some acceptance that Māori also have some stake – provided they do not want too much of 'our' resources or (even worse) some form of independence from 'us'. Second, when migrants come here they should not only accept 'our' culture, but should very definitely speak 'our' language – English.

This chapter, while acknowledging that language is *never* fully separated from culture, examines the languages policy and practice of New Zealand, particularly as these apply to the primary school sector. After this introduction, there are five further sections. The first examines the current situation of languages, using figures from the 2001 census, and updates from Statistics New Zealand to document the languages 'profile' in New Zealand. It also introduces some of the key issues concerning languages, both nationally and internationally in the first decade of the twenty-first century.

The chapter then analyses some very important moves by community language and professional interest groups in the 1980s and 1990s, who worked hard, but unsuccessfully, to develop a national languages policy in New Zealand. It refers to the more successful development of a languages policy in Australia, and offers some reasons why a comprehensive national policy has not, to date, been developed in New Zealand.

The next section presents recent data on language learning in New Zealand schools and (much more briefly) other institutions in an attempt to establish the extent of such learning and to see if there is a 'logic' or rationale for it, given current social and national needs. There are brief comments on the range and selection of languages, particularly in respect of possible 'languages policy' issues raised in the previous section.

The recent and highly significant Second Language Learning Project (SLLP), implemented in 1995–98, is summarised in the section that follows, which is based on a comprehensive evaluation of the SLLP carried out in 1997–98 by a team headed by the author (Peddie *et al.*, 1998).

These sections together demonstrate the complexity of trying to reach straightforward decisions about language policy in what is a highly contested field, and the chapter ends by examining a possible way forward. It accepts that the continuing neo-liberal policy of decentralisation and minimal government spending (evident in several governments and coalitions since the mid-1980s) will mean that a comprehensive and well-funded *national* policy on languages is most unlikely to emerge. But it also argues that central government still needs to adopt a clearly articulated 'strategy' over at least the next five years to ensure that New Zealand's rich language resources are sustained, further developed, and recognised as a significant social, cultural and economic asset.

Language and Languages in New Zealand

New Zealand is increasingly a multi-ethnic and multilingual society, and its linguistic 'balance' has shifted quite sharply since the mid-1980s. In turn, this shift has led to some fierce political and community debates about who should be 'allowed' to migrate to New Zealand. This section gives a brief overview of the language scene in New Zealand, based primarily on data from the national census in 2001, but with additional information drawn from other sources (Statistics New Zealand, 2002a).

New Zealand is still thought of by many as quite a 'British' country. The truth is that New Zealanders come from an increasingly wide variety of backgrounds. In 2000 (though earlier numbers have fluctuated), New Zealand accepted comparatively many more migrants than Australia did (NZ Immigration Service, 2001a; DIMIA, 2001). Significant numbers of these people have come from Asian or other non-English-speaking backgrounds. They have added to the richness of the culture of a small nation that was already moving – some would argue, very slowly – towards an acceptance of its main bicultural heritage; between the *tangata whenua* (people of the land), the Māori, and the Anglo-European (often referred to

Table 1.1 Ethnic identification: 'Usually resident' population

Total Population (2001)	**3,737,280**	
Total Responses to Ethnicity	**7,705,494**	
'New Zealand European':	**2,696,724**	c72%
'British' (various categories)	106,470	
(Other) European groups	71,466	
New Zealand Māori	**526,281**	c14%
Pacific Island Peoples:	**c248,000**	c6.6%
Samoan	115,017	
Cook Island Māori	51,486	
Tongan	40,719	
Niuean	20,148	
Fijian (but not Fiji-Indian)	7,041	
Tokelauan	6,204	
Asian Peoples:	**c243,000**	c6.5%
Chinese (all)	105,467	
Indian (including Fiji-Indian)	62,643	
Korean	19,026	
Filipino	11,091	
Japanese	10,023	
South African:	14,913	

Source: New Zealand 2001 Census (Statistics New Zealand, 2002b)

as *Pakeha*[1]). The data in Table 1.1, drawn from the 2001 Census of New Zealand, give a summary indication of the major groupings in New Zealand in that year. It should be noted that *all* ethnicities were recorded, which is why the total number of responses is more than twice the total population.

Tables such as this one need very careful interpretation, particularly when making comparisons with earlier census data, as the census ethnicity question in 2001 was changed from the one used in 1996 (Statistics New Zealand, 2002b). While the figures above are in some cases (reportedly) very close to the 'true' numbers of individual residents, others are quite obscure. The 23,500 who said 'European' and the 16,500 who said 'British' are arguably likely to include a number of New Zealand-born Pakeha/European, and perhaps some South Africans still holding British passports; whereas the 35,000 who said 'English' are quite likely to have been born in England. The latter situation is likely also to be true for the more than 13,500 'Scottish' and the nearly 12,000 'Irish'. For those groups who do not commonly intermarry (e.g. the Chinese), or who are very new arrivals (e.g. the Koreans), the figures in the table are likely to be a fairly accurate indicator of the number of 'New Zealanders'.

Of the non-Anglo-Celtic European groups in New Zealand, the Dutch is the largest group, with the census showing some 27,500 Dutch. Others estimate that as many as 80,000–100,000 New Zealanders could be of Dutch descent (e.g. Schouten, 1992: 257). There are over 21,000 'Australians', but more than 50,000 people were *born* in Australia (Bedford, 2003). No other Anglo or European group numbers over 10,000 (although the Germans come close with over 9,000). This is partly because many New Zealanders migrating in the nineteenth century from, for example, Scandinavian countries, would no longer identify such countries as markers of their ethnicity. Mainly white South Africans have arrived in significant numbers in recent years and, with continuing migration, the total was perhaps closer to 20,000 by the end of 2002.

Migrant groups from Pacific Islands with close links to New Zealand arrived in large numbers in the 1960s and 70s. For some decades, there have been many more Tokelauans and Niueans living in New Zealand than in their home countries. Two-thirds of these Pacific Island peoples live in greater Auckland, helping to make this conurbation the largest Polynesian city in the world.

Table 1.1 shows that the Samoans are a very large group, and for some 20–30 years they have been the largest non-Anglo/Māori ethnic group. But, as can also be seen from the table, the total number of Asian New Zealanders was close to the Pasifika (Pacific Island peoples) total and, with continuing Asian migration, is likely to have surpassed it by late 2002. In particular, the number of ethnic Chinese was closing rapidly on the total originating from Samoa. Again, given recent migration figures, the total for ethnic Chinese will have almost certainly moved ahead of the Samoans within a year of the 2001 census.

Chinese migration is very interesting – and complex. There were Chinese in New Zealand in the nineteenth century, but numbers stayed moderately low, mainly because New Zealand (like Australia), introduced discriminatory laws that made Chinese migration very difficult (NZ Immigration Service, undated). In the 15 years following the 1986 census, however, the Chinese population grew by more than 500%. Migration of Chinese, often under business migrant schemes, especially the 'Investor Category' has continued and, as a percentage of new residents, post-census figures are still rising. In the year 2001–2002, for example, Chinese represented 64% of the Investor Category, up from 46% in the previous year (NZ Immigration Service, 2001b, 2002).

The earlier Chinese often spoke Cantonese/Yue or other southern languages, but more of the recent arrivals speak Modern Standard Chinese (Mandarin). 'Chinese' refers here to the ethnic group, and includes several thousand from Taiwan, Hong Kong and South-East Asia; but the vast majority of more recent migrants are from Peoples' Republic of China.

The ethnic Indian population has also risen sharply in recent years and in 2001 was about four and a half times its 1986 figure. Contrary to popular belief, this is *not* because large numbers of ethnic Indians migrated from Fiji following the military coups there. The 2001 census revealed fewer than 2000 Fiji-Indians out of a total of over 60,000. The recent arrivals have migrated mainly from India, but also from Malaysia, Singapore and other parts of Asia. Those from India represented the largest group (24%) of the 31,359 people approved for residence under the 'General Skills' Category in 2001–2002 (NZ Immigration Service, 2002: 1). These data suggest that the total ethnic Indian population may have exceeded 70,000 by the end of 2002, making Indians very decisively the fifth largest group in New Zealand.

The Indian peoples of New Zealand speak a wide variety of languages, including Gujarati, Punjabi, Bengali, Tamil and (increasingly) Hindi. There are also more than 7,000 Sri Lankans, but only just over a thousand from both Bangladesh and Pakistan.

Another smaller, but fast-expanding, Asian group, most of whom have arrived since the early 1990s, is the Koreans, with an estimated total population of at least 20,000, almost all of whom are living in Auckland. With the sharp economic downturn in Korea during 1998, and earlier changes in New Zealand migration rules, Korean migration slowed between 1997–99, but has since increased again. The number of Filipinos has begun to rise, while the Japanese are another small but fast-growing group. In complete contrast to the situation in Australia, there are fewer than 3,500 Vietnamese, a figure that is lower than comparable earlier census figures, reportedly owing to continuing cross-migration to Australia.

The debate about 'Asians' referred to earlier, however, seems to ignore two other very important points. First, the total numbers of Asian tourists and visitors has increased significantly in recent years, mainly owing to an increase in tourists from Korea and China. Indeed, visitors from Japan, China and Korea in the year up to September 2002 totalled almost 300,000 (Tourism Research Council, NZ, 2002). Second, the number of Asian and especially Chinese full fee-paying (FFP) international students in New Zealand has sky-rocketed since the late 1990s. In 2001–2002, just under 32,500 student visas were issued to Chinese (NZ Immigration Service, 2002: 85), while an unknown number were also taking English-language courses of less than three months on visitors' visas. The University of Auckland had more than 3000 FFP students in 2002, more than 50% of which were Chinese. Throughout Auckland and in other key target areas (such as Christchurch or Wellington), there are also numbers of Chinese students in private education providers. Added to these Chinese figures, the NZ Immigration Service reports that in 2001–2002 more than 12,000 student permits were issued to South Koreans, 4500 to Japanese, and more than 10,000 to other Asian groups (NZ Immigration Service, 2002).

A large number of these Asian students are based in Auckland. Thus, when 'your average Kiwi bloke' walks down Auckland's Queen Street (the main shopping street), it is highly likely that a significant number of the 'Asians' he sees are *not* migrants at all.

How are these migration and related data reflected in language statistics and languages policy? English is certainly the standard language of trade, social intercourse, commerce, government and education. Since 1987 *te reo Māori* (the Māori language) has been an Official Language, recognised in Parliament and the courts (see next section). In recent years, there has been a major revival of te reo Māori and Māori culture in New Zealand, with much greater attention being focused on the language and cultural rights inherent in the principles of *te Tiriti o Waitangi* (the Treaty of Waitangi), signed by a number of prominent Māori chiefs and the British Crown in 1840.

Just over 160,000 people recorded in the 2001 census that they spoke some te reo Māori. But a closer examination of non-Māori recorded as Māori-speaking suggests that most of these in fact listed 'Māori' as one of their ethnicities (Galbraith *et al.*, 2002). This confirms much earlier work by Benton, which showed that very few non-Māori were fluent in te reo Māori (Benton, 1979). But another very important way of interpreting the census

Table 1.2 Languages spoken in New Zealand in 2001

Te reo Māori	160,527	Hindi	22,749	Serbo-Croatian	5,946
English	3,425,301	Japanese	19,938	Russian	5,550
Samoan	81,033	Korean	15,873	Punjabi	5,541
French	49,722	Spanish	14,676	Min	5,526
Yue/Cantonese	37,140	Afrikaans	12,783	Niuean	5,478
German	33,981	Gujarati	11,145	Khmer	4,992
Dutch	26,280	Cook I. Māori	9,375	Malay	4,941
NZ Sign Lang.	27,285	Italian	7,215	Thai	4,620
Nthn Chinese	26,514	Arabic	7,959		
Tongan	23,046	Tagalog	7,827	None/unclear	257,355

Note: the terms used in the table are those of the 2001 Census. 'Northern Chinese' means Standard Chinese/Mandarin; 'Serbo-Croatian' was treated as a single language; while 'Punjabi' is the spelling used in census reports.
Source: (Statistics New Zealand, 2002a)

data is to note that fewer than a third of all who were recorded as Māori in 2001 claimed to be able to speak te reo Māori (see Tables 1.1 and 1.2).

Many recent arrivals continue to speak their own languages. Signs in hospitals and other public buildings are increasingly in several languages (often including te reo Māori, Samoan and, more recently, Chinese). Unlike Australia, however, New Zealand has no official languages policy giving direction or special assistance to the teaching, learning or maintenance of languages other than English. Some assistance with learning English is given to those with language backgrounds other than English but, despite a sizeable boost in recent government budgets, the per capita amount is still well behind that of Australia. The issue of languages policy in much more detail in the next section.

Table 1.2 gives the 2001 census figures for all languages recorded as spoken by more than 4,500 New Zealanders (or just over 0.1%). It should be noted that the census question asked about languages 'in which you can have a conversation about a lot of everyday things'. This is clearly not the same as asking about languages normally spoken on a daily basis, nor is it a measure of genuine fluency. Note that the total number of responses was only 4,429,347 (less than 1.2 times the total population. This suggests that a significant percentage of the population, almost certainly over 80%, is monolingual (and, based on earlier census data, monolingual in English).

This table also needs some interpreting. The numbers in (especially) French, German and Japanese will to a certain extent represent school and tertiary-language learners as well as native speakers, so the numbers of fluent/native speakers are likely to be markedly fewer than the figures in Table 1.2. Similarly, all numbers are 'as recorded' and give no guarantees of genuine proficiency in the language.

Third, the numbers in some cases appear to be lower than migration and other population data might suggest. In the case of Chinese languages, more than 80,000 ethnic Chinese have arrived in New Zealand since the 1986 Census. The total of 69,180 speakers of the three Sinitic languages listed in the table (Cantonese/Yue, Northern Chinese/Mandarin and Min), does not seem to reflect this. But a further 24,000 simply indicated 'Sinitic', without specifying further which language, while several smaller groups recorded that they speak other (specified) Sinitic languages.

Fourth, the table shows that some languages that could be valuable for New Zealand's economic growth (see Peddie, 1991), are modestly well represented (e.g. Japanese, Korean), and others are now starting to rise (e.g. Arabic, Russian, Spanish and Thai). Finally, the reasons for so many New Zealanders not answering the language question on the census remain unclear, although 'None' does of course include infants who are too young to talk (some 76,000).

More important for this book, such a table naturally gives no indication of possible shifts in language use for some of the key groups. Research conducted over a number of years, both locally and internationally, and particularly by Clyne and his associates in Australia (e.g. Clyne & Kipp, 1991), has shown that inter-generational shifts towards dominant English become significant, often as early as the second generation, and especially within certain recognisable language groupings (e.g. Germanic and Scandinavian languages). In other words, it cannot be assumed that, because we had some thousands of speakers of a language in 2001, the same numbers, even in 10 to 15 years, will continue to speak that language. Such changes will depend in part on migration patterns, future policies relating to languages and other sociological and geographical variables (e.g. settlement patterns, family reunion policies and targeted migrant schemes).

Languages 'Policy' in New Zealand

New Zealand is a curious case on the world scene. As noted earlier, the predominant language of social communication, business, law and daily life is English, but the only *legally* official language is te reo Māori (*Māori Language Act*, 1987). Furthermore, New Zealand does not have, nor has it ever had, a national policy on languages. This section offers a very brief historical overview of language use and language 'policies' in New Zealand, from the times of the first missionary schools in the early nineteenth century to the much more recent attempts to develop a national languages policy in the late 1980s and early 90s. Possible reasons behind those policy moves are explored, and some reasons are offered as to why there is still no national languages policy. The discussion is located within the contexts of globalisation of recent neo-liberal politics in New Zealand. It also includes a very brief commentary on moves towards the revitalisation of te reo Māori.

While there are ongoing debates about the specifics, it is clear that Māori arrived in what is now generally referred to as 'New Zealand' some 500–800 years before Europeans started to arrive. When European settlers began to arrive in some numbers, and the missionaries from England started to introduce schools in the early nineteenth century, they regularly taught through the medium of Māori language, but promoted Christian and European values. As other schools opened, the teaching was increasingly delivered in English. Māori were quite comfortable with the latter approach, and there were several petitions to Parliament in the 1870s requesting that formal (Pakeha) education be conducted *only* in English, even in the 'Native Schools' (Simon, 1998). As New Zealand society at that time was one in which all Māori were fluent first-language speakers of te reo Māori, this was not surprising.

But over 70–80 years the languages scene changed dramatically. The Land Wars, which began in the 1840s and lasted through to the 1870s, and the dramatic fall in the numbers of Māori by the end of the century significantly decreased European settlers' perceptions of the importance of te reo Māori (Simon, 1998). This language decline continued until a remarkable revival began in the second half of the 20th century.[2]

Meanwhile, as the new settlers established (particularly) secondary schools for Pakeha, the languages taught were all European. The few secondary schools existing late in the nineteenth century tended to offer such languages as Latin, Greek and French for boys, and Latin, French and sometimes German or Italian for girls (Murdoch, 1944; Peddie, 1984).

From the 1930s, the government acknowledged that some attention ought to be paid to Māori culture, but the place of te reo Māori remained unclear, and there was certainly no hint of a 'policy' relating to languages in New Zealand.

With the establishment of the original European Economic Community in 1957, and the acceptance 18 years later of the United Kingdom as a member, New Zealand began to realise that trade links had to be built with new markets. A natural region to consider was the Asia-Pacific. Yet, despite the fact that such trade virtually demanded expertise in a number of languages, New Zealand (and to a lesser extent Australia), was slow to grasp the need for a comprehensive national policy on languages or, at the very least, a forward-looking policy on languages in education. This situation was exacerbated by the fact that the numbers of students taking languages in secondary schools had dropped alarmingly since the late 1960s (Peddie, 1984).

The advent of a significant report on a languages policy for Australia (Senate Standing Committee on Education and the Arts, 1984), was followed by the development of Australia's first national policy in 1986, and its subsequent adoption in May, 1987 (Lo Bianco, 1987). This provided a strong impetus for a movement within New Zealand towards the same end.

A central figure here was a mid-level policy officer in the (then) Department of Education, Chris Hawley. Over a period of several years, he worked tirelessly to persuade the Department of the need for comprehensive policy development. His efforts paid off when he secured funding for an in-service week held at the (then) North Shore Teachers' College in 1989. A significant group of educators and languages representatives gathered together and planned a document that could be presented to government, along the lines of a similar submission made in Australia (PLANLangPol, 1983).

The outcome was the development of a very important document, *Towards a national policy on languages* (National Languages Policy Secretariat, 1989), which late in the same year was presented by a representative group to the (Labour) Minister of Education, Philip Goff. The Minister was positive, but requested a resubmitted document, showing how other Ministries might be affected. The revised document was presented in early 1990.

This too was well-received. The outcome was an announcement made on behalf of the Minister by the Associate Minister of Education, Noel Scott, at the first National Conference on ESOL and Community Languages Education, held in Wellington in August, 1990. Two key quotations encapsulate the significance of this announcement:

> Until now, issues associated with languages in New Zealand have been dealt with in an ad hoc way ... Without common goals and a co-ordinated framework around which policies can be developed and programmes implemented, it has been difficult for the government to respond comprehensively to language issues. (Goff, 1990: 7)
>
> I am pleased to announce formally today that the government has

agreed to develop and fund a national languages policy ... A budget of more than $100,000 will be provided this year to allow the Ministry of Education to contract an appropriately qualified person to formulate the policy. (Goff, 1990: 8)

This was followed by a most interesting turn of events. Late the same year, with nothing actually actioned, there was a change of government, and The National Party took office. A rapidly-organised deputation met with the new Minister of Education, Dr Lockwood Smith. To the surprise of many, the new Minister agreed to proceed with the development of a national policy, and guaranteed the funding that had been promised by Labour.

Dr Jeffrey Waite, a (Pakeha) member of the Māori Language Commission, was duly appointed. A suitable time frame was agreed, and Waite began the difficult task of ascertaining New Zealanders' views. It must be acknowledged that he did this with commendable diligence and energy. Major *hui* (meetings) were held in New Zealand's three largest urban areas (Auckland, Wellington and Christchurch) while a large number of visits and other meetings were held throughout the country. By late 1991, Waite had produced a first version of his policy proposals, based on the enormous amount of data he had collected. This document was never released.

Then (it appears) politics and possibly other unseen influences began to operate. While Waite did have an Advisory Group drawn from a number of Ministries, and one must assume that this group was broadly in favour of what he proposed, this first version was not accepted by government. Waite was instead asked to reformulate the document, a first and then a second time (the latter with the help of a professional writer). When the final version appeared, it was in the form of a 'Discussion Document' (Waite, 1992), and no formal recommendations – reportedly an important part of the original version – were included.

The document then was sent out for public submissions. A moderately small number were received, perhaps because so many people in the 'languages community' were quite satisfied with what they saw. The in-house analysis of submissions, obtained by the present author under the Official Information Act, showed that there were only 129 separate submissions, along with 94 duplicated submissions from a TESOL organisation, and 349 signatures on a petition arguing for a much more prominent place for Latin. Only three submissions came from Māori. The in-house analysis suggested that there was no real consensus among those who had sent in their ideas, although a careful reading of the analysis indicated that most were strongly in favour of the general thrust of the document.

Waite proposed that there were six interrelated key areas to consider (Waite, 1992: Part 1, 18–22):

(1) revitalisation of the Māori language;
(2) second-chance adult literacy;
(3) children's ESL and first language maintenance;
(4) adult ESL;
(5) national capabilities in international languages;
(6) provision of services in languages other than English.

What happened next remained largely a mystery until some years later. In March, 1993, the present writer wrote to the Minister to enquire what the situation was in relation to the development of a national languages policy. The reply from the Minister's Office (ironically dated 1 April) was that 'the national languages project remains on the work plan of the Ministry of Education'. But as this writer was soon to discover, and for which action Shackleford (1996) was later able to provide solid evidence, the Minister cancelled the national languages project only a month later, replacing it with three and then four much more specific projects.

The three original areas were: further assistance for English to Speakers of Other Languages (ESOL) programmes, the encouragement of language learning at a younger age, and the setting up of the Asia 2000 project (Shackleford, 1996). Shortly after, the fourth area, the fostering of te reo Māori, was shifted from *Te Puni Kokiri* (the Ministry of Māori Development) back to the Ministry of Education, suggesting that *all* language issues should be dealt with as challenges only for *education*.

Why was the development of a national languages policy abandoned? To give an adequate answer would require a chapter in itself. Suffice it to say that it seems to have been a combination of factors, including: hesitation over the place of te reo Māori in a national policy; the rapidly-changing demography of New Zealand, which made firm decisions over languages difficult; the relative lack of understanding by business of the advantage of international languages in trade; and economic uncertainties, including a neo-liberal policy of limiting government spending and localising decision making (Peddie, 1997; see also Benton, 1994; Peddie, 1996).

In the current political climate, irrespective of which party holds power, it is unlikely that New Zealand will see a reversal of the neo-liberal approach to policy. Within this approach, which ideologically supports weaker centralised direction, but stronger centralised monitoring and accountability, government still appears to be trying to foster more language studies in schools in general and the primary sector in particular (see later). But schools are likely to be unwilling or unable to take such encouragement seriously when no long-term policy and no universally available targeted funding (other than for te reo Māori) is in place.

Languages in Education

This section presents an introductory sketch of languages in New Zealand education, then gives an overview of current language learning. The latter includes:

- an overview of te reo Māori and Pasifika languages in education;
- a brief overview of languages in the secondary and tertiary sectors;
- the situation of languages teaching in the primary sector.

In all cases, figures presented are for 2001 unless otherwise signalled.[3]

Historically, European and classical languages (French, Latin, Greek) were offered in New Zealand secondary schools and university colleges, with an unchallenged assumption that languages should be taught in schools mainly to upper-stream academic students (Murdoch, 1944; Peddie, 1984). That picture started to change in the 1960s and 70s when approaches to language learning began to alter in both the secondary and tertiary sectors.

First, secondary schools began to abandon the traditional approach of offering set courses for 'academic' and 'other' students. More specifically, it was no longer the case that the 'brightest' secondary school students studied two second languages, 'average' students studied one, and 'low-stream' students did not study any other language (Peddie, 1984).

At about the same time, New Zealand universities gradually changed their degree requirements relating to second languages. Thus in the period 1960–80 (for example), universities throughout New Zealand removed the requirement that a student graduating with a BA must have a language other than English (or otherwise an extra 'reading knowledge' course), and the requirement that law graduates must have Latin. This arguably had a 'backwash' effect on (particularly) more academic secondary schools, who typically promoted languages, and who also provided a large proportion of the entrants to the universities.

Other factors have probably continued to influence the drop in the numbers of students studying the traditional European languages. For a number of years, for example, the pattern of ethnicity of school students has been changing. In 2001 only 63% of all school students were (NZ) European/Pakeha; 20.4% were Māori, 8% were Pasifika (almost half of whom were Samoan), and just under 6% were Asian.

In some New Zealand schools, and especially in Auckland, large numbers of languages (40–50) are spoken on a daily basis, but by only very small numbers of students. This clearly creates major problems for a school that wishes to cater for its ethnic/language minorities, but equally clearly cannot possibly offer teaching in all of the represented languages.

Nevertheless, New Zealand is one of only a handful of countries where a second language is not legally or in practice compulsory in the school sector. Such compulsion is not restricted to non-English-speaking countries, as Canada, England and Wales, and almost all States in Australia, have some form of requirement for learning a second language.

What is the current situation of languages in education in New Zealand? First, let us consider Māori-medium education and the learning of te reo Māori.

In 2001 there were 9594 enrolments in Māori language and culture pre-schools (*te kohanga reo*). This is the first time since 1992 that the total has dropped below 11,000 (the peak in recent years was 14,514 in 1993). This has to be considered a matter of serious concern. While the Māori population continues to expand, the significantly lower numbers of students in these Māori-immersion pre-schools means that fewer students could be seeking immersion or bilingual programmes in primary schools, and that a decreasing percentage of very young Māori are learning their language.

In 2001, 27,865 primary and secondary school students (3.8% of all students) were in Māori-medium education for more than three hours a week. About a fifth of these students (5016) were in the 59 *kura kaupapa Māori* (schools that deliver the national curriculum in Māori, and within a Māori cultural context). Again, the data give rise for concern. While the number of *kura kaupapa Māori* has steadily increased, the number of *students* remains very low, with an average of approximately 85 students in each school.

These data also mean that just over 3% of all 'regular' school students were in Māori-medium education for more than three hours a week: it needs to be stressed again that Māori students constitute just over *20%* of the total school population.

Over 20% of *all* school students were studying te reo Māori, but the vast majority studied the language for less than three hours a week. Note that 'less than three hours a week' could mean as little as one or two brief sessions. Also, in programmes other than Māori-medium education, significant numbers of those involved are not Māori.

Overall, the 2001 data from the Ministry of Education show that only 26.8% of Māori students were either in Māori-medium programmes, or studying te reo Māori for more than three hours a week. Put another way, nearly three-quarters of all Māori students were *not* studying their language to the extent where this study might be expected to lead to a reasonable level of competence. Preliminary figures for 2002 show a very similar pattern.

In secondary schools, the number of students learning te reo Māori (in any type of programme) in the years 1999 to 2002) has been between 20,000 and 22,000. This is down from around 25,500 in the mid-1990s. The confirmed 2001 figure represents fewer than 10% of the total 2001 secondary enrolment.

What of language education for Pasifika students? In 2001 just over 2500 early childhood students were in Pasifika language nests, which collectively teach in several of the Pasifika languages. But this figure is the lowest in ten years, and is well down from peaks (approaching 4000) in the mid-1990s.

More importantly, Pasifika language learning in both primary and secondary schools is very limited. Pasifika students comprise over 6% of all school students, and about half of them are of Samoan origin. In 2001, and in 20 schools, just over 1600 students were in Pacific-medium education, with almost three-quarters of these students learning at least some of the time in Samoan. However, this total represents only 2.8% of all Pasifika students. Furthermore, fewer than 5% of Pasifika students in schools were learning a Pasifika language. While the figures are a little better for Samoans, the numbers are still well under 10%, with fewer than 1000 students learning Samoan in secondary schools. Again, unpublished figures for 2002 show little change.

Before turning to other languages in the primary sector, it is useful to set a further context by looking at the broader secondary and tertiary languages scene.

In the secondary schools (Years 9–13) in 2001, just over 61,000 students studied a second language (other than te reo Māori). This represents just under a quarter (24.5%) of the secondary school population. Over the 10 years to 2001, the total numbers have fluctuated between approximately 60,000 and 66,000 (the unpublished figure for 2002 is just under 63,000)

But these figures are somewhat misleading. While around half of students in Year 9 (the first year of secondary education), typically study a second language, only 10–12% of Year 13 students are still taking at least one other language. Furthermore, many of the students in Year 9 do not receive a year-long course. As 45–55% of the students in all of the main languages *are* Year 9 students (note that the comparable figure for te reo Māori is also 49%), this means that only 10–15% of secondary school students are getting more than a *very* minimal exposure to second language learning.

For the past 20 years, the secondary school languages scene has been dominated by two languages, Japanese and French. While the balance has shifted from French to Japanese and now back to French (in 2001, 23,816 studied French and 19,981 studied Japanese), the two languages have quite typically accounted for 65–85% of all secondary language learners. This is an intriguing mix; the traditional foreign language of 'culture' and 'diplomacy', and the newer language of 'trade'. In fact, both of those characterisations are significantly open to question. French would seem to have no stronger claim than several other languages, while teaching Japanese to a very modest level in schools is hardly likely to improve trade (Peddie, 1991).

The numbers of students learning Spanish in secondary schools have risen steadily in recent years (to 4407 in 2001 and over 5,000 in 2002), while the numbers learning Chinese rose to 1767 in 2001, but dropped to fewer than 1500 in 2002. Together, moreover, these languages are studied by fewer than 2.5% of students, more than a third of whom are in Year 9. Other languages of actual or potential commercial importance such as Indonesian, Russian, Arabic and Korean are studied by few or no students in secondary schools. Similarly, neither of the Indian languages with significant numbers of speakers in the community (Hindi and Gujarati), is offered in schools.

A wide range of languages is taught in (especially) universities and polytechnics, but there are problems in ascertaining accurate numbers. It is difficult even to obtain reliable numbers of tertiary-level students learning English as a second language as up to late 2002 legislation did not require institutions offering English language courses of less than three months to be registered. In other institutions the problem is just as complex. While students enrolled in 'languages' can easily be accessed, it is less easy to establish the numbers of students who are taking language courses as opposed to literature and other cultural courses.

Finally in this section (and important for the current volume) what is the situation of languages in the primary sector? The primary years (Years 1–8) have recently shown a modest increase in numbers of students engaged in second language learning, but there are still significant areas of concern. Just below 13% of all primary school children in 2001 were learning a language other than te reo Māori or English, but more than four out of five of these children were in Years 7–8.

In Victoria, Australia, 'language learning' is counted for statistical purposes if the language is offered for 2.5 hours a week or more – equivalent to approximately 190 hours a year in New Zealand terms. But in New Zealand, more than 40% of the 'language learners' receive fewer than

15 hours a year – a negligible amount compared with what is required to give even a good foundation for later learning. Compared with the standard in Victoria, fewer than 3% of all New Zealand primary school students (13,640 out of a total enrolment of 484,058) were taught a second language for more than *30* hours a year – the only figure currently recorded.

The main languages (other than te reo Māori) taught in primary schools in 2001 were Japanese (22,446), French (15,185) and Spanish (11,925). These three languages accounted for almost 80% of primary level language learners. The 2002 figures show a rise for Spanish and French, but the overall picture is largely unchanged. The data show that there is no clear 'pattern' of language learning in the primary sector; rather, it is a serendipitous mix of 'traditional', community and international languages.

Just as importantly, evidence from the Second Language Learning Project (see below), shows that there are very few trained language teachers in primary schools, with the possible exception of schools that cater for both secondary and primary students. In such schools a secondary-trained language teacher may also be teaching in Years 7–8, or even at earlier levels.

The Second Language Learning Project

A reasonably clear answer to the question above is offered by the research findings summarised in this section, which describes the most significant government initiative affecting languages (other than te reo Māori) in the primary school sector since decisions relating to te reo Māori were taken in the nineteenth century. The main thrust of this initiative occurred between 1996 and 1998, although some more tightly prescribed funding was offered from 1999.

The Second Language Learning Project (SLLP) was a $4.8 million project of the Ministry of Education, announced in mid-1995. In brief, it aimed to extend the teaching of second languages in schools, especially in terms of earlier starting points. Thus, it was an important development of one of the four initiatives that followed the 1993 cancellation of national languages policy work in the Ministry (see page 19). It was officially aimed at Years 7–10, but in practice the chosen focus for most participants was Years 7 and 8, the last two years of the primary school sector.

In the major project discussed here, schools bid for funding to be provided from the beginning of 1996 to the middle of 1998. After the bids had been considered, the SLLP began operation in at first 28 and later (from 1997) 29 'clusters' of schools, with cluster sizes ranging from (in a few cases) individual schools up to one cluster of 15 schools.

The schools offered languages in various ways, including: secondary school language teachers working in primary (here, including intermediate) schools, various forms of distance technology; and the use of part-time tutors, including native speakers and (in one or two cases), teachers from the tertiary sector or from private language institutions. Each cluster had a 'lead' school and an overall SLLP co-ordinator. Clusters were required to evaluate their own programmes, and to report to the Ministry on a range of matters through regular 'Milestone Reports'.

In mid-1997, a team from the University of Auckland was contracted to conduct an independent evaluation of the SLLP, carried out over the following fourteen months. This evaluation involved analysis of a range of written materials, attendance at a series of Regional Cluster Meetings held in 1997, a schools questionnaire, and two series of visits to a selection of clusters and schools.

The cluster visits included interviews with key personnel, observation of some lessons and, in appropriate cases, completion of a questionnaire relating to education technology. In all, visits were made to 12 of the 29 clusters, including both urban and rural, North and South Islands, large and small clusters. With access to all Milestone Reports and in some cases to additional material made available by schools, the evaluators were confident that they were able to present a sound – while not absolutely complete – picture of the strengths and weaknesses of the SLLP (Peddie *et al.*, 1998).

The major findings of the evaluation are summarised in the five subsections that follow: teaching and teachers, education technology, programme issues, finance, and plans and prospects for the continuation of second languages teaching in the primary sector. A very large number of other significant issues are discussed in the full report, but in the paragraphs that follow it is possible to highlight only the most important of these findings.

Teaching and teachers

The evaluators observed a number of lessons in several languages, taught by a range of what they called 'tutors', to distinguish the language teachers from the regular classroom and other teachers associated with the project. As might be expected, some of these lessons were excellent, while some were quite unproductive in terms of language learning. Overall, the main concern of the evaluators was that a combination of a limited time for learning and a lack of understanding of good communicative teaching often led to lessons that were sometimes entertaining, often enjoyable, but not always effective.

The evaluation report then considered the professional development (PD) needs of the tutors. The evaluators found that in many of the clusters the budget for PD was underspent – and in one or two clusters it was not even touched. Yet the untrained tutors in particular were concerned that they had had few opportunities for PD. The report discusses a range of issues relating to PD, proposing that a substantial programme could have led to far more effective teaching for *all* of those involved in the SLLP. Such a programme could easily have involved some of the expert teachers in the project assisting others, but in practice this occurred in only two clusters.

Education technology

Several clusters were involved in teaching by audiographics, a system that combined computer links with a 'Polycom' (a device allowing shared voice links) and shared drawing and other facilities. Broadly speaking, excellent teachers produced excellent lessons using this technology, while tutors who were less able to realise the potential of the same technology produced lessons that were at best mediocre. The use of technology in other classrooms was mixed, and much less frequent than had been expected. There were some outstanding CD-ROM and other resources available, but not all schools were aware of this, and the tutors needed PD and on-going technical and educational support to get the most out of using such material.

The evaluation noted the potential for on-going forms of language teacher PD to be conducted via distance technology, and discussed the importance of developing further quality packages, such as the *Hai!* Japanese language video series (Ministry of Education, 2000) for New Zealand use. At the same time, it would not be cost effective to ignore well-tested programmes available overseas – especially those developed in Australia.

Programme issues

The various delivery models were reviewed, with the conclusion that none was perfect, but that – as expected – the greater the language teaching skills of the teacher delivering the lesson, the more effective the learning. This highlighted the risks involved when some clusters planned that their regular classroom teachers, after only a very brief exposure to the target language, should take over from what were sometimes much better qualified language tutors.

A very wide range of other issues was discussed under this heading. These included: language selection and continuation, the goals of school language programmes, a number of factors (such as timetabling) relating to programme organisation, selection of students and dropout policies, the need for resource sharing and resource development for the primary sector, the important need to carefully consider teacher supply and continuity, the various roles taken by the classroom teachers during SLLP lessons; the crowded nature of the Year 7 and 8 curriculum and subsequent issues for language teaching at this level, and issues relating to the articulation of programmes between the primaries and local secondary schools.

Of these, four issues are selected for brief comment here. First, a number of the schools in the SLLP were already offering languages prior to the project, but the SLLP gave them the opportunity to expand their programmes and to increase the learning time for their students. Second, the provision of language teachers is a long-term issue that both the Ministry and schools will (still) need to address if language programmes are to become a more regular feature of the primary sector. In particular, the Ministry will need to consider ways of attracting fluent second-language speakers into pre-service teacher education programmes (see below). Third, none of the schools visited in the SLLP had seriously considered the teaching of one or more subjects *in* a second language as a way of avoiding adding to the 'crowded curriculum'. Yet almost all of the SLLP schools very strongly supported the continuation of a languages programme. Finally, almost all of those interviewed in the schools were adamant that their limited-time language courses *were* valuable, even though expert local and overseas views on such 'taster' approaches tend to be uniformly negative.

Financial issues

The evaluation used the concept of cost per student year (C/SY) as a measure of comparability across clusters. Although it did not take into account variables such as the teaching time offered, the cluster budget for 1997, divided by the number of students receiving an SLLP programme in that year, gave a somewhat crude (but arguably defensible) basis for comparison. The C/SY varied from $70 to $1365, with a modal range of $125–325. Sources of variation tended to relate to one or more of four main variables: staffing costs (including hourly rates and the number of hours claimed); the number of students involved in the programme, as very small numbers often (but not always) meant a higher C/SY; the costs of certain education technology options; and the level of purchase of resources, especially computer resources.

The evaluation also found that a number of schools noted that they had supplemented the programme budget by giving extra time or resources above the Ministry-provided budget. These must be added to the 'real' project cost. Yet, despite this, several clusters were able to save substantial sums from the Ministry budget in order to allow them to continue teaching languages for at least the remaining six months of 1998, after their formal participation in the SLLP had ended.

The evaluation report looks at three ways of estimating the cost effectiveness of the SLLP. It concluded that, even though some definite improvements could have been made, the SLLP was nevertheless a generally cost-effective exercise, producing a number of planned and unplanned benefits and outcomes.

Prospects and plans

The views of participants in the SLLP, including staff, students, principals and parents, were overwhelmingly positive. A surprising 72% of responding schools believed that languages were an *essential* part of the primary school curriculum. Just over half of the 60 schools responding to a further question stated that they were planning to continue teaching languages after the SLLP concluded. Those who were not and/or were uncertain tended to signal finance as the major reason, although concerns about the availability of quality languages staff were another significant factor. Both of these issues are almost inevitable when there are no clear policies on teacher education, curriculum imperatives, or ongoing financial incentives to support what – at least in this initiative – many primary schools decided they definitely wanted.

The evaluation report ended with some proposals for the development of a broad policy strategy for languages in the primary school, backed by a programme of research that would aim to ensure that maximum benefits, both educational and financial, would be enabled by such a strategy. It also signalled several 'key issues' for Ministry consideration.

The extension of second language learning in New Zealand primary schools

This was strongly favoured by almost all the participant schools in the SLLP. Issues such as general sustainability, continuity of language and of teacher supply, and articulation with secondary schools, all suggested that a carefully designed and properly researched strategy is now needed to capitalise on the demonstrated desire for languages. This would need to take into account the 'crowded curriculum', and should consider carefully such options as compulsion (gradually introduced), and bilingual schooling (to avoid adding directly to the current curriculum).

The key to good language teaching is the teacher

The key to any good teaching is excellent – and extensive – pre-service *and* in-service professional development (PD). The SLLP demonstrated that new initiatives that do not place these truths at the heart of planning will inevitably achieve very mixed results. In the SLLP this was particularly telling in the case of the specially hired part-time tutors and native speakers, both groups of whom (with a few notable exceptions), were mainly untrained as language teachers. Despite their linguistic skills, their often extensive lesson preparation and their obvious enthusiasm, the technical skills of several of these tutors displayed a serious need for PD in language teaching and in classroom management. It was recommended that the potential of PD by distance in such cases should be explored urgently by the Ministry.

At the same time, the SLLP demonstrated quite clearly that spending an hour or two a week over two and a half years watching a qualified language teacher, and learning along with the students, was *very* unlikely to produce an adequately skilled new language teacher.

The potential of education technology

Education technology in the field of languages (as elsewhere in the curriculum) had, and continues to have, enormous potential to assist the learning of languages. Both by distance and in the classroom, education technology has a range of valuable uses, especially if high quality multimedia and other programmes are developed, or purchased from overseas. Equally high quality on-going educational and technical support also needs to be available. As found in the SLLP, even when expensive modern technology was provided, a bad lesson was still a bad lesson. With technology (including software and multimedia) developing so rapidly, effective pre-service teacher education and on-going in-service PD in this area remain absolutely essential.

The reassessment of curriculum goals

The evaluation of the SLLP highlighted the need to reassess language curriculum goals and programmes as more primary schools take up teaching in this area. Teachers in such schools need to be made aware of the key findings of a very considerable body of research and overseas experience in language learning. This research points to such things as: the need for adequate time overall for language learning, the need for regular (daily) sessions, even if these are brief, and the importance of understanding what is involved in communicative teaching methods. This curriculum reassessment should be linked into a wider review of the role of introductory 'taster' courses and where – if anywhere – these might best be located in the school system. Language teachers have long understood that such courses can be considered as preparation for serious language learning only when they are *immediately* followed by more substantial programmes.

Articulation issues

The report noted that articulation issues between and among the various sectors of schooling needed to be considered further. The SLLP evaluation highlighted the positive effects of inter-sector cooperation, while at the same time signalling some of the difficulties involved. The Year 7–10 sector was and is the most complex, with a number of different types of school servicing students in these years; so both curriculum and organisational issues need to be explored in a coherent and planned manner. The issues include such matters as selection of languages, choice of texts and other resources, the availability of advanced classes, and opportunities to take one or more new languages after the first years of language study.

Project guidance and planning

The gap between what the Ministry originally wanted and what schools were able to fund in their own SLLP programmes affected the outcomes directly. The evaluation showed that the extreme range of costs per student year (C/SY) came in part from contracts that were independently negotiated in ways that led directly to some of these variations. Schools clearly have different needs in programmes of this kind, and also need the freedom to explore best practice for their local conditions. As well, some schools needed a higher C/SY than others because of specific geographic or population factors. But the range of parameters in the areas of both costs and reporting requirements in the SLLP apparently led to difficulties for the evaluation team, especially in their efforts to make valid and reliable comparisons between programmes.

Teachers also complained of a lack of forward planning in terms of what would happen when the SLLP finished. What in fact *did* happen is that further money was provided in the years immediately following. Citing the evaluation findings, the Ministry explicitly ruled out bids that asked for teacher salaries. This resulted in practice, however, in schools (at least for 1999) simply asking for resources such as CD-ROMs, other forms of software, books and other language materials. No schools asked for language teaching PD for their teachers.

Incidental benefits

Projects like the SLLP often produce a wide range of benefits to education, both central and incidental. In the section on cost effectiveness (Peddie *et al.*, 1998: Section 6), the evaluation report listed a number of such benefits from the SLLP. For example, schools regularly commented on the new understandings gained between the secondary and primary sector, and the benefits of the professional contacts that many clusters enjoyed.

Projects and planning for the future

Finally, the ways in which schools entered the final phase of the SLLP suggested that both schools and the Ministry needed to work together to see what could be done to maximise the value of the opportunities afforded by the SLLP. The Ministry had made the funding realities very clear to schools from the earliest stages of the evaluation. Nonetheless, a number of teachers and principals expressed anger and frustration over what they saw as the unnecessary end of a curriculum project that they strongly believed had been both organisationally successful and educationally effective. It is unclear how the SLLP could have prevented or resolved these dissatisfactions, but the implications of the evaluation data were that a much stronger focus on pre- and in-service teacher development and on-going planning for languages programmes would have been extremely useful components of a refocused project. Ironically, in no interviews did SLLP principals or teachers argue for a rethinking of pre- or in-service teacher education, so that primary-trained teachers could enter schools with a specialism in a language other than English.

The SLLP was a significant initiative in the area of primary sector languages. It offered a number of positive developments, but missed some important opportunities. Yet, despite the positives, subsequent trends in enrolment show that the SLLP itself appears to have played a relatively modest part in quite substantial primary sector languages enrolment fluctuations since 1995. Similarly, shifts in secondary school language enrolments since the mid-1990s do not appear to be linked to outcomes of the SLLP. Even for Spanish, where rises in primary numbers have been reflected in the secondary sector, there is no evidential link, as Spanish was taught in only a handful of SLLP schools. To sum up, the outcomes of this major initiative again reinforce the need for a much more comprehensive and forward-looking national policy strategy (Peddie, 2001).

The Way Forward?

This final section considers the implications of what has been discussed in this chapter. Briefly, New Zealand society is now linguistically far more complex than it was even 20 years ago. It seems defensible to argue that this complexity is, however, dwarfed by on-going debates in both the political and the public arenas relating to the place of English and (especially) te reo Māori. The neo-liberal moves of decentralisation and the diminished government responsibility of the last twenty years have been key factors in determining that New Zealand does not have a comprehensive languages policy. There has been a modest uptake of language studies in the elementary school sector but, even when well-intentioned and substantially-funded moves are made, the problems arising from a lack of central policy and planning are still critical. Thus, both the statistical data and the outcomes of the SLLP evaluation demonstrate that a 'local' (school-based) model does not and cannot solve New Zealand's language challenges in education (Shackleford & Peddie, 1996).

What then should be the way forward?

First, it is clear that the hands-off approach of successive recent governments has not been helpful. The New Zealand primary school sector in particular is arguably less likely to understand the challenges and benefits of a second-language programme without both a clear central policy or strategy, and quality input through targeted professional development programmes. This is in part because primary schools have traditionally not been involved in the teaching of languages other than English, perhaps mainly because the curriculum has never required this.

As noted earlier, the current neo-liberal ideology would seem to rule out any possibility of the development of a comprehensive national languages policy, and/or an adequately funded initiative for the primary school sector. Nevertheless, this does leave open the possibility that the government could target resources into languages education if it were convinced that there would be sufficient economic, social and political benefits from doing so. In other words, the government could, even within its own current agenda, develop a clear languages *strategy* that could address many of the issues raised in this chapter. Such a strategy would need to be jointly developed by the major parties, and set in place initially for at least five years in order to address teacher education and supply issues in particular.

In terms of the primary school sector, what might such a strategy look like? With a fast-changing population, and on-going economic imperatives, such a strategy could include the following:

- a clear statement by the government and the Ministry of Education about the importance of languages in the primary sector;
- the introduction of an eighth 'essential learning area' (namely, a second language) as an outcome of the 2001–2002 'national curriculum stock take';
- a programme to ensure that students with a language background other than English acquire an excellent command of New Zealand English (as well as some understanding of New Zealand's official language, te reo Māori);
- targeted funding for minority language communities to enable them to offer language retention programmes;
- targeted funding to assist *trained* primary teachers who are fluent or native speakers in another language to gain language teaching skills (a strategy that is used successfully in Victoria, Australia);
- targeted funding both for languages within pre-service teacher

education, and to encourage schools in the primary sector to employ teachers who are already primary trained, and have language-teaching skills.

As argued convincingly by Lo Bianco in Australia about 15 years ago, language competencies of migrants can be seen as a problem, as a challenge or as a resource (Lo Bianco, 1989). In New Zealand, it appears that, while successive governments *do* want to promote the learning of languages in the primary education sector, there is no obvious acceptance of the policy implications of this desire. Thus there is no clear and rational strategy to ensure that comprehensive and effective language programmes are put in place. While many of the chapters that follow report significant local successes in language learning initiatives, the over-arching need for a carefully constructed and centrally-determined languages policy remains to be addressed.

Notes

1. The term 'Pakeha' is politically and ideologically contested. It currently commonly refers to people in New Zealand whose ancestry is British/European, but some of these people see it as an insulting designation. With the immigration from the 1960s of significant numbers of Pasifika peoples and the more recent sharp rise in Asian migration, other 'non-Māori' terms may also need to be developed.
2. For an excellent overview and discussion of the fall and rise of te reo Māori, see Spolsky (in press).
3. Unless otherwise noted, all figures in this section are drawn from the annual *Education Statistics of New Zealand* (NZ Ministry of Education, Annual), or from unpublished data and updates supplied by the Statistics Section of the NZ Ministry of Education. Special thanks are due to the Ministry Information Officer Sue McGeough for her timely and friendly assistance.

References

Bedford, R. (2003) New Zealand: The politicization of immigration. Online document: http://www.migrationinformation.org/feature/print.cfm?ID=86.
Benton, R. (1979) *Who Speaks Māori in New Zealand?* Wellington: New Zealand Council for Educational Research.
Benton, R. (1994) Towards a language policy for New Zealand. *New Zealand Annual Review of Education* 4, 161–73.
Clyne, M. and Kipp, S. (1991) Language maintenance and language shift in Australia. *Australian Review of Applied Linguistics* 19, 1–19.
DIMIA (2001) Migrant/refugee numbers arriving in Australia by migration stream: For settlers in Australia 2000. Department of Immigration and Multicultural and Indigenous Affairs [Australia]. Online at: http://www.immi.gov.au/settle/data/reports/Numbers%20by%20Migration%20Stream.htm.

Galbraith, S., Ngaha, A. and Starks, D. (2002) *Māori in New Zealand: Who Speaks Te Reo?* Seminar, Department of Māori Studies, The University of Auckland, December 3.

Goff, P. (1990) Speech to 'Living languages in Aotearoa.' Unpublished speech notes for an address (given by the Hon. Noel Scott) at the Wellington College of Education, 28 August.

Lo Bianco J. (1987) *National Policy on Languages.* Canberra: Commonwealth Department of Education/Australian Government Publishing Service.

Lo Bianco, J. (1989) Making language policy: Australia's experience. In R.B. Baldauf and A. Luke (eds) *Language Planning and Education in Australasia and the South Pacific.* Clevedon: Multilingual Matters.

Māori Language Act (1987) Wellington: Government Printer.

Ministry of Education (2000) *Hai! (kit): An Introduction to Japanese.*Wellington: Ministry of Education.

Murdoch, J.H. (1944) *The High Schools of New Zealand; A Critical Survey.* Wellington: New Zealand Council for Educational Research.

NZ Immigration Service (undated) History of New Zealand immigration. Online document: http//www.immigration.govt.nz/workshop/hist.htm.

NZ Immigration Service (2001a) Tourism and migration 2000. On WWW at: http://www.stats.govt.nz.

NZ Immigration Service (2001b) Trends in residence approvals (Vol. 1). Online document: www.immigration.govt.nz/research_and_information/reports/.

NZ Immigration Service (2002) Trends in residence approvals: 2001/2002 (Vol. 2). Online at: www.immigration.govt.nz/research_and_information/reports/.

NZ Ministry of Education (annual) *Education Statistics of New Zealand.* Wellington: Ministry of Education.

Peddie, R. (1984) 'Females and foreigners': Factors affecting the status of foreign language teaching in New Zealand secondary schools. In R. Burns and B. Sheehan (eds) *Women and Education* (pp. 123–40). Proceedings of the 12th Annual Conference of the Australian and New Zealand Comparative and International Education Society. Melbourne: ANZCIES.

Peddie, R. (1991) Comparative studies in education: Lessons for New Zealand? In *Education Models from Overseas* (pp. 1–12). Wellington: New Zealand Planning Council.

Peddie, R. (1996) What's the use? Languages policies in Australia and New Zealand. In R. Hunter (ed.) *Dilemmas and Responsibilities for Educators (Tradition, Change and Progress in National and International Contexts)* (pp. 163–78). Proceedings of the 24th Annual Conference of the Australia and New Zealand Comparative and International Education Society. Brisbane: ANZCIES.

Peddie, R. (1997) Why are we waiting? Languages policy development in New Zealand. In W. Eggington and H. Wren (eds) *Language Policy (Dominant English, Pluralist Challenges)* (pp.121–46). Amsterdam/Philadelphia: John Benjamins/ Language Australia.

Peddie, R. (2001) Languages in New Zealand elementary schools: Key to the future or 'Just another lesson'? *World Studies in Education* 2 (2), 85–96.

Peddie, R., Gunn, C. and Lewis, M. (1998) *Starting Younger: The Second Language Learning Project Evaluation.* Report to the NZ Ministry of Education. Auckland: Auckland UniServices Ltd/The University of Auckland.

PLANLangPol. (1983) *A National Language Policy for Australia.* Sydney: The Committee, Professional Languages Association for a National Languages Policy.
Schouten, H. (1992) *Tasman's Legacy: The New Zealand–Dutch Connection.* Wellington: New Zealand–Netherlands Foundation.
Senate Standing Committee on Education and the Arts (1984) *A National Language Policy.* Canberra: Australian Government Publishing Service.
Shackleford, N. (1996) Languages policy and international languages of trade and tourism; Rhetoric and reality. Unpublished MEd. thesis: The University of Auckland.
Shackleford, N. and Peddie, R. (1996) Congruence and dissonance: Aspects of languages policy development in Australia and New Zealand. Paper presented at the World Conference of Comparative and International Education Societies, Sydney, Australia, July 1–6.
Simon, J. (ed.) (1998) *The Native Schools System 1867–1969. Nga kura Māori.* Auckland: Auckland University Press.
Spolsky, B. (in press) Reassessing Māori regeneration. *Language in Society* 32 (4).
Statistics New Zealand (2002a) 2001 census of population and dwellings. Online document: http://www.stats.govt.nz/census.htm.
Statistics New Zealand (2002b) Change in ethnicity question; 2001 census of population and dwellings. On WWW at: http://www.stats.govt.nz.
Tourism Research Council, New Zealand (2002) International visitor survey. Online document: http://www.tourism.govt.nz/research/res-ivs.html.
National Languages Policy Secretariat (1989) Towards a national policy on languages; *Hei Putake mo Tetahi Kaupapa Reo mo Aotearoa.* Unpublished Paper. Wellington: National Languages Policy Secretariat.
Waite, J. (1992) *Aoteareo: Speaking for Ourselves* (Parts 1 and 2). Wellington: Ministry of Education.

Chapter 2

A Community Elder's Role in Improving Reading and Writing for Māori Students

TED GLYNN AND MERE BERRYMAN

Background

Education developed from within the world view of a dominant majority culture has all too often failed to understand and ignored or belittled indigenous minority beliefs and practices (Bishop & Glynn, 1992; Cummins, 1989; Cummins & Swain, 1993; Scheurich & Young, 1997; Skutnabb-Kangas & Cummins, 1988; Glynn & Bishop, 1995; Glynn *et al.*, 1992), and so has contributed to the political and economic marginalisation of the indigenous minorities (Stokes, 1985; Bishop & Glynn, 1997; Jackson, 1998; Durie 1998). In New Zealand, the Treaty of Waitangi signed in 1840 between the British Crown and Māori (the indigenous people of New Zealand) promised partnership in government, protection of precious resources (including language and culture) and participation in all benefits arising from British citizenship. However, political and economic relationships between Māori and non-Māori soon fell well short of these promises. The Māori population was rapidly outnumbered by waves of colonial settlers, and the proportion of land under Māori collective ownership rapidly diminished as a result of land wars and biased legislation.

Like all indigenous peoples, Māori had their own processes for defining, accessing and protecting knowledge before European contact (Matheson, 1997). Education through the medium of the English language provided a means for early colonial and settler governments to assimilate Māori into European culture and society (Codd *et al.*, 1990). For nearly a century the state education system took little or no account of Māori language, cultural values and practices, nor of the collective tribal organisation of Māori society. Essential elements of Māori identity and well-being were belittled, or were totally absent from curriculum and pedagogy. While writers such as Ladson-Billings (1995) and Scheurich and Young (1997) contend that schools need to adopt pedagogies that are congruent with the pedagogical practices of minority cultures, success in New Zealand schools for Māori students was expected to come at the cost of leaving their language and culture at home (Glynn, 1998). This colonisation process has been so pervasive that many current Māori grandparents and parents neither speak their own language, nor fully understand traditional cultural knowledge and practices. Furthermore, official reports consistently show that disproportionate numbers of Māori students are suspended or expelled from school because of perceived behavioural difficulties, and many of them complete their schooling without achieving any formal qualification (Ministry of Education, 1994, 1995, 1996).

Various reasons have been advanced to explain why Māori have not gained the same benefits from education as non-Māori. These have included the absence of Māori language and culture from the curriculum (Selby & Karatea-Goddard, 1996) and from the classroom settings in which Māori children participate (Bishop & Glynn, 1999). Another reason advanced is that many teachers approach their students as if they have all come from the same cultural group, or all have the same parental and home resources. Many teachers do not understand, and so cannot build upon, the different knowledge bases that their students bring to school. In addition, the New Zealand education system traditionally has provided little opportunity for Māori people to problem-solve some of these issues. This is seen in the fact that only very recently have Māori been recognised as having the authority to determine what aspects of Māori language and culture should be included in the national curriculum, and how these should be represented and legitimated. The state education system has defined success for Māori students largely in terms of learning the culture and language of non-Māori (Hollings, 1992; Ministry of Education, 1994; 1995; 1996).

However, over the past two decades Māori have been exerting greater control over education as a means of reclaiming their traditional identity, language, and cultural values and practices (Walker, 1990; Smith, 1990; Smith, 1992; Keegan, 1996). In the 1980s *kōhanga reo* (language nests for pre-school children) emerged as a result of strong grassroots Māori initiatives for the development of education through the medium of Māori and from within a Māori world view. The 1989 Education Act formally established *kura kaupapa Māori* (Māori-immersion primary schools) as an alternative form of state schooling. Many of these schools are now establishing secondary classes, and a number of *whare kura* (Māori-immersion secondary schools) have emerged. There are now several *wānanga* (Māori tertiary institutions) as well as Māori-medium classes within mainstream schools. Māori are now developing approaches to education that challenge the traditional dominance of a Western world view (Smith, 1990; Smith, 1992; Bevan-Brown, 1998).

Whānau and the Māori World View

Since 1840 there have been continuous threats and disruptions to the organisation and functioning of Māori society. These include the Land Wars (between 1860s and 1880s) that dispossessed many Māori of their tribal resources bases, as well as subsequent legislation that undermined collective ownership of land and enfranchised only the holders of individual land titles. A more recent disruption was the effects of industrialisation in the 1950s and 1960s, which saw the departure of young Māori from their traditional rural tribal way of life to new urban lifestyles. The increasing family dysfunction within contemporary New Zealand society continues to impact negatively on Māori society. Nevertheless, the whānau (extended family) has survived, and is still regarded by Māori as an essential and integral part of Māori society. However, the traditional notion of whānau defined in terms of kinship has evolved to include Māori from other whānau or other *iwi* (tribes) who share a *kaupapa Māori* world view (i.e. one that represents Māori cultural values, aspirations and practices), and who form an association based on a common interest (Smith, 1995). Māori are now looking to traditional collective whānau structures to intervene and assist in revitalising their language and culture, especially within education.

Collaborative Storying and Narrative Inquiry

Ethnographic perspectives on research emphasise the importance of the relationship, rather than the distance, between those conventionally labelled 'researcher' and 'subject'. Further, they highlight the significance of the social and cultural contexts in which such research takes place (Glynn *et al.*, 1997). Storying is a traditional cultural practice preferred by indigenous people for the maintenance and legitimation of their own knowledge (Cole, 1998; Te Hennepe, 1993). However, many indigenous people are no longer prepared to let their stories be defined and reconstructed in the language and culture of the researcher (Te Hennepe, 1993; Bishop, 1996; Bishop & Glynn, 1997; Smith, 1999). Heshusius (1994) challenges researchers to strive to overcome their egocentric tendencies of the past and seek acceptance by, and participation into, the consciousness of those whom they are researching. In order to become more collaborative and less impositional, she maintains that researchers should try to participate in the consciousness of the storyteller. This requires researchers to listen actively and carefully if they are to silence their own internal theorising and thus represent the stories with accuracy. Heshusius (1994: 18) sees participatory consciousness leading to a point where the 'reality is no longer understood as truth to be interpreted, but as mutually evolving'. This means that the researcher's understanding of a story, and his or her ability to represent that story with accuracy and authenticity, emerges from continued sharing of lived experience with the storyteller.

Bishop (1996) describes a methodology of narrative inquiry as a process based on a series of semi-structured interviews that are recorded and transcribed. Transcripts then serve as the basis for further inquiry through reflective discussion and collaborative validation. In this way, interviews form part of a co-constructed written record of the narrative. Bishop describes how participants repeatedly revisit the topic of inquiry through spiral discourse. Narrative inquiry therefore arises out of an autonomous and synergistic partnership that minimises the distance between researcher and researched.

Narrative enquiry may therefore be seen as an effective methodology for addressing cultural aspirations and identifying culturally-appropriate solutions because it recognises that the people and their communities are essential participants in the research process (Bishop, 1996). Their lived experience and their own ways of knowing and sharing knowledge bring validity to the research process (Te Hennepe, 1993; Cole, 1998). Narrative inquiry maintains and respects the integrity of storytellers and the knowledge and culture that they represent. It allows researcher and researched to co-construct narratives. Hence it offers an approach that might highlight how the research process and outcomes may be understood through the agency of key research participants rather than through the agency of the researchers alone.

The Rotorua Home and School Literacy Project

The Rotorua home and school literacy project (Glynn *et al.*, 2000, 2002) was designed to utilise and strengthen within school communities the whānau relationships and organisational structures that operate within Māori society. The project aimed to help schools work more collaboratively with whānau to improve the literacy achievement of eight- and nine-year-old students experiencing difficulties with reading and writing. Māori was the predominant cultural group among the students involved. Nine primary schools in the New Zealand provincial city of Rotorua participated in the project, in which home–school liaison workers were trained to help the schools develop a literacy partnership with students' parents or whanau (Glynn, Berryman & Glynn, 2000). Participating schools contacted parents or whanau members and sought permission for their children to participate in the project, and within each school students were randomly assigned to one of two groups: either the home– school group (programme) or to the school group (control).

Parents and whanau members completed two separate one-day training sessions with the research team and the home-and-school liaison workers. These sessions covered first the reading procedures (Glynn *et al.*, 1979; Glynn & McNaughton, 1985; Glynn 1995; Harawira *et al.*, 1993; McNaughton *et al.*, 1987), and then the writing components of the programme (Jerram *et al.*, 1988). Training took place in settings initiated by the schools, and valuable flexibility was achieved through schools collaborating and allowing parents to access any of the training settings, whether in their own school or in one of the other schools.

Following analysis and scoring of audiotapes and writing samples, the research team and the home-and-school liaison workers provided detailed feedback to parents on their implementation of the reading and writing strategies. This feedback was carried out in a group context, so that parents heard feedback on the tutoring of other parents as well as on their own tutoring. A fuller description of parent training in the reading strategies is provided in Chapter 3. These sessions also allowed opportunities for addressing concerns that arose as parents and family members become more skilled in implementing the programme. Information from these feedback sessions provided data on how effectively the parents implemented the programme, prior to gathering data on students' progress throughout each of the phases.

The Development of Collaborative Partnerships in One School

Throughout the project it was noticeable that people in one particular mainstream primary school were operating differently from people in the other schools, even though all the schools served communities of similar socio-economic status, and had a similar teacher and student ethnic mix. The great majority of students and their whānau in this school, as well as many of their teachers, their principal and members of the school Board of Trustees were from one *hapu* (sub-tribe), Ngati Whakaue. This school had an unequivocally higher visibility of Māori cultural values and practices and Māori language use. For example, the formal training sessions in this school began with a *whakatau* (formal welcome) to all *manuhiri* (visitors), conducted in both Māori and English. Whānau training always began and ended with *karakia* (prayer). The school principal saw his role as humbly seeking advice and support from his *kaumatua* (tribal elders) on the school's Board of Trustees, rather than requiring them to respond to directives or requirements from him as the expert or the professional leader. Once the formal whānau training led by the researchers was completed, the school continued to conduct an ongoing series of *hui* (meetings conducted according to Māori protocol) that were very well attended by parents and often took place independently of the research team.

Parents in this school took a particularly active role in the project, in helping each other's children and in the everyday life of the school. One parent took responsibility for exchanging the student reading material. Parents supported each other in their tutoring tasks and made a concerted effort to continue tutoring through holiday periods. These parents also expected and welcomed a higher level of participation from their liaison worker, their teachers, and from the researchers than did parents in other schools. They produced more audiotapes than any other parents in the project. The parents, liaison person and staff, (whether of Māori or non-Māori descent), operated in a far more connected and collaborative manner than did participants from other schools. They displayed a high level of understanding and competence in Māori-preferred ways of working and communicating.

The liaison teacher in this school was Hiro, a grandmother of Te Whānau a Apanui descent (a different tribe from that of the school principal and many of the school staff and parents) who had spent the past 33 years raising her family and working in Rotorua and as a *whaea* (senior Māori woman) was widely known and respected within the Māori community. She was also a teacher widely respected for her extensive experience in both English- and Māori-medium teaching. As a Resource Teacher of Māori, Hiro was employed to provide advice to teachers in all areas of the curriculum as they relate to things Māori. Because of her language and cultural expertise and her *mana* (acknowledged authority and standing), Hiro succeeded in getting Māori parents 'on board the *waka*' (canoe) and becoming active in the home-and-school project

We first met Hiro two years ago at the start of the project, and established a close relationship based on mutual respect and trust, sharing personal as well as professional knowledge and experience. We have met regularly to reflect on the process of working in collaboration with the parents both during and after the project. Some of our meetings were taped and transcribed. Following each transcription, we tried to share our understanding of what we had said. This process typically helped us to raise additional questions and to challenge assumptions, leading to new transcriptions. We returned these to Hiro for verification, and again reflected on them together.

In this way we attempted to participate in Hiro's story and to co-construct meanings from the shared narratives. From our shared narrative we identified several cultural concepts (discussed below) that helped us understand our collaborative interaction with the teachers and whānau members and led to establishing a successful home and school partnership. This narrative therefore details the impact that the research project has had on the students and whānau members with whom Hiro has worked, and also on Hiro herself. This narrative served to help evaluate the project as well as to inform future research.

Elements of Effective Partnerships with Māori Whānau

Affirming culture

The first and most essential element identified was that this school not only understood but also affirmed the cultural background of its students and their families. We believed that this school strengthened the *wairua* (spiritual well being and self-esteem) of its Māori students and whānau by affirming them in the home, at school and in the community. While Hiro may have been too *whakama* (self-conscious) to speak directly about her own knowledge and expertise of the people, their language and *tikanga* (preferred customary practice), she provided many examples of this in her interaction with both teachers and families in the project. Her narrative shows that she was continually modelling the use of this knowledge and experience to improve the learning outcomes for the people in her group.

Hiro: I was a sort of liaison officer. I would sort of keep in touch with the parents concerned and with their children and with you but besides keeping touch with the parents, I also had to encourage them to come forward 'cause a lot of our Māori parents are a bit shy and that was a problem with a lot of them. They were keen enough in their own way but they were just shy, took a while to come to the meetings, but when they did come they were fine.

It's just *patipati* (encouragement), I call it. You know, give them a little *awhi* (support) and rub on the back and just have a quiet little *kōrero* (talk) to them and most of the time they open up.

Sharing cultural beliefs and understandings

As educators, we often think that we gather information to inform educational policy, and persuade administrators to improve educational practice. However, our efforts may nevertheless undermine indigenous languages and cultures by discouraging indigenous voices from being heard and by preventing indigenous people from participating in education from within their own world view. We do this despite our growing appreciation that human learning and human development are hugely influenced by the detailed social and cultural contexts in which they occur (Vygotsky, 1978; McNaughton, 1995). Through the shared beliefs and common cultural understandings that Hiro held with whānau, she was able to engage successfully with Māori teachers and parents in this school.

Hiro: One of the other coordinators had difficulty getting a couple of the parents on board. But I think the problem there was because there was lack of communication between the teacher and the senior teacher in charge of those bilingual children. Some of the children were in the bilingual class. There was no consultation with her and she could have been a big help if the coordinator had asked her, but she wasn't asked.

Mere[1]: Why was it so important that she be asked?

Hiro: She (the bilingual teacher) knew those parents very well and she would have been able to help make the coordinator's road a bit easier. It wouldn't have been such a heavy job, getting them to come on board.

Mere: Do you know how she felt about not being asked?

Hiro: Ah all she said was just 'well I wasn't asked, but *kei te pai* (that's fine) because I've got plenty of work'.

Some teachers have got the knack of getting around teachers without causing big hassles. Sometimes you need a bit of *awhiawhi* and a bit of *patipati* as we said last time. But some (teachers) tend to sort of take the approach that you've got to try and lay the law down. And some of our Māori parents back away from that. That approach sort of worries them so they go backwards. They won't come forward.

While this situation was also of concern to the researchers, we knew at the time that intervention would have been misinterpreted and possibly result in further hurt and recriminations. All we were able to do was try to alleviate the concerns of the bilingual teacher and access the parents from their home. These home contacts subsequently proved to be some of the most successful researcher–home relationships. The harsh reality for us both was observing how teachers' pre-judgement of parents (for example, concluding they were uncaring or apathetic if they did not attend meetings called by the school) could perpetuate the marginalisation of minority cultural groups.

Inviting community participation

When asked what advice she would give to other coordinators, Hiro clearly considered that schools should invite, rather than require or demand, community participation. They should then continue to value and nurture all connections with their community.

Hiro: The way they approach their parents. You are not there to lay down the law. You are there to get them on side and to see the benefits of this training to help their children. Looking at it from the angle of the children rather than you telling them that they've got to do this and they've got to do that.

You don't need to have power and control. Work together collaboratively. Yes, that's where the focus should be.

Hiro explained how she herself had invited community participation and how this had led to gaining parental trust.

Hiro: I put aside my Wednesday afternoons for them and my room. They knew they could come here and I also told them to ring me if they had any problems.

And I was at the other end of the telephone whenever they needed me. If they needed me for anything like that, to do with the programme, just ring me up. If I'm not here leave a message at the school. And I always tried to respond to their needs and I think they came to trust me and because they knew whenever they had a query I was able to answer it. If I couldn't I would find someone who could, either from you or someone else and then I'd answer it. I think that trust was a big thing.

Providing ongoing positive support

Hiro used her own personal experience to ensure that the whānau were always provided with ongoing encouragement, support and positive feedback. Although she found this a particularly challenging task, she also found it very rewarding as she saw the parents continue to come back for more.

Hiro: I enjoyed doing it because they were responsive. They wanted it. I didn't push it down their throats. They came asking for it. And as I said earlier there were times when I said, oh here we go again when I saw one mother coming. And I'd think now what does she want. But I pushed all of those thoughts aside and listened to what she had to say or ask.

Mere: She (the mother) had some wonderful skills but she was quite negative about whether she could make the programme work.

Hiro: Well she was also unable to see where she was herself at that time. That was the biggest problem I felt at that time. I don't know whether she had high expectations of her son or what he should be doing. I feel she has really benefited from this programme a lot because it made her step back and look at herself and her son.

Yes, she had been chasing me up (recently) and saying to me 'What's happened to our books, aren't we doing it any more?' I said 'I have been busy this term because of contracts", I said 'But if you like, we'll pick it up again next term'. She said 'yes please'. So we're continuing.

Parents were supported to successfully complete all tutoring tasks set by the research team, even when this meant Hiro's own personal time was imposed upon.

Hiro: One school holiday, there were three of them whose tapes had not come in so I suggested to them they tape them in the holidays and I would go round and pick them up 'cause they sort of live within arms reach of each other and I arrived at his place and he's busily cleaning his yard when he saw me he went and taped his son read. That didn't matter, I had all the time in the world, I waited and when he finished I went round to the other one and picked up there, she had it all. One hadn't done it 'cause he (the son) had gone off to the bush for his holidays so she promised to do it when he came back and then the other one I picked up so I had those.

Sharing control

The researchers and Hiro all believed that to establish an effective home-and-school partnership it was essential to give parents some control over determining the context and direction of their learning, including how and with whom their results were to be shared. Balance of power, shared control and reciprocity between learning and teaching roles, are seen as elements of responsive, social contexts that promote independent learning (Glynn, 1985). They are also embodied in the Māori notion of *ako* (a term that combines the concepts of teaching and learning as a unified whole). It was evident that a key to parents' support of the project had been Hiro's own personal commitment to responding to their concerns and meeting their needs, rather than simply directing them to ensure their compliance with the project requirements. Hiro ensured that resources were always ready for them, that there was a space to meet where they felt comfortable and safe. Given the many competing demands made on parents' time and energy. Hiro also ensured that the time set aside for them remained suitable and convenient. When asked why she thought none of her parents had dropped out, Hiro replied:

Hiro: Perhaps because we had our regular meetings. Sometimes I'd set a time for meetings on a Wednesday afternoon and it usually tied in just before they came to collect their children. I didn't want to hold a meeting in the morning so that they'll come from where ever they were, have the meeting, and then go home. I fitted the meeting in after lunch before three o'clock so that they could stay and pick up their children and they didn't mind doing that because it wasn't inconveniencing them and sometimes it would be just one or two. Might be the whole lot. But if some were having problems then I would have a meeting with just one person at a time. I didn't have them all together at once. I had, say, this mother up here who's still in the office helping, I'd say have her stay for half an hour. The first half hour 1:30 pm to 2:00 pm and then I'll have someone else from 2:00 pm to 2:30 pm or whatever or might even be shorter time and I gave them that time as their own.

Mere: Right. So you actually had the group meeting and I attended some of those but you also had some individual meetings.

Hiro: Yes, 'cause I felt well if they were shy about some of the things they were doing and weren't too confident, well on a one to one they would open up and they wouldn't be embarrassed in front of other people.

Hiro had taken a personal interest in, and got to know very well, each of the families with whom she worked. She spoke about them from a personal perspective. Even though the programme had begun 18 months prior to this interview and some of the families had left the area, Hiro still had close contact with most and spoke in depth about them all. Not only had Hiro shared in their work and successes, she had also shared in their pain and their grief.

Hiro: Well there was one grandfather, who was having problems with his ex partner, and that child got hi-jacked by the ex and that grandfather had worked so hard.

> Yep and that was sad when he came to tell me that his grandson had been taken away by his grandmother, his ex.
>
> And then there was one, a parent that had all the time in the world but he was too busy playing spacey games to listen to his own child read.
>
> And there was one mother who felt that she was not that good at Māori but she persevered, borrowed dictionaries and everything. This made them work.
>
> No, the father wasn't in the home, but mum was lovely.
>
> Then there was another one. Mum wasn't in the home but dad was working with the child. That was the difficult one 'cause he (the child) was taught in bilingual, taught to read in English first and then he came to immersion'. He learnt English first. Then he came here and straight into immersion. So that was a big step for him, he needed a fair bit of help for a start. And the father just needed help in sort of calming down not losing it. But dad turned out really good. He's now at Hamilton. He went to Hamilton to train as a teacher.

Sharing common lived experiences

The families Hiro worked with became part of her life and she part of theirs. This was not just a relationship that was restricted to the research project, and to the specific training and feedback sessions. It went beyond that. Values of individual achievement and competition between individuals that are dominant in the majority culture were gradually replaced by values of collective achievement and collective responsibility for the well-being of the extended family. Rather than seeing themselves as individuals, participants were developing relationships and patterns of organisation similar to those applying within a traditional Māori whānau. They had begun to operate along lines where Māori expectations for people to identify themselves collectively applied. Through their participation in the project, whānau members were affirming their cultural identity and validating the cultural understandings that came from experiencing the world from within a Māori frame of reference (Bishop & Glynn, 1997). The aspirations of the school and families were consistent and complementary.

Mere: So was this just advice about the reading and writing?

Hiro: No, whatever they asked.

Mere: Why do you think they came to you?

Hiro: As I said, I think they trusted me. You build up that rapport with them by what you do and how you do it. You don't just necessarily give directions. I'm just used to doing things hands on, showing by example. I'm not a lecture type person. So perhaps they saw what I was doing and with what I was doing and that made them happy too. We'd have a cup of tea or coffee. Down here or in the staffroom they were at home. They didn't feel uncomfortable they felt safe.

Well they sort of formed their own whānau and helped each other too. That didn't matter that they weren't brother and sister and that word *whanaungatanga* (interconnectedness through relationships) came out very strongly with that group of parents, with their 'network' going. We also had to share cassette players, recorders so one of them would finish with it, and go round the corner and pass it on to the next one down the street. And so they did the rounds and the school supplied the recorders. I didn't have to go and pick them up from each one. They would just pass them on to the next one. And I got them all back at the end of the programme. So that was excellent. And they helped each other in that way. Well even with the responsive writing. That's another way that whanaungatanga came out because as we said last time, they got sick of waiting for the teacher and they took control. I mean I started (by just) listening but the busier I became, they decided that they would take control and they did.

Mere: So there was an element of trust with you, What about with each other?

Hiro: Yes I think so. There was that there too. It came and was developed through that whanaungatanga, because they were helping each other there were no hidden agendas. They were all on the same wavelength and I think the trust developed out of that.

Mere: What is whanaungatanga for you?

Hiro: It's being part of a family. Not necessarily blood ties. Having that family feeling working together is part of a whānau. And might all be from totally different areas but when you get together you all work towards the whānau goal, helping each other. Doesn't necessarily have to be brother, sister, mother, father.

Mere: One of the things that amazed me was that they were actually just as interested in everybody else's child as they were in their own.

Hiro: I think it was to give them something to compare with maybe. I could be wrong but just to see how their child was doing while there was another person's child to compare with. Not so much against, as with.

Mere: Right. Because I got the impression that they wanted the benefits to come to all of the children within, as you say they did form their own whānau. So they wanted all of the children who were part of the whānau to benefit.

Hiro: Yes.

Mere: That strong whānau network that had developed, I haven't seen it in any of the other places. How do you think you got it?

Hiro: That's the way our school is. Well we've got about 90% (Māori). At that stage we only had about eight pakeha children and the rest were Māori ... And that's the way our school is run. It's run like a big whānau whether you are in mainstream (English medium) or immersion (Māori medium). Everything is whānau.

Reciprocity of learner and teacher roles

Pere describes *ako* in terms of the reciprocal and continuous interchange between the teacher and learner role as part of traditional Māori educational practice (Pere, 1982). It was clear that Hiro and her school were manifesting these values and beliefs. They believed families should and could become involved in the formal education of their children. With Hiro's help, it was not long before these parents, who had up until then been the learners, reciprocated the teacher role. This could have been a potential source of conflict but, because of Hiro's experience, the *mana* (acknowledged authority and understanding) of the parents as well as the mana of the teachers was maintained. Teachers and parents were able to learn alongside and from each other. The common and central focus was on sharing the responsibility for student progress.

Hiro: I like seeing people who are not in the education sector (parents and other whānau members) latching on to things in education and seeing the benefits.

Mere: Do you think those parents latched on?

Hiro: I think so. The majority of them, I would say. The hardest part was getting them into that routine of working with the teacher. Mind you it was hard getting the teacher into the routine too.

When it came to the responsive writing and brainstorming ... Well it ended up the parents decided they'd do it at home.

They took control of the responsive writing project away from the teacher because they got sick of waiting for him and I can understand that, being a parent and a grandparent myself. But I can also understand the teacher who was only new to our school so he was still getting to know his children and still settling in. Some (teachers) don't take long you know, some only take five minutes but some take longer and I think that may have been where the difficulty was.

Mere: You had a really strong group of parents?

Hiro: Oh yes very strong. They knew what they wanted and they demanded it and if it wasn't forthcoming well that's what they did. They took it away. And they operated it themselves but they hounded me, to you know keep them up with it.

Mere: Did you feel like you were piggy in the middle?

Hiro: No because the teacher was fine about it and so were they. They were quite happy. As long as there was someone there to do it, it didn't have to be the teacher. And it just kept going. I just felt that the teacher would need to sort of get himself faster into a routine. Yes some take a bit longer than others.

This example of collaborative problem solving provided an opportunity for the co-operative and active learning roles of the teacher and whānau to be exchanged.

Learning authentic life skills

An element of the learning that Hiro saw as being crucial was the learning of independent living skills, not only for the children but also for their whānau. Hiro talked about one mother in particular who because of this experience finally began a concerted effort to learn the Māori language herself and who has also become a valued assistant in the school. This mother grew not only in self-confidence but also in self-efficacy.

Mere: The mother you are talking about was actually one of the mums that I thought was shy. She's certainly not shy now!!

Hiro: Oh heck, no. She runs that office (school) up there when the office ladies are away.

Mere: She really became ...

Hiro: ... confident, her self-esteem is up there (indicating with hand). That's what I like to see, confident in her own ability. Once she got her confidence she was in charge of getting the books and doling them out.

We kept an exercise book and we recorded what books we had given to each one and then we had a date when those books had to be back in and if I wasn't around I'd ask her if she didn't mind and she said 'no, I'll do it' and she'd chase them up with their brown envelope with books so the kids could just go to the office, and bring the envelopes up there.

Because she grew in confidence she is still busy in the school. She's tied up, we've got a brand new photocopier, this is how good she is, and it's one of those with a memory and you punch it in. Well she's the chief operator. Besides the office lady, she is the only one who knows how to operate everything. She came here voluntarily and now there are some things she gets paid for. If one of the office ladies is away, she steps in, then she gets paid. She has just grown in confidence in her capability. It's all been hidden in there, and it's just coming out.

Mere: So has that been as a result do you think of participating in this research?

Hiro: I reckon that participating in this programme has been a big part of it and the other part big part of it has been the staff and our principal, the way they treat her like an equal and not like a ... (body language expression indicating that she means in a disparaging manner).

Providing authentic learning contexts

This context for learning was real and meaningful for Hiro and the whānau. Whānau members were fully engaged with Hiro in helping their children to be more successful in reading and writing at school.

Mere: With some of the parents that you worked with although we were targeting one child in their family would you have seen any benefits to others in the family?

Hiro: Yes my Mother parent helper. She's got another son so he ended up on the programme too, on the side, and that didn't worry me. It was of benefit to that one any way.

Hiro had also learned strategies that would assist her to help other parents and teachers. Initially when asked what aspect of the programme made her want to participate she identified that she had wanted to learn the reading tutoring procedures as well as the assessment procedures that the researchers would be using to monitor the programme.

Hiro: Well I had heard a little bit about it so I was getting excited too and that's why I pushed John to ask if we could go first in the first group 'cause it sounded exciting. Anything to help our children and our parents help their children. It's always a value.

We needed the *Tatari Tautoko Tauawhi* (Pause Prompt Praise). And we needed to up-skill our parents in that procedure as well so that they (parents) could support our kids and our teachers.

There wasn't much assessment for our Māori (medium) children. I've always felt we're still playing catch up. Our mainstream schools, they have heaps of resources. We're still catching up, with teachers, trained Māori-speaking teachers plus Māori resources for our *rumaki* (total Māori immersion) classes and we still haven't caught up so I feel anything like that will help with that anyway.

I'd actually like to take the senior staff on that *whakaputa whakaaro,* (structured brainstorming), *tuhi atu tuhi mai,* (responsive writing) one day at a *hui* (meeting) – just take them through that. Because that's excellent for them.

A further element that ensured collaboration between home and school was specifically targeting the learners' own experiences at a level where they were able to achieve successfully with appropriate support. For Hiro this element applied to learners at all levels. For students it meant giving them opportunities to raise any issues about the research as well as on-going assessment to ensure reading was at an appropriate level for instruction.

Hiro: The parents, no not just the parents but the children too, because when, throughout the programme I felt that they needed to go up a level or the book was too difficult then I gave them a *pukete panui haere* (running record) and we'd talk. And that was also my time when I could talk to the children. And if they had anything to tell me, I'd listen and let them talk.

For teachers it meant professional development in literacy and assessment strategies. Hiro become one of the 28 people targeted in a nation-wide project that trained Resource Teachers of Māori to train classroom teachers in *Ngā Kete Kōrero* (assessment framework for reading in Māori). She was also invited to several *Poutama Pounamu* (Education Research Centre) training hui. Being part of these projects gave us as researchers a better insight into the importance of accurate assessment of student progress and effective literacy programmes, not only for teachers and students but also for the strengthening of whānau.

Hiro: Yes, well the spin off from that is when like we've just had professional development for teachers on Ngā Kete Kōrero and trying to, you know, remind our new, newer teachers, you know the older ones aren't so bad, the senior teachers they know what they're doing but the ones that are fairly new to the service trying to get through to them that you don't just give a child a book for reading time. You need to talk about it before hand. There're all the things you need to talk about. There's new vocab. They latched on to that because there may be some strange words. And in those books, you do get some strange words depending on who wrote the book.

Yes and sort of getting across to them that that's when you introduce those words because those children may not have heard those words. That you need to prepare them (the children) first.

Follow Up

It is now almost four years since the research study was begun in this school, and about two years since the above interviews took place, so we asked Hiro what was happening now. We have found that the whānau has continued to grow. More and more people have got on board the *waka* . This is clearly evident in the role they have played in the production of two separate videotapes that present the experience of the whānau and the school in the whole research process. The first video (Berryman *et al.*, 2001a) illustrates the various cultural qualities of the home-and-school partnership in this school. These cultural qualities are conveyed through the stories and voices of students, parents, grandparents, teachers, principal and other school staff. They include whanaungatanga, *rangatiratanga* (the way in which all participants, including the principal, are guided by the authority of kaumatua) and *manaakitanga* (the very real duty of care that all participants demonstrate towards each other). The second video (Berryman *et al.*, 2001b) provides a detailed close up of parents using the Pause Prompt Praise tutoring procedures with children from the community. It also provides detailed examples of parents receiving specific feedback from a home–school liaison teacher on the accuracy of their tutoring. This video serves as an effective training tool that has strong 'street credibility' among families in this school community. They are able to see members of their own community successfully tutoring reading with children who are also members of their own community. Both videos validate and affirm Māori culturally-preferred ways of speaking, acting and theorising about their children's learning to read at home and at school.

Making these two videotapes allowed the authors to continue to develop their research relationship with Hiro and other staff in this school. This has led to their close involvement in a further research project *Tukuna kia rere* ('let it fly free') aimed at increasing the depth and richness of the Māori language offered to students who are making the transition from *kohanga reo* to this mainstream primary school.

Hiro's positive attitude, her sense of humour and spontaneity, and her strong commitment to the community continue to ensure that the benefits of effective home and school partnerships remain for whoever may need them.

Hiro: This lady, this old lady who is working on the mainstream side, she was a parent helper in Carol's class and she's just continued working in whatever class needs her. So Carol gave her to me and she just loves it.

I got a big buzz. Because you trained me in the actual programme and I can now carry on and run this programme in our own *kura* (school). That's what we're doing but just in regard to the reading side at the moment. That's all we want to build up at the moment. The reading side.

Mere: And the benefits?

Hiro: Oh heaps and heaps. You learn how to get on with different kinds of people and you also learn how to compromise. Even though there may be times when you feel like you want to introduce a number eight boot (laughter). But you don't. You sort of, exercise control.

At our most recent meeting with Hiro, we discussed this almost completed-chapter. Hiro legitimated our representation of her story by agreeing to have her name used throughout the chapter.

Conclusion

The traditional position of the researcher in Western research is one of distant interpreter and narrator. This practice de-constructs the subject's way of knowing and replaces it with the researcher's own (Heshusius, 1994).

Narrative inquiry enabled the researchers in this project to offer Hiro a more collaborative and legitimate way of rediscovering or creating new knowledge and ensuring the authenticity of the story. By being invited to share in Hiro's narration, the distance between the researcher and research subject was reduced and the researcher was permitted a closer insight into the participant's consciousness.

Connelley and Clandinin (1990) maintain that the collaborative relationship goes beyond mere contact to a relationship that more resembles friendship. It was *whanaungatanga* rather than friendship that underpinned the collaborative relationship between Hiro, the people from her school and the research team. Even before they had met, cultural links and whānau connections were already being established.

This whānau reached decisions through group discussion and consensus. Individual experience and strengths were utilised to ensure that all whānau members, students, parents and the school wide community contributed to decision making. Mutual trust and respect strengthened the relationship. Because everyone shared common goals and aspirations about improving students' reading and writing, everyone was 'on board the waka'.

Time and commitment from both home and school to establish and maintain these relationships was freely given. The way this school worked to maintain these relationships with its whānau was fundamental to the success of the home–school collaborative partnership.

Time and commitment from both Hiro and the researchers was also fundamental to establishing understanding and trust in the process of narrative inquiry so that collaborative storying could emerge. Until this happens the research may not move beyond reporting the partial truths described by, among others, Te Hennepe (1993).

Educators and researchers must continue to seek alternative approaches to educational research that are consistent with the values and beliefs of the research participants. This project needed to be conducted in ways that represent the cultural preferences, practices and aspirations of Māori people. Māori families and teachers within this school actively contributed to improving the literacy achievement of their own children. Their success played an integral part of the increasing knowledge and skill base of this whānau. Collaborative storying provided a culturally safe and appropriate way to address the research questions and understand the findings of the project. Collaborative storying ensured that the research methodology and the way in which the research group worked was understandable within a Māori world view, while maintaining the integrity of the people, their knowledge and their culture.

Notes

1. Here, and elsewhere in the chapter, Hiro's interviewer is Mere Berryman.

References

Berryman, M., Glynn, T. and Glynn, V. (2001a) *Me hoki whakamuri kia haere whakamua: Building Culturally Competent Home and School Partnerships* [videotape]. Wellington: William & Associates, for Specialist Education Services.

Berryman, M., Glynn, T. and Glynn, V. (2001b) *Pause Prompt Praise: Building Effective Home and School Partnerships* [videotape]. Wellington: William & Associates, for Specialist Education Services.

Bevan-Brown, J. (1998) By Māori, for Māori, about Māori: Is that enough? Paper presented at the Te Oru Rangahau Māori research and development conference, Palmerston North.

Bishop, R. (1996) *Collaborative Research Stories: Whakawhanaungatanga.* Palmerston North: Dunmore Press.

Bishop, R. and Glynn, T. (1992) He kanohi kitea: Conducting and evaluating educational research. *New Zealand Journal of Educational Studies* 27(2), 3–13.

Bishop, R. and Glynn, T. (1997) Researching in Māori contexts: An interpretation of participatory consciousness. *Journal of Indigenous Studies* (in press).

Bishop, R. and Glynn, T. (1999) *Culture Counts: Changing Power Relations in Education.* Palmerston North: Dunmore Press.

Codd, J., Harker, R. and Nash, R. (1990) *Political Issues in New Zealand Education* (2nd edn). Palmerston North: Dunmore Press.

Cole, P. (1998) First nations knowing as legitimate discourse in education. Paper presented at the annual conference of the New Zealand Association for Research in Education, Dunedin.

Connelley, F. and Clandinin, D. (1990) Stories of experience and narrative enquiry. *Educational Researcher* 20 (June–July).

Cummins, J. (1989) Empowering minority students: A framework for intervention. *Harvard Educational Review* 56 (1), 18–36.

Cummins, J. and Swain, M. (1993) Empowerment through biliteracy. In J. Tinajero and A. Ada (eds) *The Power of Two Languages: Literacy and Biliteracy for Spanish Speaking Students* (pp. 9–25). New York: MacMillan, McGraw-Hill

Durie, M. (1998) Real lives: What it means for Māori. *New Zealand Journal of Disability Studies* 5, 28–35.

Glynn, E.L., McNaughton, S.S., Robinson, V.R and Quinn, M. (1979) *Remedial Reading at Home: Helping You to Help your Child.* Wellington: New Zealand Council for Educational Research.

Glynn, T. (1985) Contexts for independent learning. *Educational Psychology* 5 (1), 5–15.

Glynn, T. (1995) Pause Prompt Praise: Reading tutoring procedures for home and school partnership. In S. Wolfendale and K. Topping (eds) *Family Involvement in Literacy: Effective Partnerships in Education* (pp. 33–44). London: Cassell.

Glynn, T. (1998) Bicultural challenges for educational professionals in Aotearoa. Inaugural lecture, University of Waikato. *Waikato Journal of Education* 4, 3–16.

Glynn, T., Berryman, M., Atvars, K., Harawira, W., Kaiwai, H., Walker, R. and Tari, R. (1997) Research, training and indigenous rights to self determination: Challenges arising from a New Zealand bicultural journey. Paper presented at the International School Psychology XXth Annual Colloquium, School Psychology: Making Links, Making the Difference, Melbourne, Australia.

Glynn, T., Berryman, M. and Glynn, V. (2000) Reading and writing gains for Māori students in mainstream schools: Effective partnerships in the Rotorua Home and School Literacy Project. Paper presented at the 18th World Congress on Reading, Auckland.

Glynn, T., Berryman, M., Grace, H. and Glynn, V. (2002) The power of culturally preferred pedagogy in a community and school literacy partnership. Paper presented at the Addressing Difficulties in Literacy Conference, Centre for Curriculum and Teaching Studies, The Open University..

Glynn, T. and Bishop, R. (1995) Cultural issues in educational research: A New Zealand perspective. *He Pukenga Korero* 1 (1), 37–43.

Glynn, T., Fairweather, R. and Donald, S. (1992) Involving parents in improving children's learning at school: Policy issues for behavioural research. *Behaviour Change* 9 (3), 178–185.

Glynn, T. and McNaughton, S. (1985) The Mangere Home and School Remedial Reading Procedures: Continuing research on their effectiveness. *New Zealand Journal of Psychology* 15(2), 66–77.

Harawira, W., Glynn, T. and Durning, C. (1993) *Tatari Tautoko Tauawhi: Hei Awhina Ttamariki ki te Panui Pukapuka*. Tauranga: New Zealand Special Education Service.

Heshusius, L. (1994) Freeing ourselves from objectivity: Managing subjectivity or turning toward a participatory mode of consciousness. *Educational Researcher* 23 (3), 15–22.

Hollings, M. (1992) Tino rangatirotanga in mainstream schools. Paper presented at the annual conference of the New Zealand Educational Administration Society, Wellington.

Jackson, M. (1998) Research and the colonisation of Māori knowledge: A keynote address. Paper presented at the Te Oru Rangahau Māori Research and Development Conference, Palmerston North.

Jerram, H., Glynn, T. and Tuck, B. (1988) Responding to the message: Providing a social context for children learning to write. *Educational Psychology* 8 (1 & 2), 31–40.

Keegan, P. (1996) *The Benefits of Immersion Education. A Review of the New Zealand and Overseas Literature*. Wellington: New Zealand Council for Educational Research.

Ladson-Billings, G. (1995) Toward a theory of culturally relevant pedagogy. *American Education Research Journal* 32 (3), 465–491.

Matheson, D. (1997) Research the whānau: Renew the whānau. *New Zealand Education Review*. Wellington: Victoria University Press.

McNaughton, S. (1995) *Patterns of Emergent Literacy*. Melbourne: Oxford University Press.

McNaughton, S., Glynn, T. and Robinson, V. (1987) *Pause, Prompt and Praise: Effective Tutoring of Remedial Reading*. Birmingham: Positive Products.

Ministry of Education (1994) *Nga Haeata Matauranga*. Annual report on Māori education 1993/94 and strategic direction for Māori education 1994/95. Wellington: Learning Media.

Ministry of Education (1995) *Nga Haeata Matauranga*. Annual report on Māori education 1994/95 and strategic direction for Māori education 1995/96. Wellington: Learning Media.

Ministry of Education (1996) *Nga Haeata Matauranga*. Annual report on Māori education 1995/96 and strategic direction for Māori education 1996/97. Wellington: Learning Media.

Pere, R. (1982) Ako: Concepts and learning in the Māori tradition. *Working Paper No. 17*. Hamilton: Department of Sociology, University of Waikato.

Scheurich, J. and Young, M. (1997) Coloring epistemologies: Are our research epistemologies racially biased? *Educational Researcher* 26 (4), 4–16.

Selby, M. and Karatea-Goddard, D. (1996) *He Arotakenga o nga Hoataka Whakapakari Kaiwhakaako Māori. An Evaluation of Professional Development Programmes in Māori Education*. Wellington: Ministry of Education.

Skutnabb-Kangas, T. and Cummins, J. (eds) (1988) *Minority Education: From Shame to Struggle*. Clevedon: Multilingual Matters.

Smith, G. (1990) Taha Māori: Pakeha capture. In J. Codd, R. Harker and R. Nash (eds) *Political Issues in New Zealand Education* (pp. 183–187). Palmerston North: Dunmore Press.

Smith, G. (1992) Tane-Nui-A-Rangi's Legacy: Propping up the sky:Kaupapa Māori as resistance and intervention. Paper presented at the Joint Conference of the New Zealand Association for Research in Education and the Australian Association for Research ion Education, Deakin University Australia.

Smith, G. (1995) Whakaoho whānau: New formations of whānau as an innovative intervention into Māori cultural and educational crises. *He Pukenga Korero: A Journal of Māori Studies* 1 (1), 18–35.

Smith, L. (1999) *Decolonising Methodologies: Research and Indigenous Peoples*. Dunedin: Zed Books Ltd and Otago University Press.

Smith, R. (1991) Professional ethics in education: Some issues in ethics at work. Paper presented at the conference on Issues in the Workplace and in Education, Auckland Institute of Technology, Auckland.

Stokes, E. (1985) Māori Research and development. A discussion paper prepared for the Social Sciences Committee of the National Research Advisory Council. Hamilton: University of Waikato.

Te Hennepe, S. (1993) Issues of respect: Reflections of first nations students' experiences in post-secondary anthropology classrooms. *Canadian Journal of Native Education* 2 (2).

Vygotsky, L. (1978) *Mind and Society: The Development of Higher Psychological Processes*. Cambridge, MA: Harvard University Press.

Walker, R. (1990) *Ka Whawhai TonuMmatou: Struggle Without End*. Auckland: Penguin Publishers.

Chapter 3

Reciprocal Language Learning for Māori Students and Parents

MERE BERRYMAN AND TED GLYNN

Introduction

Hohepa, Smith, Smith and McNaughton (1992) assert that the acquisition of linguistic knowledge is interdependent with the acquisition of cultural knowledge. This view is shared by socioculturalists working from a Vygotskian paradigm (Vygotsky, 1978). Participation in structured social activities within a cultural context, where the users are active rather than passive participants in the process, enables learners to acquire both linguistic and sociocultural knowledge. As the linguistic and sociocultural knowledge structures the learning activity, the activity can then create and recreate the linguistic and sociocultural knowledge of the participants.

Glynn (1985a; 1985b) supports an increased emphasis on social contexts for learning, and highlights the powerful reciprocal learning that can occur within natural interactions between parent and child, or between peers. Such learning contexts are often characterised by opportunities for children to initiate learning interactions and opportunities for reciprocal skill gains between the teacher and learner (the participants in the interaction). Further, it is more likely that responsive rather than corrective performance feedback is being given. *Ako* has been defined by Metge (1983: 2) as a 'unified co-operation of learner and teacher in a single enterprise', and draws no clear line of distinction between the teacher and learner. Ako would therefore provide the type of learning environment that could promote the learning outcomes characterised by responsive, social contexts for learning Glynn (1985a). Rangimarie Pere describes the process of ako as, 'both learning and teaching, where the child is both teacher and learner' (Pere, 1982). Ako as a process does not assume any power relationship between teacher and student, but instead serves to validate dual learning or reciprocal learning experiences.

The balance of power between teacher and learner can be achieved through co-operative learning where turns are taken, on an equitable basis, both at initiating and responding in learning interactions, so that there is true sharing of the task. Ako highlights a Māori cultural perspective from which to view and rationalise the reciprocal learning gains for tutor and tutee reported in behavioural research studies of peer tutoring (Houghton & Bain, 1993; Houghton & Glynn, 1993). The notion of tutor and tutee can be aligned with the concept of *tuakana* (elder), *teina* (younger) in which the relationship is based on the cultural obligations that come from being part of a *whānau* (immediate or extended family). The older or more able person has the cultural obligation to help the younger or less able child, but both come to the task with existing skills and knowledge. The interchange of learner/teacher roles (ako) provides opportunities to practise collaborative and collective learning within a culturally salient context (Smith, 1995).

Smith (1989), cited in Quintero and Huerta-Maeras (1990), affirms the need to re-think the significance of the social context in which literacy is best learned and the methods of instruction used. He writes that 'individuals become literate not from the formal instruction they receive, but from what they read and write about and who they read and write with' (Smith, 1989: 353). Quintero and Huerta-Maeras (1990) were able to successfully enhance the development of literacy and biliteracy skills of a group of parents and children. Parents were empowered to utilise and connect the specific newly acquired literacy activities to their own lives in order to improve their children's literacy development. Wolfgramm, McNaughton and Afeaki (1997) also found that Pacific Island parents in New Zealand were very keen to participate in their children's education. Collaboration between school and community is being encouraged by the reforms recommended by the New Zealand Literacy Experts Group (1999) and the recent changes to the National Education Guidelines and the National Administration Guidelines (Ministry of Education, 1999a, 1999b).

McNaughton (1995) emphasises that, for effective learning to take place, the positive social relationships between children and parents and teachers are crucial. They highlight the importance of the responsive social and cultural contexts in which learning takes place. McNaughton and Glynn (1998) contend that collaboration, in the context of home-and-school partnership, should ideally involve the sharing of expertise between educators and student caregivers. Further, they argue that this expertise requires shared understanding of the goals and processes that result in shared actions that lead to reciprocal understandings and mutual benefits. The interactive tutoring context and the acquisition of linguistic and cultural knowledge is considered in this chapter in the context of the implementation of *Tatari Tautoko Tauawhi* (Glynn *et al.*, 1993; Berryman *et al.*, 1995), which is a one-to-one Māori reading tutoring programme for older remedial readers derived from an English language tutoring programme, Pause Prompt Praise (Harawira *et al.*, 1993).

Training of tutors is a crucial factor in the successful implementation of tutoring procedures. All twelve studies reviewed by Glynn and McNaughton (1985), and most of the studies employing Tatari Tautoko Tauawhi, report using either single or multiple training sessions, where the tutors were taught the three tutoring procedures (pause, prompt and praise) at the same time. Tutors were then encouraged to practise the procedures with a tutee. One study reported on the effect of learning the components of pause, prompt and praise separately and successively (Houghton & Glynn, 1993). As each component was learned, it was then practised in the tutoring context. Evidence of the component being successfully used by the tutor during practice led to training in the next tutoring component until the tutors had mastered all three tutoring components. By presenting the training in more manageable learning chunks, Houghton and Glynn (1993) were able to be more inclusive in their choice of tutors. Separate and successive training components proved an effective strategy that enabled less able readers to become competent reading tutors.

This present study, which was part of the home-and-school literacy project described in Chapter 2, sought to explore the potential of two parents who were highly competent in their parenting role. Nevertheless their level of competency in their children's language of instruction (Māori) was below that of the children. While parents were more knowledgeable (*tuakana*) in terms of their understanding of the reading tutoring process, they were less knowledgeable (*teina*) in terms of their skill in te reo Māori This study documents the tutors' implementation of the tutoring procedures prior to and then after specific training (with the support of cue cards). This study also monitored the tutors' use of Māori language in their tutoring, and whether this use extended beyond the specific tutoring context. Finally, the study discusses how each pair (parent and child) benefited.

Method

Experimental Design

The overall research study employed a multiple baseline design. This allowed for built-in evaluation of the programme through comparison measures across small groups of target and control students in three separate sets of three schools. Repeated measurements were taken over a two-year period across all students and at two-term intervals from pre-programme to post-programme. The study design incorporated multiple-outcome measures of reading: book level, reading rate, reading accuracy and oral comprehension in English or in Māori. It also incorporated multiple-outcome measures of writing: writing rate, audience appeal and language competency in English or in Māori. Narrative information was gathered by interviewing participants on their ideas about the programme and what they thought they had learned from the programme

The study reported here describes the tutoring interactivities between two mother–son pairs from one of the first three schools. This component was added to the design of the main study because mothers were found to be using English language to support their sons' reading in Māori. For these two parents, the reading tutoring procedures of previewing the reading material, providing *tauawhi* (praise) and providing the three different types of *tautoko* (prompt) were reintroduced separately and sequentially. This was done using Māori language cue cards together with on-going feedback from audio-taped tutoring sessions over approximately one and a half school terms.

Procedure

The authors met with community groups, local *iwi* (tribal) representatives, school principals, members of Boards of Trustees, and other school representatives. A general discussion about reading at school and at home led to the group identifying that parents in the community were an under-valued and under-used resource in the schools' endeavour to advance the literacy levels of their students. The researchers spoke about possible home-and-school partnerships that could provide worthwhile solutions, and the community groups present indicated a willingness to provide support and resources. This information was taken to a meeting of the local School Principals Association, where the chairperson encouraged schools to participate. At a third meeting, principals, community people and researchers set the final parameters of the project. One of the important contributions made by schools was the selection of their home–school liaison worker. How these people were regarded by both the home and school community was critical to the success of the programme (see Chapter 2).

Participants were children aged between seven and nine years, from either English- or Māori-medium school settings, with identified reading and writing problems. Their parents agreed to allow them to be part of the study. Baseline data involved the gathering of information on the children's reading achievement in Māori or in English using 3-minute oral reading samples to assess their reading accuracy and reading rate. Oral cloze and recall questions were also used to assess the students' oral comprehension of the stories they had read. Data on students' reading included book level, reading accuracy, reading rate and comprehension.

Students were divided randomly into a control (home) and target (home–school) group. Parents of the target students were invited to join in the project themselves. They attended two training and practice sessions before they utilised the procedures with their own children. One session trained parents in either the Pause Prompt Praise or the Tatari Tautoko Tauawhi reading tutoring procedures, while the second session trained them in two supportive writing procedures (not discussed in this present chapter). In the first fortnight of programme implementation with their children, the parents supplied the researchers with taped reading tutoring sessions. The tapes were analysed, and served as the means by which home–school liaison workers provided specific feedback to tutors on their use of the procedures. They also provided data on the accuracy of parents' implementation of given procedures (treatment integrity).

Participants

Collaborative feedback sessions provided opportunities for building directly on the prior tutoring experiences of the parent tutors. In this way, new knowledge about the tutoring procedures was reciprocally developed and co-constructed by the home–school liaison worker, the tutors and the researchers. These sessions were critical to the further development of tutoring competencies. This chapter focuses on two parents who used no Māori on their first tutoring audiotape, even though their children were reading in Māori. These parents received additional training using the technique of sequential introduction of training components (Houghton & Glynn, 1993) in an attempt to support greater use of Māori in their tutoring.

Training

The parent tutors were trained to first of all preview and review the story to be read. They were also trained to use three different and specific reading prompts, depending on the type of error made by the reader:

- The first type of prompt, *pānui tonu/whakahokia* (read on/read again), is used when the reader comes to a word that he/she does not know and could not read meaningfully without assistance. It focuses the reader on a search within the text for information about word meaning. Tutors ask readers to read on to complete the sentence or, if the word occurs near the end of the sentence, to go back and start again.
- The second type of prompt, *kia ata titiro ai* (look carefully at the word), is used when the word the student reads makes sense, but is not the

word used in the story (meaningful word substitute). The tutor prompts the reader to make use of any letter-sound information available within the word.

- The third type of prompt, *kia marama ai* (to make meaningful), is used when the word produced is a substitute that does not make sense in the context of the sentence or story. The tutor prompts the reader to think about what was happening in the text and to think of a more meaningful word.

While the first two types of prompt require only short, repetitive phrases that are easily learned, meaning prompts require greater language sophistication and expertise. The tutor needs to understand what is happening in the story in order to help the reader to make sense of what he/she is reading. Effective meaning prompts need to be salient to the context of the error and/or to the story itself. Although some formulaic phrases can be used to introduce meaning prompts, they depend on the tutor being able to highlight key ideas about the word, the sentence or the story, and to express these ideas in language that is appropriate to the text and to the student.

The two mothers, who received the additive cue card training from the researcher, also met weekly with the home–school liaison worker, Hiro, who ensured that they were using books that were at appropriate levels for their sons and that they themselves could read and understand all the words in the books. Taped tutoring sessions provided the basis for specific responsive and corrective feedback on their use of the Māori language cue cards supplied to support their tutoring. Feedback sessions also provided opportunities to develop and co-construct the tutoring pathway ahead ('feed-forward') for these two mothers and in turn for their sons' learning.

After each feedback session, the next cue card was introduced, modelled and practised. Cue cards were presented in order from the easiest to the most difficult. The first two cue cards, given immediately prior to Tape 2, provided examples of praise statements and read on or read again prompts. The cue cards given before Tape 3 gave examples of visual letter prompts and preview starters, and those given before Tape 4 gave examples of starters that could be used for meaning prompts. If tutors asked for additional cues, assistance was given orally. The cue card training followed the order given above so that the two parents had sufficient time and experience to build their confidence and language base before attempting the more challenging meaning prompts. However, when parents were unable to give a prompt in Māori, they were encouraged to continue to prompt using English. The audiotapes also provided evidence of the tutors' increased efforts to introduce Māori language into their tutoring sessions.

After twelve tutoring weeks, all students (both in the home–school programme and in the school programme) were assessed again using all assessments.

Settings

Parents carried out all reading tutoring sessions in their own homes at times that had been previously negotiated with their children. Tutoring took place at least three times each week for 15–20 minutes. Each tutoring pair taped one of their sessions every two to three weeks and feedback was based on scoring the tapes. Tutors received written and oral feedback from the home–school liaison worker in collaboration with the researchers.

Materials

This study used published Māori texts that could be placed within the framework of the *Ngā Kete Kōrero* (the kits of language) book levels (Ngā Kete Kōrero Framework Team, 1996). Each parent was supplied with a box of books selected at school by the home–school liaison worker at the appropriate level previously identified by researchers. During training, parents learned how to recognise when a book was at an appropriate level of instruction for tutoring by the simple method of pre-counting 50 words before tutoring and then identifying the number of errors made by their tutee. If the reader made between 3–5 errors within the 50 pre-counted words, the book was considered to be at an appropriate level for tutoring. Parents took increasing responsibility and control over which books were selected and when they could be exchanged. If they chose to, they could select new books themselves from the appropriate book level.

Measurement of tutors' programme implementation

The measures of the tutors' implementation of the programme were as follows:

Preview/review

This was measured as the number of discrete verbal utterances (in either Māori or English) given by the tutor to introduce the story title, to name characters, to explore the sequence of events, to link to the background of the reader, to introduce difficult words prior to the reading, or to explore the reader's understanding of the text after reading. The percentage of discrete verbal utterances that were given in Māori was calculated.

Measures of prompts

These were the number of prompts contingent on reading error or omission given by the tutor after a 3–5 second delay (Houghton & Glynn, 1993).

The number of prompts given in Māori was expressed as a percentage of the total number of prompts given in either language.

Measures were taken of three types of prompts: read on/read again, visual ('look carefully'), and meaning. The number of each prompt type given in Māori was expressed as a percentage of the total number of that prompt type given in either language.

Successful prompts were defined as the number of tutor prompts given, in either English or Māori, that led to the student correcting the error. The number of successful prompts given in Māori was expressed as a percentage of the total number of successful prompts given in either English or Māori, and the percentage of prompts given in Māori was then calculated.

Praise

This was the number of instances of specific verbal praise, given in either English or Māori, that followed reader self-corrections, prompted such corrections, or was given as general praise. The percentage of all praise statements given in Māori was also calculated.

Reading behaviour and measures

Reading behaviours were also defined. Correct reading was the number of words read that were identical to the words in the text. Words read that were not identical to those in the text were errors. Self-corrections were errors that were spontaneously and independently corrected by the reader, while prompted corrections were errors that were corrected after appropriate tutor prompting:

- *reading rate* was measured as the rate of correct words per minute and the rate of incorrect words per minute;
- *reading accuracy* was measured as the percentage of words read correctly;
- *comprehension accuracy* was the percentage of oral cloze items and oral comprehension recall questions responded to correctly;
- *book level* referred to the Ngā Kete Kōrero level assigned to a book that the reader could read to reader accuracy criterion of 90% accuracy or to a comprehension criterion of 40%.

A native Māori speaker made a comparison analysis of each audiotaped three-minute reading assessment and tutoring session so that inter-scorer agreement with the researcher could be calculated.

Results

Tutor implementation of procedures

Table 3.1 shows the percentage of reader errors that each parent tutor (Tutor A and Tutor B) was able to prompt (following appropriate delays) to successful correction, either in English or in Māori. After the first basic Tatari Tautoko Tauawhi programme training session provided for all tutors, both tutors were able to use the delay-then-prompt technique to help tutees correct their errors: Tutor A did this with all tutee errors, while Tutor B did it with 33%. Following the first set of cue cards (read on/praise) and feedback training immediately prior to Tape 2, Tutor A prompted 86% of tutee errors to correction, while Tutor B improved her percentage to 100%. After the training sessions before Tape 3 (visual/preview) and also after those prior to Tape 4 (meaning), each tutor was prompting 100% of tutee errors to correction.

The percentage of errors that were taken to prompted correction using Māori language alone is shown in Table 3.2. After the first basic training session provided for all tutors, neither tutor prompted in Māori. However following the cue card and feedback training session immediately prior to Tape 2, Tutor A achieved 83% of successful prompted corrections in Māori,

Table 3.1 Percentage of successful prompted corrections in English or Māori

	Tutor A	*Tutor B*
Basic training	100%	33%
Read on/praise cue card	86%	100%
Visual/preview cue card	100%	100%
Meaning cue card	100%	100%

Table 3.2 Percentage of successful prompted corrections in Māori

	Tutor A	*Tutor B*
Basic training	0%	0%
Read on/praise cue card	83%	88%
Visual/p review cue card	89%	90%
Meaning cue card	100%	100%

Table 3.3 Tutor use of each of the three prompt types

	Tutor A			*Tutor B*		
	Prompt types			*Prompt types*		
	Read on	*Visual*	*Meaning*	*Read on*	*Visual*	*Meaning*
Basic training	75%	0%	25%	100%	0%	0%
Read on/praise cue card	30%	30%	40%	79%	21%	0%
Visual/preview cue card	44%	44%	11%	70%	30%	0%
Meaning cue card	75%	0%	25%	80%	20%	0%

and Tutor B achieved 88%. After the second session, Tutor A achieved 89% of successful prompted corrections in Māori and Tutor B achieved 90%, and after the final session, both tutors achieved 100% of successful reader corrections in Māori.

Table 3.3 shows the overall distribution of the three prompt types given by each tutor in either English or Māori; they are shown in the order that training was given. After the first basic training session provided to all tutors, Tutor A used read on/read again prompts most frequently (75%) and meaning prompts next (25%). Tutor B relied solely on read on or read again prompts. Following the training session before Tape 2 (when the read on cue card was provided) Tutor A used a combination of all three prompts, while Tutor B again used the read on/read again prompts most frequently (79%) and also the visual prompts (21%), but no meaning prompts. After the training session before Tape 3 (when the 'look at the word' cue card was provided) Tutor A continued to use a combination of all three prompts, while Tutor B again used the read on/read again prompts most frequently (70%) and the visual prompts next (30%), but still no meaning prompts. Following the final training session (when the 'think about meaning' cue card was provided), Tutor A still used the read on/read again type prompt for 75% of the prompts, but now used the meaning prompt for 25%. Tutor B continued to use the read on/read again prompts most frequently (80%) and the visual prompts next (20%), but still did not use meaning prompts.

Table 3.4 shows the percentages of each of the three different prompt types given in Māori. After the first basic training session, neither tutor gave any prompts in Māori. After the training session in which the read on/read again prompt and praise cue cards were provided, Tutor A used a

Table 3.4 Overall percentage of three prompt types given in Māori

	Tutor A			*Tutor B*		
	Prompt types			*Prompt types*		
	Read on	*Visual*	*Meaning*	*Read on*	*Visual*	*Meaning*
Basic training	0%	0%	0%	0%	0%	0%
Read on/praise cue card	30%	30%	40%	79%	14%	0%
Visual/preview cue card	44%	44%	0%	70%	20%	0%
Meaning cue card	75%	0%	25%	67%	33%	0%

combination of all three prompt types in Māori. Tutor B used the read on/read again and visual prompts in Māori, but not the meaning prompts.

Following the training session when the 'look carefully at the word' prompt and preview cue cards were provided, both tutors used a combination of the read on/read again and the visual prompts in Māori but not the meaning prompt. After the final training session, when the 'think about meaning' cue card was provided, Tutor A used the read on/read again type prompt in Māori for 75% of the tutee errors and the meaning prompt for 25%. Tutor B continued to use a combination of read on/read again (67%) and visual prompts (33%) in Māori, but no meaning prompts.

Table 3.5 presents the percentage of different types of tutee errors alongside the percentage of prompt types (following delayed attention) offered by the tutors in either English or Māori. There are four discrete sets of data, one following each taped tutoring session (Tapes 1 to 4). The tutee error data presented in the second column shows that, for Tape 1, all Tutee 1's errors were of the meaningful word substitute type that would best be responded to with the visual delayed prompts ('look carefully at the word'). In contrast, all Tutee 2's errors were of a type that would best be responded to with prompts that helped the reader with meaning. After the basic training, Tutor A responded to 75% of these errors with read on/read again prompts and to 25% of them with meaning prompts. Tutor B responded to all errors with read on /read again prompts.

After the next training session, both tutees displayed all three types of error, and the tutors needed to use their full range of prompts if they were to make the best tutoring response. Tutor A used a fairly balanced range of the three tutoring prompts, while Tutor B used only two of the three tutoring prompts and relied mainly on the read on/read again prompt (79%).

Table 3.5 Types of tutee error and types of tutor prompts (following delayed attention) in either Māori or English

	Tutor A response		*Tutor B response*	
Error/prompt types	***Error***	***Prompt***	***Error***	***Prompt***
After basic training (Tape 1):				
Read on	0%	75%	0%	100%
Visual	100%	0%	0%	0%
Meaning	0%	25%	100%	0%
After read on/praise cue cards (Tape 2):				
Read on	17%	30%	38%	79%
Visual	50%	30%	25%	21%
Meaning	33%	40%	38%	0%
After visual/review cue cards (Tape 3):				
Read on	0%	44%	50%	70%
Visual	0%	44%	38%	30%
Meaning	100%	11%	12%	0%
After meaning-prompt cue cards (Tape 4):				
Read on	67%	75%	0%	80%
Visual	0%	0%	0%	20%
Meaning	33%	25%	100%	0%

In the third tutoring session (following training with the 'look at the word' prompt and preview cue cards), all of Tutee 1's errors required the tutor to help with meaning, while Tutee 2 made all three types of error, which required the full range of prompts. Tutor A, less appropriately this time, continued to use all three prompt types, while Tutor B again used only two of the three tutoring prompts and again relied mainly on the read on/read again prompt (70%). On this occasion, neither tutor was matching the type of prompt closely with the type of error.

Table 3.6 Percentage of discrete tutoring utterances given in Māori made by her tutee

	Tutor A				*Tutor B*			
	Tutoring procedure				*Tutoring procedure*			
	Preview	*Prompt*	*Praise*	*Review*	*Preview*	*Prompt*	*Praise*	*Review*
Basic training	0%	0%	0%	0%	0%	0%	0%	0%
Read on/praise	0%	90%	71%	0%	0%	85%	5%	0%
Visual/preview	100%	89%	89%	0%	70%	90%	75%	82%
Meaning	100%	100%	100%	80%	89%	100%	100%	60%

In the final session, Tutee 1 made two different types of errors (67% read on; 33% meaning), while Tutee 2's errors were mainly of a type that would best be responded to with meaning prompts. Tutor A now used a pattern of prompts that best matched the pattern of errors of her tutee (75% read on, 25% meaning). Tutor B again used only two of the three tutoring prompts (80% read on, 20% visual), and again relied mainly on the read on/read again prompt, regardless of the types of error her tutee made.

Table 3.6 presents the percentage of discrete tutoring utterances given in Māori during the basic training (Tape 1) and during the additive component cue card and feedback training phases of the study (Tapes 2, 3 and 4). It shows four of the different tutoring components taught during training (preview the story; delayed attention prompt to tutee errors; praise, specific or general; review what has been read). After the basic training sessions, Tutor A and Tutor B provided none of their tutoring responses in Māori.

After the second training session (when the read-on prompt component and praise cue cards were provided), Tutor A gave 90% of her prompt statements and 71% of her praise statements in Māori, but none of her preview or review statements. Tutor B gave 85% of her prompt statements and 5% of her praise statements in Māori, but also gave no preview or review statements in Māori. After the next training session (when the 'look at the word' prompt component and preview cue cards were provided), Tutor A gave all her preview statements, and most of her prompt statements and her praise statements in Māori, but gave no review statements in Māori. Tutor B gave most of her preview statements, prompt statements and praise statements in Māori, and her use of Māori had generalised to review statements (82%), which were not specifically supported by cue cards at that time.

Following the final training session (when the 'look at the meaning' prompt cue card was provided), Tutor A gave all her preview statements and all her prompt and praise statements in Māori. Her use of Māori had also generalised to review statements, 80% of which were given in Māori. Tutor B gave most of her preview statements and all her prompt and praise statements in Māori, and her use of Māori once more generalised to 60% of her review statements.

Student reading achievement

Assessment examples of the two tutees' reading in Māori are shown in Table 3.7. Data for Tutee 1 and Tutee 2 appear on the table above the mean data for the group of home–school programme students, who were tutored at home by fluent Māori-speaking family members. Immediately below the mean data for the home–school group is the mean data for the school group, who worked on the school programme alone, without input from parent tutors.

Pre-programme and programme data are shown for four different reading measures:

- *book level* – there are 11 different reading levels in the Ngā Kete Kōrero framework ranging from early emergent (Level 1: Kete Harakeke A) to fluency (Level 11: Miro);
- *comprehension* – the percentage of cloze and oral questions correct;
- *correct rate* – the number of words read correctly per minute:
- *incorrect rate* – the number of incorrect words per minute.

Reading rate improvement is shown both as increases in correct reading rate and as decreases in incorrect reading rate.

Table 3.7 shows that Tutee 1 moved up four reading levels during the programme. Even though he was reading texts at a much more difficult level at the end the programme, he maintained his level of comprehension (54%). His correct reading rate improved slightly (from 26 to 28 correct words per minute) while his incorrect reading rate decreased slightly (from 4 to 3). Tutee 2 also moved up four reading levels during the programme and also improved his comprehension score (from 89% to 95%). It is interesting that he slowed down his rather rapid reading rate from 55 to 36 words per minute. However, his incorrect reading rate also went down from seven errors per minute to two. Taken together, these data suggest that this student was reading more difficult books with greater care, with fewer errors and better comprehension.

The home–school group mean showed the same increase in book level (from 6 to 10) as achieved by Tutee 1 and Tutee 2. However reading these

Table 3.7 Reading in Māori

	Pre-Programme	*Programme*
Book level		
Tutee 1 home–school	6	10
Tutee 2 home–school	6	10
Mean home–school group	6	10
Mean school group	6	8
Comprehension (%)		
Tutee 1 home–school	54	54
Tutee 2 home–school	89	95
Mean home–school group	68	50
Mean school group	35	35
Correct rate (words per minute)		
Tutee 1 home–school	26	28
Tutee 2 home–school	55	36
Mean home–school group	41	33
Mean school group	36	63
Incorrect rate (words per minute)		
Tutee 1 home–school	4	3
Tutee 2 home–school	7	2
Mean home–school group	6	3
Mean school group	4	2

more difficult texts resulted in a decrease in comprehension for the home–school group (from 68 to 50), while both Tutee 1 and Tutee 2 increased their comprehension scores. The home–school group mean indicated a decrease in correct rate (from 41 to 33 words per minute) and an accompanying decrease in incorrect reading rate (from 6 to 3 errors per minute).

The school group mean showed a smaller increase in book level (from level 6 to level 8), which was less than that for Tutee 1, Tutee 2 or the home–school group (from 6 to 10). On book level 8 the school group maintained comprehension at 35%, but almost doubled their speed of reading, increasing their correct word rate (from 36 to 63) while decreasing their incorrect word rate (from 4 to 2). Taken together, these data suggest that the school group students were reading texts at a lower level of difficulty than the home–school students, but at a much faster rate and with less comprehension.

Discussion

As reported in the previous Tatari Tautoko Tauawhi studies (Glynn *et al.*, 1993; Glynn *et al.*, 1996), the concurrent training strategy, in which all three tutoring components were taught concurrently, was an effective method for training peer tutors to understand and implement the tutoring procedures. These findings are consistent with those for English language tutors trained in the English Pause Prompt Praise procedures (Glynn & McNaughton, 1985; Wheldall & Mettem, 1985). However, in the present study the sequential, rather than concurrent, introduction of each component (Houghton & Glynn, 1993), together with specific feedback (Henderson & Glynn 1986), enabled the two tutors who were less-proficient speakers of Māori to provide effective support to their own children who were learning in Māori.

The additional training component in this study meant that training continued over a longer period of time than the general training component used in previous studies. It involved more focused modelling of the different types of prompts, and the use of five separate cue cards for the two tutors. Corrective and responsive feedback on the tutors' use of each type of prompt, and on their use of Māori language in their tutoring, took place following each of the three consecutive taped tutoring sessions. The additional training component also provided more frequent and more intensive meetings with the home–school liaison worker, who had a very strong commitment to supporting parents from this community.

Both parent tutors reported increased enthusiasm and confidence in their ability to support their children with the school reading programme. In addition, they were increasingly able to provide this support in their children's language of instruction. These tutors both shared with the researcher that Māori was the language of instruction for their children at school, and they strongly supported their children learning through the medium of Māori. However they acknowledged also that feelings of insecurity had prevented them from seeking opportunities to speak the language themselves. They believed this additional training in Tatari Tautoko Tauawhi helped to improve their confidence and self-efficacy.

They began to believe that they could speak and understand some Māori and they could now provide better support for their children.

At first, owing to their heavy reliance on the cue cards, these tutors felt that their tutoring in Māori was a little contrived. Support and feedback from the home–school liaison teacher and the researcher were systematically provided and, as the tutors' confidence in the cue card examples grew, so too did their confidence to experiment with their own phrases and with combining these phrases. Each tutor began to more actively collect and learn a few more new words in Māori. Once they began using Māori in their tutoring, they began to receive positive feedback not only from the home–school liaison worker and the researcher, but also from their own children, who helped by providing new words. Both parents showed that they were able to extend their use of Māori to the unsupported review component of their tutoring. Both tutors also reported that they were using more Māori in the home and in the community.

Data in Tables 3.1 to 3.6 show that the additional training procedures developed to further support these two tutors resulted in an improved quality of tutoring over the twelve week period. After the initial general bilingual training session, tutors learned to provide delayed attention, and were able to prompt all errors to correction (Table 3.1). However, none of their prompts was given in Māori (Table 3.2). Moreover, neither of the tutors was using the full range of prompts that they had been trained to give (Table 3.3), and the types of prompt they provided did not match closely with the type of tutee error (Table 3.5). After the first cue card and feedback training session (data from Tape 2 on Tables 1 to 5) there was immediate evidence that tutors were prompting and praising in Māori, and that they were able to use a wider range of tutor prompts. The next two taped tutoring sessions reveal that their tutoring skills continued to improve. As well as using Māori in their prompting and praising, they also began to use it in their previewing and reviewing of the story (Table 3.6).

Prompts used by tutors (Table 3.4) confirm that the read on/read again and visual prompts were the easiest prompts to learn, and that meaning prompts were the most difficult to learn, especially in Māori. The data in Table 3.5 also show that, after additional training, these tutors began to respond to their tutee errors with the most appropriate type of tutor prompt. Tutor A managed to use a more balanced range of the three different prompt types in Māori, but Tutor B used no meaning prompts in any of her taped tutoring sessions. Data in Table 3.2 show that both tutors were able in Māori to successfully prompt to correction all tutee errors. Effective use of all three types of prompt enabled these parents to help their children correct all errors.

Table 3.7 shows how the reading behaviour of the two tutees improved markedly over the 12 weeks of home tutoring. Both students progressed by four reading levels to being able to read much more difficult texts. At this higher text level, Tutee 1 maintained the same level of comprehension and also maintained his correct and incorrect reading rates. Tutee 2 improved his comprehension at the higher text level; he lowered his rapid reading rate and decreased his incorrect rate, now reading with far fewer errors.

These gains compare very favourably with the mean gains of the rest of the home–school students who were being tutored by family members who spoke Māori more fluently. The mean for the home–school students shows an increase of four reading levels, but with a slight decrease in comprehension accuracy and a further improvement in reading rate (correct reading rate decreased, but students were reading with far fewer errors). In contrast the mean for the school group (students who did not have home tutors) showed an increase of only two reading levels. At this level comprehension was maintained, correct reading rate had improved and the incorrect rate had also improved (students were reading with far fewer errors). Clearly, the student reading progress that resulted from the support given to Tutee 1 and Tutee 2 by their less fluent mothers shows that the home tutoring was helpful and effective.

Conclusion

Data in this study demonstrate that two parents who were less proficient in Māori than their children could nevertheless be supported to provide effective reading tutoring for them. Presenting the training in more manageable chunks, providing additional training support in the form of cue cards and providing more focused and personalised feedback sessions were effective strategies for assisting less fluent tutors. These sessions proved critical to the further development of language competencies that in turn supported the tutoring. Tutors were authentically focused on furthering their own learning in order to improve their child's learning. This authentic parent-and-child learning context (Glynn, 1995) provided a cultural context from which to view evidence of the interchangeable learner/teacher roles (*ako*) throughout the tutoring process. Parents supported their children to solve problems with their reading and, at the same time, the children's use of Māori helped the parents to learn more about the language. It also provided both parent and child with the confidence and impetus to learn more Māori and to use Māori in settings other than the home.

As well as the reciprocal development of Māori language skills, important social and cultural learning was also taking place. Not only was there responsive support within the parent–child tutoring relationship, the responsive support relationship was also evident between the two tutors and amongst the home–school tutors and the home–school liaison worker. The crucial role played by this home–school liaison worker is described in narrative form by Glynn and Berryman in Chapter 2. Participants learned about this cultural relationship, as well as from it.

This study highlights the significance of the effective learning that can take place when positive social relationships exist between tutor and tutee and the task is seen as shared rather than imposed. The findings of this study add to our understanding of the methods of training used in implementing the Tatari Tautoko Tauawhi reading tutoring procedures.

The provision of additional structured feedback support for two parents with limited proficiency in their heritage language, to enable them to be effective tutors of their own children, has particular significance in the context of language revitalisation (Glynn & McNaughton, 2002). Māori people in New Zealand, like indigenous peoples throughout the world, have had their language systematically marginalised from mainstream society, and from education in particular. Consequently, most Māori students need to learn their own language as a second language, embedded within a dominant and monolingual (English) language environment, both at school and in the wider community. However, most of these students also lack access to a parent generation that speaks Māori fluently. Such a precarious situation calls for new and effective approaches to the reclaiming of indigenous and other languages. The Tatari Tautoko Tauawhi reading tutoring programme offers one such approach. The present study suggests that Tatari Tautoko Tauawhi is able to scaffold the use of the target language within regularly-occurring and naturalistic contexts, such as parents helping their own children learn to read.

References

Berryman, M., Bidois, P., Furlong, M., Atvars, K. and Glynn, T. (1995) Tatari, Tautoko, Tauawhi: A Māori language reading tutoring programme. Item 6. *Set; Research Information for Teachers* 1, 1–6.

Glynn, T. (1985a) Contexts for independent learning. *Educational Psychology* 5 (1), 5–15.

Glynn, T. (1985b) Contexts for learning: Implications for mildly and moderately handicapped children. *Australia and New Zealand Journal of Developmental Disabilities* 11 (4), 257–263.

Glynn, T. (1995) Pause Prompt Praise: Reading tutoring procedures for home and school partnership. In S. Wolfendale and K. Topping (eds) *Family Involvement in Literacy: Effective Partnerships in Education* (pp. 33–44). London: Cassell.

Glynn, T., Atvars, K., Furlong, M., Davies, M., Rogers, S. and Teddy, N. (1993) Tatari, Tautoko, Tauawhi: Hei āwhina tamariki ki te pānui pukapuka. Some preliminary findings. *Cultural Justice and Ethics Symposium Report*. New Zealand Psychological Society Annual Conference, Wellington.

Glynn, T., Berryman, M., Bidois, P., Furlong, M., Walker, R. and Atvars, K. (1996) Bilingual gains for tutors and tutees in a Māori reading programme. *He Paepae Kōrero. Research Perspectives in Māori Education*. Wellington: New Zealand Council for Educational Research.

Glynn, T. and McNaughton, S. (1985) The Mangere home and school remedial reading procedures: Continuing research on their effectiveness. *New Zealand Journal of Psychology* 15 (2), 66 –77.

Glynn, T. and McNaughton, S. (2002) Trust your own observations: Assessment of reader and tutor behaviour in learning to read in English and Māori. *International Journal of Disability, Development and Education* 49 (2), 163–173.

Harawira, W., Glynn, T. and Durning, C. (1993) *Tatari Tautoko Tauawhi: Hei Awhina Tamariki ki te Panui Pukapuka*. Tauranga: New Zealand Special Education Service.

Henderson, W. and Glynn, T. (1986) A feedback procedure for teacher trainees working with parent tutors of reading. *Educational Psychology* 6 (2), 159–177

Hohepa, M., Smith, G., Smith, L. and McNaughton, S. (1992) Te Kohanga Reo. Hei tikanga ako i te reo Māori: Te Kohanga Reo as a context for language learning. *Educational Psychology* 12 (3 and 4), 333–346.

Houghton, S. and Bain, A. (1993) Peer tutoring with ESL and below-average readers. *Journal of Behavioural Education* 3 (2), 125–142.

Houghton, S. and Glynn, T. (1993) Peer tutoring of below average secondary school readers using Pause Prompt and Praise: The successive introduction of tutoring components. *Behaviour Change* 10 (2), 75–85.

Literacy Experts Group (1999) Literacy Experts Group report to the Secretary of Education. Wellington: Ministry of Education.

McNaughton, S. S. (1995) *Patterns of Emergent Literacy: Processes of Development and Transition*. Melbourne: Oxford University Press.

McNaughton, S. and Glynn, T. (1998) Effective collaboration: What teachers need to know about communities. Paper presented at the New Zealand Council for Teacher Education, Hamilton, October.

Metge, J. (1983) *Learning and Teaching: He Tikanga Māori*. Wellington: New Zealand Department of Education.

Ministry of Education (1999a) *National Administrative Guidelines*. Wellington: Ministry of Education.

Ministry of Education (1999b) *National Education Guidelines*. Wellington: Ministry of Education.

Ngā Kete Kōrero Framework Team (1996) *Ngā Kete Kōrero Framework Teacher Handbook: A Framework for Organising Junior Māori Reading Texts*. Wellington: Ministry of Māori Development.

Pere, R. (1982) Ako: Concepts and learning in the Māori tradition. *Working Paper No.17*. Department of Sociology, University of Waikato.

Quintero, E. and Huerta-Maeras, A. (1990) All in the family: Bilingualism and biliteracy. *The Reading Teacher* 44 (4), December.

Smith, F. (1989) Over selling literacy. *Phi Delta Kappan* 70, 356–359.

Smith, G. (1995) Whakaoho whānau: New formations of whānau as an innovative intervention into Māori cultural and educational crises. *He Pukenga Korero: A Journal of Māori Studies* 1 (1), 18–35.

Vygotsky, L.S. (1978) *Mind in Society: The Development of Higher Psychological Processes*. Cambridge, MA: Harvard University Press.

Wheldall, K. and Mettem, P. (1985) Behavioural peer tutoring: Training 16 year old tutors to employ the Pause Prompt and Praise method with 12 year old remedial readers. *Educational Psychology* 5 (1), 27–44.

Wolfgramm, E., McNaughton, S. and Afeaki, V. (1998) Story-reading programme in a Tongan language group. *Set Special 1997: Language and Literacy* (pp. 1–4). Wellington: New Zealand Council for Educational Research.

Chapter 4

Samoan Children's Bilingual Language and Literacy Development

JOHN MCCAFFERY AND PATISEPA TUAFUTI, IN ASSOCIATION WITH SHIRLEY MAIHI, LESLEY ELIA, NORA IOAPO AND SAILI AUKUSO

> *A leai se gagana, ua leai se aganuu, a leai se aganuu ona po lea o le nuu.*
> When you lose your language, you lose your culture and when there is no longer a living culture, darkness descends on the village. (Fanaafi, 1996: 1)

Introduction

The focus of this chapter extends beyond the case study of individual bilingual children to present an ethnographic report of a cohort of Samoan bilingual learners and the factors that, over time, have led to their successful bilingual and biliteracy development.

The debate over whether or not to implement bilingual education for language-minority students from low socio-economic backgrounds often seems to revolve around ideological and political issues rather than around issues of school and programme effectiveness. According to various authorities (Schlesinger, 1992; Crawford, 1992; Cummins, 2000; May, 2000), the US English Only movement appears unwilling to even consider, let alone study, the substantial longitudinal research now available on the clear benefits of bilingualism and biliteracy for many language-minority learners. For example, in the United States, Thomas and Collier (1995, 1997, 2002) have shown clear academic advantages for long-term bilingual education programmes over other forms of schooling and organisation. In New Zealand, this research is not well known (see Coxen *et al.*, 2002; McCaffery & Tuafuti, 1998) and even the New Zealand Ministry of Education has until recently advocated a Transitional Early Exit model at around Year 3 as a possible solution to Pasifika students' academic underachievement (Ministry of Education, 2002a; 2002b). A familiar claim from education officials here is that there is no research showing that bilingual education will work in New Zealand with Pacific Island communities and students. 'Consequently, an assimilationist imperative and a subtractive view of bilingualism are clearly apparent in the majority of language policies, and language education policies, aimed at ethnic minority groups' (May, 2001: 305).

This presentation of the research findings reviewed here again challenges beliefs, both within New Zealand and internationally, that fail to acknowledge the demonstrated academic benefits of long-term bilingual/biliteracy education. We present a picture of what has been achieved in one school and a vision of what can be done in many others. *O le Taiala* (which means 'the world of the navigator') is the name of the Samoan bilingual unit at Finlayson Park School in Manukau City, just south of Auckland – a district often referred to in New Zealand as South Auckland. In 2003, this Samoan bilingual unit had five classes and approximately 140 students out of a total school roll of about 900. This chapter describes and analyses the background, development and student outcomes of a ten-year project to establish in New Zealand the first full 'dual medium, dual literacy' bilingual unit, in which both English and Samoan are used as the medium of instruction and for literacy teaching. O le Taiala provides for students from Years 1 to 8. (In New Zealand schools, children are classified by year levels. Children start school in Year 1 on their fifth birthday; thus, students in Year 8 are approximately twelve years old.)

The authors take a critical empowerment position (Apple, 1999; Bishop & Glynn, 1999; Cummins, 1986, 1989; Freire, 1972; Giroux, 1997; Lankshear, 1998; May, 1999; Pennycook, 2001) and attribute the success of O le Taiala students to the application of empowerment factors from Cummins' (1996, 2000) model at all three levels: *micro* (child, family, classroom, teacher), *meso* (syndicate/unit, school) and *macro* (education system and wider society outside education).

Cummins (1989) argues that minority students are empowered or disempowered by four major characteristics of the way schools operate. These involve the extent to which:

- minority language students' home language and culture are incorporated into the school curriculum;
- minority communities are encouraged to participate in their children's education;
- education promotes the inner desire for students to become active seekers of knowledge, and not just passive receptacles;
- assessment of minority language students avoids locating problems in the students and seeks, wherever possible, to find the root of the

problem in the social and educational systems, including curriculum and assessments.

Using the first language of our children for academic learning, and working within a strong empowerment base, is in our view the quickest and most efficient way to gain conceptual and academic knowledge. Well-organised, theory-based and community-situated bilingual education is now recognised as the most powerful empowerment approach in minority education (Baker, 2001: Baker & Prys-Jones, 1998; Corson, 2001; Cummins, 1996, 2000).

The Project Team and Critical Empowerment Philosophies

This chapter is jointly authored by two teacher educators from the Auckland College of Education, and is written in partnership with the Principal, Associate Principal, Senior Teacher and staff from O Le Taiala. We are not all Samoan, but most of us are members or honorary members of *Ulimasao* (the Samoan Bilingual Education Association). All have been closely involved in the project, and have worked in partnership since its inception. We began this journey years ago with a determination to confront and address the issues of empowerment and disempowerment that we believe lie at the heart of minority language underachievement and which Samoan Bilingual Education in New Zealand seeks so determinedly and passionately to address (McCaffery & Tuafuti, 1998).

The traditional relationship between researcher and researched has never applied in our work. We have used a model of teaching and learning as a group of colleagues engaged in reflective empowerment activity (Cummins, 1989), and action research (Kincheloe, 2003). This chapter explicitly reflects the cooperative style in which the project was developed.

The authors as researchers, however, seek to move beyond uncritical action research into critical areas to question 'whose constructions of reality prevail and whose ought to prevail' (Kincheloe, 2003). As a group, we represent and present several views of that reality. We accept that this is problematic, and is itself an important issue to address in the research as an object of the study (Pennycook, 2001: 42). We seek to provide space and opportunity for others to explore and express their own 'lived realities' as members of the Samoan community in Auckland – a community whose members have faced direct, personal and institutional racism and the exercise of unequal power on a daily basis all their lives (Jones, 1991; Spoonley *et al.*, 2001).

Critical theorists (Foucault, 1980; Giroux, 1997; Kincheloe, 2003; May,

1999; McLaren, 1997; Young, 1990) argue that power constructs and controls all discourses. There is no neutrality, no equality. It dictates who may speak and when; what are legitimate topics for discussion; what are valid questions; what can or cannot be said; who are the voices of authority and who must just listen; whose reality is valid and scientific, and whose is unvalidated and unimportant. In New Zealand, as in many other Western nations, ethnic and language minorities such as the Samoan community therefore lack power and control over their own destinies (Bishop & Glynn, 1999). We argue that a major problem in having schools address issues of recognition of cultural and linguistic difference is the entrenched New Zealand hegemonic ideology that says, in essence, that sameness is the route to equality. Such a view disempowers language-minority communities by denying their right to exist as an ethnic group and denying them language and cultural rights in their new homeland. As Stephen May observes:

> the near universal response of conservatives and liberals has been one of active hostility to minority rights ... schemes which single out minority cultures for special measures ... appear immediately unjust, a disguise for creating or maintaining ... ethnic privilege ... Any deviation from the strict principles of universal political citizenship and individual rights is seen as the first step down the road to apartheid. Or so it seems. (May, 1999: 15)

To challenge such structural racism, and to prepare students for the future, we seek ways in which our processes of discussion and professional development can be used to create a safe, supportive, but critically aware, climate – a climate where staff, parents and children are encouraged to seek the best of both *Faasamoa* (traditional Samoan knowledge) and the knowledge and critical thinking of modern Western education. This includes reflection and examination of their own situation as language minority speakers.

This too is problematic as, traditionally, children in Samoan society are to be seen but not heard: to listen and obey without question is the norm, and discussion between children and adults is very rare. In addition, literacy activities for Samoan children are often first introduced in a religious setting (Sunday School, Bible studies) where any form of questioning of the text or the issues it raises is considered completely unacceptable and not seen as Faasamoa. Such traditional perspectives challenge our view that critical literacy skills, strategies and understanding are essential for children in the modern world. Our belief is that an awareness and exploration of this problem is essential to help individuals find a resolution, a blend of both traditional and modern factors to help them achieve this goal. As May (1999: 33) argues: 'Critical Multiculturalism must foster, above all, students who can engage critically with all ethnic and cultural backgrounds, including their own.'

To date, we have opted for the notion of 'critical empowerment and multiculturalism' (Cummins, 1989; May, 1999; Walsh, 1991) as the best pathway to this challenge: that is, the need to critically examine how each culture operates, and to learn to operate successfully in each environment while yet retaining a strong personal sense of Samoan identity. Further work is needed in the next phase of the project at Finlayson Park school to actively involve the children in exploring the process of how to better meet their own and their families' needs for the future. The end result of this process will, we hope, be children with a quite different range of skills and strategies, who will have redefined what it means to be Samoan young people in the modern world. To encourage such young people to engage in critical literacy, and to have their parents support that development, requires us to take our communities with us on such a journey. Polynesians have set out on many unknown journeys in the past; it is time to do so again.

Samoan Children and Bilingualism in New Zealand

Most Pacific Island communities are based in Auckland, with over 35% of them in Manukau City. This is partly because it is where most Pacific Island immigrants first settled in New Zealand; smaller but significant Pacific communities live in Wellington, the capital city. With a population at around 110,000 in 2003, Samoans comprised more than 50% of the entire Pacific Island population in New Zealand, and two thirds of them live in the Auckland region. Thus Samoan affairs dominate the New Zealand Pacific scene. The New Zealand-born children of these communities (referred to by the Ministry of Education as *Pasifika* students) account for over one third of enrolments in all schools in Manukau City, and in some schools in the western part of the district this figure is as high as 70%.

The bilingualism of Samoan children in New Zealand has become the subject of considerable professional and community interest in recent times. This is because a high level of Samoan language use continues in homes and communities while the use of several other community languages has declined over time (Lameta-Tufuga, 1994: Shameem, this volume; Tuafuti, 2000). Data from the 1996 and 2000 national censuses and from a local research project (Bell *et al.*, 2000, 2001) show that the Samoan language is currently still secure in the middle generations above 35 years of age. Most Samoan children still come to school from Samoan-speaking homes as native speakers of Samoan (Bell *et al.*, 2000, 2001; Hunkin-Tuiletufuga, 2001; Lameta-Tufuga, 1994). However, several of these researchers have also reported a small but rapidly growing percentage (perhaps around 5%) who understand Samoan but do not speak it well. As a group, these students have poor vocabulary knowledge and engage significantly in language mixing, and recently, even show evidence of using English grammatical features translated into Samoan (Bell *et al.*, 2000, 2001; Lameta-Tufuga, 1994: Tuafuti, 2000). Thus Samoan and other Pacific languages show early signs of serious erosion amongst the school-age population. There are predictions based on this and other research data that – unless bilingual education programmes are established within the next few years – several languages (notably Cook Island Māori and Niuean) will cease to have another generation of speakers (McCaffery, 2002; McCaffery & Fuatavai, 2002).

In the last five years, the comparatively low academic achievement of Pacific Island children has finally begun to receive attention from both research and intervention programmes (Coxon *et al.*, 2002; Education Review Office, 1994, 1995; Elley, 1992; Esera, 2001; Flockton & Crooks, 2000, 2001; McCaffery & Fuatavai, 2002; Ministry of Education 2000, 2001). Historically, both here and in other countries (Cummins, 1989), the blame for language-minority educational failure has been placed on the students and their families, their languages and cultures, rather than on the failure of the education system to cater adequately for them.

While Samoan appears more secure than other Pacific languages, the Auckland Samoan community, as represented by Ulimasao, is not being complacent. In 1995, it began to strategically plan and implement measures to promote the continued use of Samoan as a medium both for Samoan social and cultural life and for promoting academic learning among their pre-school and school-age population. It is significant, however, that the prime motivation for Samoan bilingual education in schools does not come at present from concerns about language loss. Rather, it is driven by powerful and deeply embedded desires in most Samoan families for their children to succeed academically at school.

Finlayson Park School

In New Zealand terms, Finlayson Park School in Manukau City is a very large multi-ethnic primary school, with more than 900 students and 35 classrooms. The ethnic composition of the school is:

63% Māori	27% Pacific Islands (26% Samoan)
5% *Palangi**	5% other immigrants and ethnic groups

* *Palangi* refers to New Zealanders of European descent

The school is classified as decile 1a, the lowest socio-economic category of the Ministry of Education's indicators for equity funding and support. In spite of this, the school has many special features not found in most New Zealand schools, especially those serving low socio-economic communities. It has a large hall funded by the community, its own purpose-built health centre, a parents and community meeting room, a computer suite, a very well-stocked library, an Early Childhood Centre/Crèche (owned and operated by the school) for the children of staff and parents working in the school, and its own school bus. It also employs its own school counsellor and social worker. The school has long-standing special programmes for students in: Special Needs, Special Abilities, ESOL, Bilingual Education, Behaviour Management, Choir, Music, Māori and Pacific Cultural groups, and a strong and highly successful team sports programme. The school's mission statement says the school strives to provide a safe and caring educational environment, which is both culturally sensitive and educationally challenging.

Like all other state schools, Finlayson Park is funded centrally by the Ministry of Education, but administered locally by an elected parent Board of Trustees that is required to ensure that the school follows National Administration and National Curriculum guidelines. Within these general guidelines there is substantial scope for local initiatives, including the teaching and use of community languages as media of instruction. This allows the Board of Trustees to be responsive to local community aspirations and to be accountable to the community for its decisions. To this end, the five Trustees of Finlayson Park make a local commitment after each election to co-opt four additional members to ensure that there is a representative of the Māori and Samoan bilingual units and each of the main ethnic groups in the school community.

The school has 92 full time and part-time staff including 45 teachers and other support professionals. Staff and children are organised into seven teaching teams or syndicates. Among them are *Te Huringa* (the Māori immersion unit), which has seven classes. There is also a dual-medium bilingual Māori/English unit with four teachers. O le Taiala has five classes, whose staff are appointed for their teaching expertise and knowledge in both Samoan and English. Almost 40% of the school's classroom teaching staff are therefore directly involved in bilingual education. The school's policies strongly support bilingualism, and value all children's home languages and cultures. All staff are required to attend professional development sessions and/or programmes on bilingualism and bilingual education, and to model respect for the languages and cultures of parents and children. There is a strong commitment to promoting tolerance, understanding and respect between members of all cultures in the school (Finlayson Park School Board of Trustees 2001). The role of the school's principal in developing a shared vision and collective commitment by all groups in the school community cannot be overestimated.

By 2003, there were more than 20 Samoan bilingual units in New Zealand schools. To the best of our knowledge, only two units had at that time chosen to develop full dual-medium biliteracy as their major strategy towards greater academic achievement for their students. None of them had been established or operated with any additional funding from the Ministry of Education as in 2003 there was no national policy in existence for Pacific bilingual education. It is our hope that policy, funding and other support measures will be in place shortly (McCaffery & Tuafuti, 1998; McCaffery & Fuatavai, 2002; NZEI, 2002). O le Taiala, then, has been largely resourced, operated and funded entirely through the hard work and determination of the Finlayson Park School community and this project team.

Empowerment and Partnership with Samoan Parents and Community

As educators passionate for bilingual education and empowerment programmes for parents and minority communities, we know from experience that it is impossible to isolate teaching from families (Bastiani & Wolfendale, 2000; Shore, 1992). We cannot teach and learn in a vacuum. As Tuafuti (2000: 12) says, 'it is impossible to teach part of a language and culture without understanding how that particular part fits into the whole Samoan family and society'.

Samoan parents want the best education for their children, and this is one of the main reasons why they migrate to New Zealand. However, when failure occurs, teachers blame the parents and their language and culture. Parents in turn blame their children. Some Samoan parents punish their children when they fail their school subjects. The parents believe that failure is the fault of the child, or themselves, and it brings shame on the family and community (Jones, 1991). Many parents want to help their children, but have no idea how to do so. Many have some ideas, but are not sure of the best way they can help their children succeed (Tuafuti, 2000). Finlayson Park School has used Cummins' model, together with parent-partnership models (Bastiani & Wolfendale, 2000; McAllister Swap, 1993; Vopat, 1994; Wolfendale, 1989), to overcome the mismatch between school culture and expectations, and Samoan culture and expectations, with a view to empowering the school's Samoan parents and community.

The same principles apply to teachers' work with Samoan students.

Teachers need to understand the place and role of the students' first language, their bilingualism, their conceptual and cultural experiences, and how these aspects can be used in the second-language acquisition process. Samoan students also have strong spiritual beliefs and need to grow socially and emotionally. They need to see these holistically validated at school. Without such understanding, schools treat students as partial people and fail to recognise their full being.

The most important empowerment strategy has been the formation and involvement of Ulimasao, the joint teacher and community, which since its inception in 1995 has aimed to:

- promote the interests, rights and involvement of learners and their parents from Pacific nations;
- provide a shared forum for parents, community and teachers to work together;
- reaffirm and encourage the language maintenance of all Pacific Island learners;
- promote bilingual education, bilingual biliteracy and academic achievement;
- assist Pacific Island educators to undertake professional study and research on bilingual education and language maintenance issues.

Ulimasao has been crucial in supporting Finlayson Park School in its quest to raise the academic achievements of O le Taiala children, strengthen their Faasamoa and assist them to be proud of being Samoan. Workshops, seminars, large and small conferences for parents, staff and community members have covered topics such as: understanding the New Zealand education system and the school, its programme, policies, organisation and operation; encouraging partnership with teachers; promoting empowerment philosophies and beliefs; voicing community concerns and developing the understanding that it is a right to ask questions and challenge the school; promoting reading and writing and Samoan literacy in the home; making first-language resources; implementing the Samoan language curriculum; promoting excellence in English and in academic development; and supporting the study of bilingual education (research, approaches, methodology, case studies, learning and teaching strategies, etc.).

Cummins (1986) argues that parents must be central and full partners with school in the education of children, not extras, left-overs, fill-ins. He cites the success of partnership 'Family Literacy' reading schemes in Great Britain as evidence of the power of teacher–parent partnership. A brief examination follows of the home–school partnership at Finlayson Park, which has drawn inspiration from the work of McAllister Swap's (1993), 'new vision partnership model'. The model's primary goal is for the 'school and community to work together to accomplish a common mission, generally for all children in school to achieve success' (McAllister Swap, 1993: 49). This is the level at which Finlayson Park School is working.

Accomplishing the joint mission requires two things. First, it requires a re-visioning of the school environment and a need to discover new policies and practices, structures, roles, relationships, and attitudes in order to realise the vision. Second, it requires collaboration among parents, community representatives and educators. Because the task is very challenging and requires many resources, none of these groups acting alone can accomplish it.

Thus a very powerful approach to achieving change has been established at Finlayson Park – one that incorporates the community centrally in the developments and encourages their vision and hopes and dreams to be central to the project. Parents want their children to succeed in both worlds – the mainstream world and their world as Samoans. In other words, they want their children to be balanced bilingual learners: academically, socially, culturally, physically and spiritually. O le Taiala therefore provides a holistic approach to supporting Faasamoa that recognises and values all aspects of the students' lives. Many other New Zealand schools are unaware, unable or unwilling to do this. The Samoan parents' vision became a shared vision among the school's principal and senior management team, the teachers, the Board of Trustees, Ulimasao, the students of O le Taiala unit and the advisers supporting the project. As Vopat (1994: 8) says, 'parents, teachers and school need to honour the primary relationship they all have in common: in learning and how to ensure its success'.

Communication between school and the O le Taiala parents is more productive and meaningful because the school has made the move to meet parents half way. Both languages, Samoan and English, have been used as much as possible in meetings, discussions, notices, assemblies and official functions and ceremonies. This strategy of bilingual communication also supports literacy in both Samoan and English for children and parents. Cultural understanding of both school culture and expectations, and the Samoan culture and parents' expectations has created broader empowerment rather than subtractive assimilation. It supports greater tolerance and acceptance of the diversity of children's backgrounds.

There are many personal development opportunities for teachers, children and parents alike. When they are able to use their first language, Samoan parents are more relaxed during workshops. They are also proactive and readily question the teachers if they do not understand notices or teachers' comments regarding their children's school reports. Parents and teachers work well together in both formal and informal settings and situations. Vopat (1994: 9) notes that: 'working together sounds great, but is really only feasible when those who are expected to be together know and feel comfortable with each other'. This comfort is evident in the relationship and partnerships between the Samoan community and O le Taiala and the whole school.

As experienced educators, we believe that children's first teachers are their parents. In the Samoan cultural context, parents – together with the whole extended family – welcome their children into the world and take them through a process of holistic learning where everyone in the extended family is involved. This is now the reality in O le Taiala.

Reading Research Conducted on O le Taiala Students

In order to build a comprehensive picture of students' achievements, we have drawn on both quantitative and qualitative information on the work of the unit and students' development in reading. Preliminary quantitative data are now available that confirm intuitions that reading levels in both languages have been rising close to students' chronological ages. The data for this chapter came from three main sources. The first two sources are research studies (Aukuso, 2002; Esera, 2001), and the third source is the school's own reading assessment data. Qualitative data came from interviews, observations and participant observation within an action research paradigm. Because the focus of this review is on the students of O le Taiala, we have placed greater emphasis on student issues and achievement in English rather than on the many Samoan achievements and other related factors that emerged from the rich sources of data we now have access to.

The Esera study

Esera (2001) describes his research as an exploratory comparative study of the acquisition of English language proficiency. He sought to identify the key language components (listening, speaking, reading and writing), policies and practices in both Samoan and English that appear to be effective in raising children's academic development. His study provides a rich source of quantitative and qualitative information on reading assessment, and many other issues.

Esera employed a Year 6 sample that comprised 20 students from different types of bilingual education in two primary schools in the same decile 1a category. School 1 described its programme as a Samoan bilingual programme in which Samoan was used as the medium of instruction for half a day a week and also intermittently when Samoan was needed to support students' learning. School 2 in Esera's study was Finlayson Park.

Unlike School 1, the O le Taiala students were in a full dual-medium programme where English and Samoan were each used for 50% of the time in all matters relating to the curriculum. For the purposes of the study, ten children from the Year 6 class in each school were randomly selected. All students (except for one student in School 1) were Samoan and came from Samoan-speaking homes. According to Esera, this close matching of students allowed valid comparisons of the effects of schooling and the different programme variables examined. Esera assessed and interviewed all the students, and also interviewed approximately 15 administrators, teachers and parents in both schools. He also observed the Year 6 classrooms in operation at both schools over several days in the middle of the school year.

The Aukuso study

Aukuso (2002) set out to describe and explore the long-term effects on students' reading progress of a seven-year dual medium, Samoan and English, reading programme. To this end, she studied two groups of 20 students, all from Finlayson Park, but in different programmes; one was O le Taiala, and the other was an English-medium programme. In order to ensure that the long-term effects of continuous participation in the biliteracy programme could be accurately assessed, only students who began at school in Year 1 were admitted to the sample. All the students were Samoan and came from Samoan-speaking homes.

Aukuso uses the term Samoan bilingual students (SBS) for the first group of 20 students from O le Taiala: five each from Years 3, 4, 5 and 6. The students' reading proficiency levels in both languages, as currently measured by New Zealand schools, were independently assessed and documented by Aukuso through the use of the IRI reading assessment measure. The IRI (Informal reading Inventory) is an informal diagnostic reading instrument, similar to a 'running record', that gives diagnostic information and a reading age or level.

The parallel group of 20 students came from the English-medium mainstream part of Finlayson Park School; five each from Years 3, 4, 5 and 6: Aukuso refers to these as Samoan mainstream students (SMS). They formed a matched control group allowing a more accurate assessment of the effects of the O le Taiala bilingual programme on English reading achievements. As students are enrolled in either bilingual or English-medium programmes by Samoan parental choice, the matched control group was purely fortuitous and avoided the usual concerns associated with assigning students to control groups.

Data from both groups of students were collected early in the school year by Aukuso. and discussed, compared, evaluated and verified in partnership with the school's senior staff member responsible for the school's student assessment processes. The data were then further analysed and interpreted in the light of research from the work of Cummins and Nichols-McNeely (1987) and Collier (1995).

The school's own reading assessment data

The Finlayson Park School Project Team comprised the staff of the school and the authors of this report. Standard school reading assessment data were gathered from four participant O le Taiala. classes of approximately 25 students each. Data were collated from the beginning and end of the school year, for students in Years, 5, 6, 7 and 8. Longitudinal data for these students over several years were also available. However, only the end-of-year data are reported in this chapter.

Findings

Findings from the Esera study

Esera (2001: 138–146) reported that the O le Taiala students at Finlayson Park (School 2) were achieving significantly higher levels of oracy and literacy in both languages than their counterparts in School 1. Esera states that the achievement of students from O le Taiala in English 'suggested that average reading age for all classes was above the chronological age of the children' (Esera, 2001: 122).

In School 1, standardised English Reading Vocabulary scores from the Progress and Achievement Tests (Reid & Elley, 1991) showed all Samoan-speaking students achieving at less than the 40th percentile. In reading comprehension, 70% of the students scored less than the 50th percentile. 'Students' reading levels were well below national norms' (Esera, 2001: 84). Concerning writing skills, Esera states: 'In general the writing lacked form and structure ... nearly all the students had difficulties putting their thoughts into language' (Esera, 2001: 92).

Esera argued that his study has identified key factors that can be used to promote successful bilingual/biliteracy programmes. He attributed the high level of success, including success in English reading and writing, in Finlayson Park to the following factors (not ranked in any order of priority), all of which were strongly in evidence in O le Taiala.

- The continued use of Samoan language and literacy throughout the entire eight years of primary school as essential for facilitating and maintaining the acquisition of high levels of English literacy;

- The acknowledgement and valuing of the student's first language in the unit and in the wider school, which emphasised positive effects on students' academic performance, their behaviour and their sense of self.
- High levels of teacher fluency and competence in Samoan, together with teacher knowledge, teaching skill and ongoing professional development involving continuing study about bilingual education.
- Regular discussion and reflection by all involved, together with support from the Project Team's Advisory and research staff.
- The organisation of a unit as a team, a separate syndicate from the mainstream school, together with a close physical proximity of all the classes; this allowed and encouraged teachers to work collaboratively.
- The high levels of professional interest, support and commitment from the principal and senior staff to articulate and promote a bilingual and biliteracy vision.
- A clearly articulated school-wide bilingual policy, achieved by shared understanding among students, parents, and teachers alike.

Esera also reports important benefits from having a clear policy on language use that keeps the languages separated during instruction by time, place, person or purpose (Cummins, 2000; McCaffery & Fuatavai, 2002). The random code switching between English and Samoan used in School 1 proved to be unhelpful. Finally, the effective engagement and empowerment of parents in and through the programme at Finlayson Park school was found also to be an essential component.

Findings from the Aukuso study

The following three figures (4.1–4.3) from Aukuso (2002) present her major data on reading development at Year 6 gathered during the first three months of the New Zealand school year. They will be discussed in detail in the summary section below.

In brief, the average scores of the Samoan Bilingual Students (SBS) in the Aukuso study demonstrate reading proficiency to grade age norms and chronological ages in both Samoan and English in Years 5 and 6. For the purpose of clarity in the following discussion, the SBS will be referred to as the O le Taiala students.

The programme appears to assist O le Taiala students to achieve higher individual reading levels by Year 6 (as well as consistently higher average reading levels) than the Samoan Mainstream Students (SMS). O le Taiala students are therefore acquiring literacy in both Samoan and English, with their biliteracy having a significant positive impact upon their acquisition

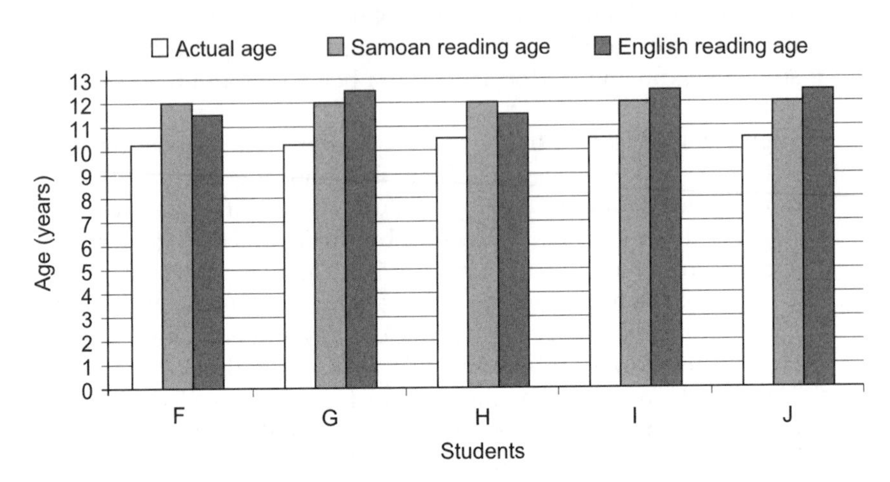

Figure 4.1 A comparison of reading levels/ages in both Samoan and English with chronological ages of five Year 6 Samoan bilingual students (SBS) from O le Taiala

Source: Adapted from Table 6.8 (Aukuso, 2002: 54)

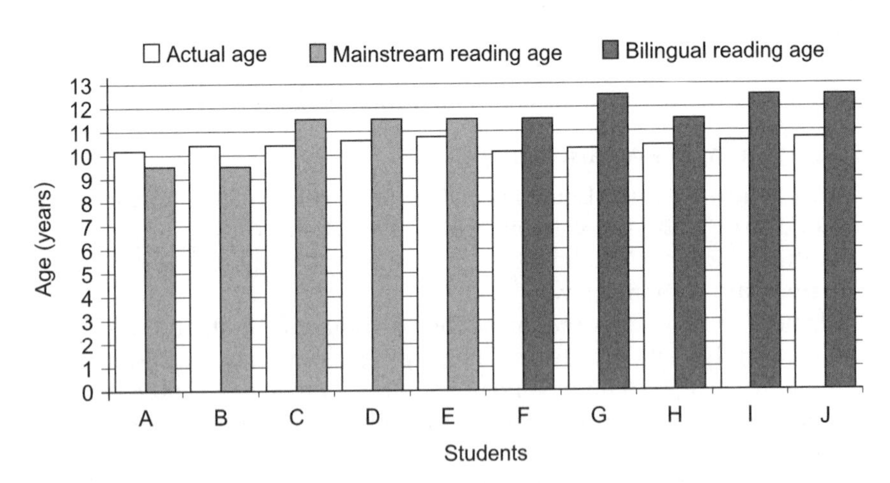

Figure 4.2 A comparison of English reading levels of five Year 6 Samoan Bilingual Students (SBS) and five matched Samoan Mainstream Students (SMS)

Source: Adapted from Tables 6.15 and 6.16 (Aukuso, 2002: 60)

of English. They had completed three years of intensive literacy instruction in their first language, Samoan, before the introduction of English reading, yet still managed to reach chronological age norms in English some two years later. Aukuso argues that this is further evidence that the interdependence language transfer model proposed by Cummins & Nichols-McNeely (1987) has validity as an explanation for the ability of O le Taiala students to transfer deep structure cognitive strategies from their first to their second language.

Sociocultural factors described in the study also appeared to be very important in the students' academic achievement. In spite of coming from low socio-economic backgrounds, the empowerment approach adopted by the school appears to have helped overcome the now familiar and often reported low academic achievements of Pacific Students in New Zealand Schools (Elley, 1992; Esera, 2001; Ministry of Education, 2002a; Smith & Elley, 1997: 112).

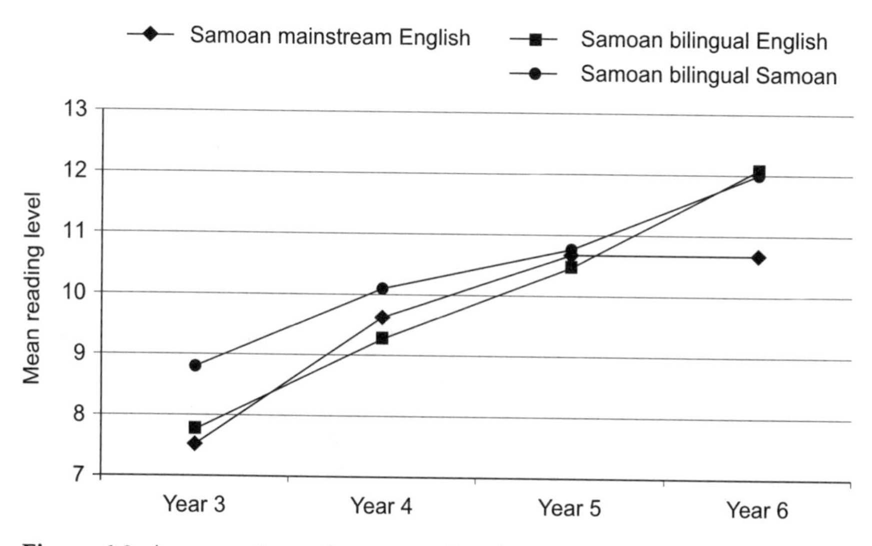

Figure 4.3 A comparison of mean reading levels in Years 3 to 6 between 20 Samoan mainstream students (SMS) and 20 Samoan bilingual students (SBS)

Source: Adapted from Table 6.17 (Aukuso, 2002: 62)

These conclusions affirm the effectiveness, identified in local and international research, of long-term, well-organised and sensitively operated dual-medium biliteracy approaches and models.

Findings from the Finlayson Park Project Team

The third source of quantitative data is from Finlayson Park School itself. For a number of years, the school has monitored all childrens' progress twice a year using an Informal Reading Inventory or IRI (Smith & Elley, 1997: 91–93). These results cover all students in Years 5 to 8 who have been at Finlayson Park over the full school year, which in New Zealand is from February to December. The school data therefore include students who are relative newcomers to the school and to the bilingual programme. In spite of the presence of these newcomers, the school data also show that O le Taiala students by Years 6 to 8 consistently read at levels at or above their English chronological reading ages and grade-age norms. The Project Team's data are shown in Figure 4.4 – note that the mainstream programme runs only to Year 6, while the English programme for bilingual students begins in Year 3 and runs until Year 8.

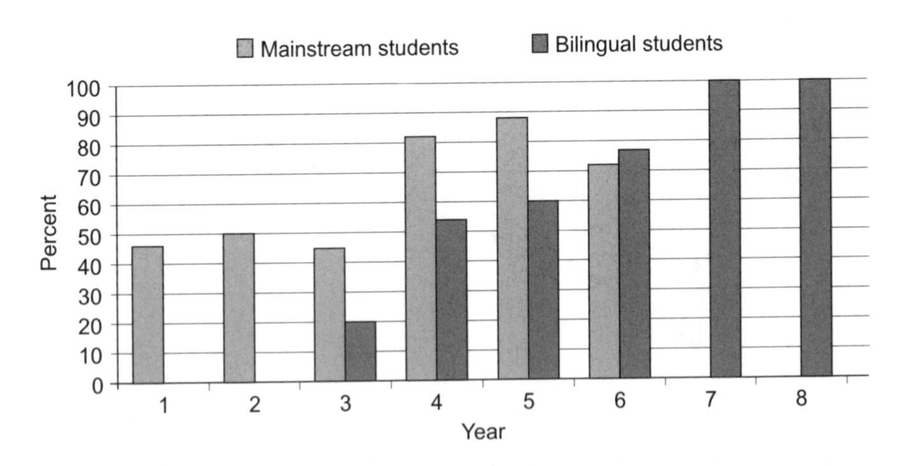

Figure 4.4 The percentage of Samoan mainstream students (SMS) and Samoan bilingual students (SBS) at the end of the school year who are reading in English at or above their chronological ages

Summary and Interpretations

All sources of reading assessment data were compared and reviewed by the School Project Team and the general conclusions that were drawn are presented below.

Reading in Samoan

Bearing in mind the limitations of the current Samoan IRIs (see below), the Aukuso study indicates that O le Taiala students, on average, reached Samoan chronological reading ages around Year 3. By Year 6, the Samoan reading levels for all students were approximately 1–1.5 years above their chronological ages, and continuing to rise rapidly. Their Samoan reading levels remained significantly ahead of their reading levels in English until midway between Years 5 and 6: at this point, the gap closed rapidly. Esera's study draws similar conclusions. No Samoan reading data are available yet for Years 7 and 8.

Reading in English

During Year 5, the mean English reading levels of O le Taiala students showed significant improvement: an improvement of almost 2 years reading level in one school year. According to the Aukuso data, they caught up with the SMS (Samoan mainstream students) in March–April of Year 5. They then overtook the SMS: their average reading level being 10 months above their chronological age. The gap between bilingual and mainstream students then appeared to accelerate as the students moved further into the Year 5 programme. Towards the end of Year 5, the English reading levels of the O le Taiala students caught up with their Samoan reading levels. These findings are consistent with other international research on biliteracy development showing that biliteracy success in the second language takes five to seven years to achieve (Cummins, 2000; Thomas & Collier, 1997, 2002). Esera's data show that chronological age/grade age norms were reached around Year 5.

At the beginning of the school year in Year 6, according to the Aukuso study, 100% of the O le Taiala students read above their chronological ages, on average by 1.75 years (Figure 4.1). The bilingual students were all younger than students in their matched mainstream Year 6 sample. Figure 4.2 also shows a consistent lift in the reading levels of Year 6 O le Taiala students, whereas the spread of SMS levels was far wider, with some still reading below their chronological ages. Esera's (2001) data also demonstrated that by Year 6 all of O le Taiala students were reading above their chronological age.

At the end of Year 6, according to the school reading assessment data (Figure 4.4), 6% of O le Taiala students were reading in English at their chronological age and 71% were reading above it: a total of 77%. Those children who were not achieving these levels were all late transfers in to the programme, either from Samoa or from English-medium schools. Among the SMS, a total of 72% were reading at (45%) or above (27%) their chronological age. Esera's comparative data for the other mainstream school, School 1, showed that most students there were reading well below their chronological ages (Esera, 2001: 84).

By Year 7, according to school data, all O le Taiala students were reading above their chronological ages. Comparisons with SMS can be made only up to Year 6, as mainstream students leave Finlayson Park at the end of Year 6 and attend an intermediate school for Years 7 and 8 before going on to high schools. The results for this group of SMS from Year 3 onwards, are, however, very good in comparison with nationwide average New Zealand literacy results for Pasifika students (Elley, 1992).

In Year 8, according to school data, all O le Taiala students who have been there for more than two years are reading in English at their chronological ages.

O le Taiala's Year 1 foundation students, who began when the unit started in 1996, complete the full eight years of the programme at the end of 2003: they constitute the Year 7 SBS reported above. According to the school records, 100% of them read above their chronological age. At the time of writing, more complete results for these foundation students at Year 8 were not available, and the full effects of the biliteracy programme await our further attention.

Additional comment

The focus of the above discussion has been on the O le Taiala students. However, as earlier noted, the reading achievements at or above chronological ages for the *mainstream* Samoan students (the SMS group) at Finlayson Park School were 82% in Year 4, 88% in Year 5, and 72% in Year 6. These figures are significantly higher than School 1 in Esera's (2001) study and also significantly higher than the national data on mean Pasifika literacy achievement (Elley,1992: Flockton & Crooks, 2000, 2001). We believe the reasons for this need further investigation. Perhaps the true effectiveness of the bilingual/biliteracy programme may be revealed by further comparative work with similar students in programmes in the many mainstream schools that do not have the school-wide empowering approaches, policies and programmes that prevail at Finlayson Park.

Sources and Limitations of Reading Assessment Data

The data on students' reading levels or reading ages gathered from all three sources relied heavily on the Informal Prose Inventory (IPI), now called the Informal Reading Inventory (IRI) (Smith & Elley, 1997: 91–93). These are running records taken on a series of passages of high-interest material, graded in levels of difficulty and followed by comprehension questions. Increasing numbers of commercial publishers now produce IRIs for schools in New Zealand. Schools most frequently use the IRIs to place students within a one-year band. An example is the graded reading materials from the *New Zealand School Journal*, a Year 4–8 reading resource supplied by the Ministry of Education. These materials are graded using the Elley Noun Frequency Count (Elley & Croft, 1989, cited in Smith & Elley, 1997), which provides a reading age that is usually correct to within one level. The ability of the IRI instrument to place students at appropriate reading levels, and the additional usefulness of IRIs for diagnosis and consequent teaching, mean that the reading progress of most school students in Years 4 to 8 is recorded in the form of data from IRIs.

However, a number of factors limit the ability of researchers to compare data gathered from schools that use different IRI instruments. Neither the range of instruments nor the results have systematically been compared, and many of the IRIs currently used may not adequately deal with comprehension issues and oral vs. silent reading for testing purposes. These factors prevent most researchers from being confident about their concurrent and construct validity and their reliability in producing standardised scores that can be used in comparative studies.

Furthermore, the development and use of IRIs in Samoan reading are in their very early stages. To the best of our knowledge, the only complete set of IRIs in use is that developed by Tuafuti and the O le Taiala staff, which has been under trial since 2000 at Finlayson Park. These Samoan IRIs are based on the school's own English IRIs, which use seven comprehension questions ranging from closed direct-reference questions to open-ended inference items. However, the Samoan set, like the National Education Monitoring Project (NEMP) tests, currently uses only four questions covering both open and closed comprehension (Flockton & Crooks, 2000, 2001). The early development of a standardised Samoan reading test will probably depend on cooperation and cost sharing between New Zealand and Samoa, where there is also an urgent need for reliable literacy indicators.

Esera (2001) used his own self-selected reading material in Samoan and English to assess students in both schools. School 1 also had standardised Progressive Achievement Tests (PAT) data (Reid & Elley, 1991) available for the assessment of reading in English. However, many multicultural schools in New Zealand with large numbers of bilingual/ESOL (English for speakers of other languages) learners in formative years have been reluctant to use PAT testing, believing that – rather than signal progress and achievement – the PAT tests have norms that do not provide for such learners and simply suggest failure.

Aukuso and the Finlayson Park School Project Team used data from non-standardised IRI formats devised within the school. This material was, however, extensively trialled and cross-checked against other standardised IRI material used by the school, and found to be accurate and reliable. When the school's IRI results were further cross-checked with results from the BURT word reading test (Gilmore *et al.*, 1981), the BURT test consistently gave a higher reading age. Finlayson Park also adjusted the age band used in the beginning-of-the-year tests to reflect the increasing age of the students at the end of the year. Both these factors suggest that the school's English IRIs provide a conservative assessment of reading levels.

In the next phase of the project, we look forward to further confirmation of these early indications of solid academic success on a wider range of standardised reading measures. Among the instruments that have been applied by the school from 2003 onwards is a new standardised reading test, STAR (Elley, 2000). This is proving to be a very reliable measure and will be used either to cross-check results or as the primary data collection instrument.

Other Positive Features of O le Taiala

The report on Finlayson Park School by the Education Review Office (2002) speaks very highly of the school's achievements and those of O le Taiala and its students. Specific positive features noted by the school and external researchers (Aukuso, 2002; Esera, 2001) as outcomes of the bilingual programme relate to the students, their parents and the school staff.

Student attendance on a daily basis in the bilingual unit is considerably higher than that of Samoan children in similar schools. Moreover, transience (moving from school to school) has decreased dramatically: 90% of O le Taiala students have been at Finlayson Park since Year 1, compared with only 20% of the mainstream students. Samoan families who leave the school zone often travel long distances to return their children to O le Taiala to continue their education. The children's positive attitudes towards school, schoolwork and education are noteworthy. The unit's students have made significant achievements in external competitions, such as the Manukau district speech competitions and Australian Maths competitions. The O le Taiala students do well in sports and other cultural competitions and events, and stand out from others in this respect. They carry a great deal of responsibility both in the unit and in the wider school; many of them play senior leadership roles as counsellors, peer mediators, role models and tutors for others. Beyond the school context, these students are able to maintain an active and valued membership of their family and community organisations. Churches in particular report that bilingual children continue to attend church and youth groups, and to adopt leadership roles there too. They are able to operate biculturally, and interact confidently with other children and adults from a range of cultures and backgrounds. Support for O le Taiala from local churches and other Samoan organisations is very strong.

When enrolling children at Finlayson Park, Samoan parents are now able to observe the Samoan bilingual programme option and to discuss it with staff, and they have a genuine choice. Most are choosing to enrol their children in O le Taiala. Parent participation in and around the school has increased dramatically. There is strong parental support for educational trips and visits, fundraising and community events. Parents indicate that they feel a real sense of ownership and control over their children's education. The requests to O le Taiala from other schools and organisations for displays of bilingual work and cultural performances continue to grow. This has helped build the students' self-esteem and confidence. Finlayson Park therefore enjoys the high levels of active and close scrutiny – and positive reporting – usually found only in New Zealand schools in high socio-economic areas.

Relationships between children and their families, parents and teachers, teachers and senior management are highly valued and positive. Senior staff now find that Samoan parents have the confidence to approach the school to ask questions and seek answers. The school attracts quality teachers who want to share and participate in these bilingual values and philosophy: they have a commitment both to the Samoan community's language, and to excellence in English literacy. The sick record of O le Taiala teachers is very low in comparison with that of many other schools. Relationships within the unit are very good: the principal attributes this to happy teachers and high levels of job satisfaction.

Where To From Here? Possible Developments at O le Taiala

Bilingual assessment measures need to be developed across the curriculum at Finlayson Park. For example, formal Year 8 assessment across several subject areas in both languages would provide useful summative data on children's achievement at graduation. The bilingual unit's programme could also be evaluated by entering its students into a wider range of external competitions, such as the Australian English and maths competitions.

At the same time, work will continue on refining assessment procedures in Samoan literacy and oracy, such as translating and adapting the SEKA (School Entry Kit Assessment) and the Six Year Net diagnostic assessments and using a standardised measure of reading assessment such as STAR (Elley, 2000)

Official information for parents needs to be more readily available in both Samoan and English: a regular bilingual school-wide newsletter would be a start in this direction

The high degree of staff commitment to the school and the fostering of positive relationships among teachers, and between teachers and the parents and community, need to be continued, as should networking through Ulimasao. Qualified bilingual teaching staff and teacher aides should continue to be recruited, and one of these could be detailed to produce more bilingual resource materials in various subject areas. A booklet on O le Taiala orientation and professional competencies could also be written as a first step towards the development of a Bilingual Teacher Certificate. This certificate could then be accredited by the school, as there are currently no national professional certification standards in New Zealand for teachers in bilingual education.

There is also a need to continue to develop the links between O le Taiala and the rest of the school. The school already runs 'buddy classes' and other initiatives to encourage cross-unit and cross-ethnic friendships and to assist relationships across the school.

A broad-based critical review of the work of the unit since 1996 could be undertaken: the first Year 1 students enrolled at that time graduated at the end of 2003. Such a review could identify the strengths and weaknesses of the programme and identify issues that can be addressed over the next eight years. In addition, the authors of this chapter plan to undertake a longitudinal study of biliteracy development in O le Taiala using a combination of critical literacy philosophies and strategies derived from critical pedagogies.

Planning for bilingual education provision in the secondary sector needs to begin in earnest. There is currently no surrounding secondary/high school that is willing, or able, to provide for the children's continued bilingual development. Recent research by Thomas and Collier (2002) shows that continued bilingual education provision into secondary school is essential for high levels of academic success in that sector.

Conclusion

The students of O le Taiala are unique. They come from low-income, Samoan-speaking homes – a background usually associated in New Zealand with low levels of overall academic achievement. They have had eight years of bilingual education, and have learned to listen, speak, read and write in both Samoan and in English – the latter to levels that appear to equate with their native English-speaking peers. They demonstrate an ability to move easily and bi-culturally between the worlds of school, home and the wider community. In the opinion of the school, they are well-balanced creative, enthusiastic outgoing young people who play leadership roles both inside the school and in the local churches and community. They, their school, their parents and teachers all seek to model the principles of empowerment that the project set out as essential minimum criteria for the success of minority-language students. These principles (Cummins 1989, 1996) are restated below:

- The students' home language and culture are incorporated into the school curriculum.
- The students, parents and community are able to participate in their children's education.
- The assessment policies and measures avoid locating problems in the students and seek, wherever possible, to identify causes and explanations in the structure and operation of schools and society.

There is still much work to be done. However, the *vaa* (canoe) of O le Taiala that carries us on our journey has made great progress. O le Taiala students came to school as five year olds in 1996. In 2003, they graduated from eight years in the programme and left the school for the next part of their voyage of discovery.

It is appropriate that we conclude our case study with some of their voices:

Being an O le Taiala student is very special. It feels like a family.

I like knowing how to speak my own language so I can speak to people who can speak Samoan.

I feel comfortable speaking in two languages because all my friends speak in two languages and we all can understand what each of us is saying.

I progressed a lot in O le Taiala and I thank the teachers for it.

When I left and went to high school, I only got to speak Samoan when we were in cultural groups or when we were with a group of Samoans.

You can go to two speech competitions – Samoan and English.

I like to read and write in both languages. I would not go to mainstream because they only speak one language.

You learn how to respect your own language and culture.

My first time at O le Taiala, I didn't know that they were all Samoan. When the teacher talked in Samoan, I was kind of happy.

I consider O le Taiala a very special place because we all act as one big family; even though we do fight sometimes.

I consider myself very lucky to be in O le Taiala and I am proud to be a Samoan.

References

Apple, M. (1999) *Power, Meaning and Identity: Essays in Critical Educational Studies.* New York: Peter Lang.

Aukuso, S. (2002) O le Taiala Samoan bilingual unit: A case study of the dual medium programme in the New Zealand context. MA thesis, University of Auckland.

Baker, C. (2001) *Foundations of Bilingual Education and Bilingualism* (3rd edn). Clevedon: Multilingual Matters.

Baker, C. and Prys-Jones, S. (1998) *Encyclopedia of Bilingualism and Bilingual Education.* Clevedon: Multilingual Matters

Bastiani, J and Wolfendale, S. (2000) *The Contribution of Parents to School Effectiveness.* Trowbridge: Cromwell Press Ltd.

Bell. A., Davis, K. and Starks, D. (2000) *Languages of the Manukau region: A Pilot Study of Use, Maintenance and Educational Dimensions of Languages in South Auckland.* Manukau City: Wolf Fisher Research Centre, University of Auckland.

Bell, A. Davis, K. and Starks, D. (2001) Māori and Pacific languages in Manukau: A preliminary study. *Many Voices* 17, 8–13.

Bishop, R. and Glynn, T. (1999) *Culture Counts: Changing Power Relationships in Education*. Palmerston North, New Zealand: Dunmore Press.

Collier, V.P. (1995) Acquiring a second language for school. In *Directions in Language and Education.* Washington, DC: National Clearinghouse for Bilingual Education. Online at: http://www.ncela.gwu.edu/ncbepubs/directions/indexhtm.

Corson, D. (2001) *Language Diversity and Education.* Mahwah. NJ: Lawrence Erlbaum.

Coxon, E., Anae, M., Mara, D., Wendt-Samu, I. and Finau, C. (2002) *Literature Review on Issues Facing Pacific Education.* Auckland, New Zealand: University of Auckland for the New Zealand Ministry of Education.

Crawford, J. (1992) *Hold Your Tongue: Bilingualism and the Politics of 'English Only'.* Reading, MA: Addison-Wesley.

Cummins, J. (1986) Empowering minority students: A framework for intervention. *Harvard Educational Review* 56 (1), 18–36.

Cummins, J. (1989) *Empowering Minority Students*. Sacramento, CA: Association for Bilingual Education.

Cummins, J. (1996) *Negotiating Identities: Education for Identity in a Diverse Society*. Ontario, CA: California Association for Bilingual Education.

Cummins, J. (2000) *Language, Power and Pedagogy: Bilingual Children in the Crossfire*. Clevedon: Multilingual Matters.

Cummins, J. and Nichols-McNeely, S. (1987) Language development, academic achievement and empowering minority students. In S. Frad and W. Tikunoff (eds) *Bilingual Education and Bilingual Special Education: A Guide for Administrators* (pp. 75–94). San Diego, CA: College Hill Press.

Education Review Office (1994) *Barriers to Learning*. Wellington: Education Review Office.

Education Review Office (1995) *Annual Report*. Wellington: Education Review Office.

Education Review Office (2002) *Finlayson Park School*. Wellington: Education Review Office.

Elley, W. (1992) *How in the World Do Students Read?* The Hague: International Association for Evaluation of Educational Achievement.

Elley, W. (2000) *STAR Supplementary Test of Achievement in Reading: Years 4–6*. Wellington: New Zealand Council for Educational Research.

Elley, W. and Croft, C. (1989) *Assessing the Difficulty of Reading Materials: The Noun Frequency Method*. Wellington: New Zealand Council for Educational Research.

Esera, I.O.F. (2001) Acquisition of English proficiency by students from Samoan speaking homes: An evaluative study. MEd thesis, Victoria University of Wellington.

Fanaafi, Le Tagaloa (1996) *O la ta Gagana*. Apia, Western Samoa: Lamepa Press.

Finlayson Park School Board of Trustees (2001) *Finlayson Park School Charter*. Manukau City, Auckland: Finlayson Park School.

Flockton, L. and Crooks, T. (2000) Reading and speaking: Assessment results 2000. *National Educational Monitoring Report (NEMP) 19*. Dunedin: Otago University for the Ministry of Education.

Flockton, L. and Crooks, T. (2001) Information skills 2001. *National Educational Monitoring Report (NEMP) 21*. Dunedin: Otago University for the Ministry of Education.

Freire, P. (1972) *Pedagogy of the Oppressed*. Harmondsworth: Penguin.

Foucault, M. (1980) *Truth and Power: Selected Interviews and Other Writings 1972–1977*. New York: Pantheon.

Gilmore, A., Croft, C. and Reid, N. (1981) *BURT Word Reading Test. Teachers Manual*. Wellington: New Zealand Council for Educational Research.

Giroux, H. (1997) *Pedagogy and the Politics of Hope: Theory, Culture and Schooling*. Boulder, CO: Westview.

Hunkin-Tuiletufuga, G. (2001) Pasefika languages and Pasefika identities: Contemporary and future challenges. In C. Macpherson, P. Spoonle and M. Anae (eds) *Tangata o Te Moana: Evolving Identities of Pacific peoples in Aotearoa New Zealand* (pp. 196–211). Palmerston North: Dunmore Press.

Jones, A. (1991) *At School I've Got a Chance*. Palmerston North: Dunmore Press.

Kincheloe, J. (2003) *Teachers as Researchers: Qualitative Inquiry as a Path to Empowerment*. New York: Routledge Falmer Press.

Lameta-Tufuga, E. (1994) Using Samoan language for academic learning tasks. MA thesis, Victoria University of Wellington.

Lankshear, C. (1998) *Literacy Schooling and Revolution*. London: Falmer Press.

McAllister Swap, S. (1993) *Developing Home School Partnerships: From Concepts to Practice.* New York: Teachers College Press.
McCaffery, J. (2000) Critical literacy: A NZ response. Paper presented at the 18th World IRA Congress on Reading, Auckland. Online at www. reading.org/critical literacy.
McCaffery, J. and Fuatavai, N. (2002) Read write succeed. Keynote address to the Ulimasao First National Pasifika Bilingual Education Conference, Auckland. Available at: http://www.geocities.com/ulimasao2002/.
McCaffery, J. and Tuafuti, P. (1998) The development of Pacific Islands bilingual education in Aotearoa/New Zealand. *Many Voices* 13, 11–16.
McLaren, P. (1997) *Revolutionary Multiculturalism; Pedagogies of Dissent for the New Millenium.* Boulder, CO: Westview Press.
May, S. (ed.) (1999) *Critical Multiculturalism: Rethinking Multicultural and Antiracist Education.* London: Falmer Press.
May, S. (2000) *Language, Education and Minority Rights*. London: Longman.
May, S. (2001) *Language and Minority Rights: Ethnicity, Nationalism and the Politics of Language*. Harlow: Pearson Education Limited.
Ministry of Education (2000) *2000 Educational Statistics.* Wellington: Ministry of Education, Data Management and Analysis Division.
Ministry of Education (2001) *2001 Educational Statistics.* Wellington: Ministry of Education, Data Management and Analysis Division.
Ministry of Education (2002a) *Talanoa Ako: Pacific Education Talk.* Issues 1–4. Wellington: Ministry of Education.
Ministry of Education (2002b) A draft policy for Pasifika bilingual education. Unpublished draft. Wellington: Ministry of Education.
NZEI (2002*) Report to Annual Meeting 2002: Pasifika Bilingual Education*. Wellington: New Zealand Educational Institute.
Pennycook, A. (2001) *Critical Applied Linguistics: A Critical Introduction*. Mahwah. NJ: Lawrence Erlbaum.
Reid, N. and Elley, W. (1991) *Progressive Achievement Tests of Reading.* Wellington: New Zealand Council for Educational Research.
Schlesinger, A (1992) *The Disuniting of America: Reflections on a Multicultural Society.* New York: W.W. Norton.
Shore, I. (1992) *Empowering Education: Critical Teaching for Social Change.* Chicago: University of Chicago Press.
Smith, J. and Elley, W. (1997*) How Children Learn to Read.* Auckland, New Zealand: AddisonWesley Longmann.
Spoonley, P., Mcpherson, C. and Anae, M. (2001) *Tangata o Te Moana Nui: The Evolving Identities of Pacific Peoples in Aotearoa/New Zealand.* Palmerston North: Dunmore Press.
Thomas, W.P. and Collier, V. P. (1995) *Language Minority Student Achievement and Programme Effectiveness: Research Summary.* Fairfax, VA: George Mason University.
Thomas, W.P. and Collier, V.P. (1997) School effectiveness for language minority students. *NCBE Resource Collection Series*, 9 December. Washington, DC: National Clearing House for Bilingual Education. Online at http://www.ncela.gwu.edu/ncbepubs/resource/effectiveness/thomas-collier97.pdf.

Thomas, W.P. and Collier, V.P. (2002) A national study of school effectiveness for language minority student's long-term academic success. Center for Research on Education, Diversity & Excellence (CREDE). Online at: http://www.crede.ucsc.edu/research/llaa/1.1_final.html

Tuafuti, P. (2000) Bridging the dichotomy between modern and traditional literacies in Samoan and English. *Many Voices* 15, 10–14.

Vopat, J. (1994) *The Parent Project*. Portland, MA: Stenhouse Publishers.

Walsh, C. (1991) *Pedagogy and the Struggle for Voice: Issues of Language, Power, and Schooling for Puerto Ricans*. Toronto: OISE Press.

Wolfendale, S. (1989) *Parental Involvement: Developing Networks Between School, Home and Community*. Oxford: Alden Press.

Young, R. (1990) *A Critical Theory of Education: Habermas and our Children's Future*. New York: Teachers College Press.

Chapter 5

A Five-Year-Old Samoan Boy Interacts with his Teacher in a New Zealand Classroom

ELAINE W. VINE

Immigrant Children Learning English in Primary School Mainstream Classes

In the USA, Carrasquillo and Rodriguez (2002) take the position that immigrant children learning English should be in bilingual or ESL (English as a second language) programmes. However, they acknowledge that such students are often placed in mainstream classes, and they argue that, in their class programmes, teachers need to address the students' English language development as well as their development in subject matter content and skills.

In the UK, policy and practice have moved from placing immigrant students who speak languages other than English in 'special English' classes or centres, to including them in mainstream classes where class teachers and special English teachers teach in 'partnership' to meet the needs of all learners (Levine, 1990; Mohan *et al.*, 2001) and/or with bilingual assistants in a 'support' role (Martin-Jones & Saxena, 2001). Both English language learning and curriculum learning take place in the mainstream. In practice, the role of the language specialist is more often 'support' role than partnership' role both in primary (Martin-Jones & Saxena, 2001) and in secondary (Creese, 2000) schools.

In Australia, as in the UK, policy and practice have moved from providing separate specialist ESL classes, to ESL teachers providing language support and team teaching in the mainstream (Mohan *et al.*, 2001). Clegg (1996) documents case studies of Australian, UK, USA and Canadian primary school classrooms where ESL and class teachers work together in mainstream classes.

In New Zealand, immigrant students are usually referred to as NESB (non-English-speaking background) students, and the programmes that are provided for them as ESOL (English for speakers of other languages) programmes (Kennedy & Dewar, 1997: 300). Although the importance of first language maintenance is recognised by many staff working with NESB students (Kennedy & Dewar, 1997: 244–247), it is not recognised in *The New Zealand Curriculum Framework* (Ministry of Education, 1993), and bilingual programmes for NESB students are very rare in New Zealand. As in the USA, not even ESOL programmes or specialist ESOL support are available to many NESB students. They are placed in mainstream classes, and the mainstream class teachers have to cope as best they can. In many cases, mainstream class teachers will have had little or no access to any training in how to address the needs of NESB students. McCloskey (2002: 3) reports an estimate that 45% of teachers in the USA have English learners in their classes, but only 12% of them have any training to work with such students.

Language learning and content area learning are interdependent. The following statement appears under 'Language and Languages' in 'The Essential Learning Areas' section of *The New Zealand Curriculum Framework:*

> Language development is essential to intellectual growth. It enables us to make sense of the world around us. The ability to use spoken and written language effectively, to read and to listen, and to discern critically messages from television, film, the computer, and other visual media is fundamental both to learning and to effective participation in society and the workforce. (Ministry of Education, 1993: 10)

This 'Language and Languages' section links directly to the English and te reo Māori (Māori language) curriculum documents, which dilutes the strength of the statement. The statement should have been included in 'The Principles' section of the document, where it would apply across the curriculum. In an analysis of the New Zealand national curriculum statements, Penton (1996) found extensive language expectations, both explicit and implicit, across all curriculum areas.

The *Curriculum Framework* focuses on language as communication by including 'communication skills' as an 'essential skill'. However, Mercer argues that:

> Language is designed for doing something much more interesting than transmitting information accurately from one brain to another: it allows the mental resources of individuals to combine in a collective, communicative intelligence which enables people to make better sense of the world and to devise practical ways of dealing with it. (Mercer, 2000: 6)

In the *Curriculum Framework*, the link between language and thinking and learning is at best implicit, and at worst lost. Language in the curriculum should be seen not just as the means by which students communicate what they are doing, but also as the means by which they develop their thinking and learning.

The English that NESB students need to participate effectively in social, conversational situations is not the same as the English they need to participate effectively in academic situations (Cummins, 1994). Teachers need to ensure that NESB students are supported as they develop the proficiency to participate effectively in both types of situation.

English is used differently in different curriculum contexts (Carrasquillo & Rodriguez, 2002; Forman *et al.*, 1997; Gillham, 1986; Lemke, 1990; Mohan, 1986; Vine, 1984, 1985, 1997). Students need to learn how to use language effectively to do social studies or maths, or any other subject. Mainstream teachers need to provide for teaching and learning the language of curriculum areas for all students, but particularly for NESB students.

Learning a language takes a long time. Studies in the USA (Collier, 1987, 1989) and Canada (Cummins, 1981) indicate that, while immigrant children can develop appropriate conversational skills in two years or so, they can take four to nine years to reach an adequate level of academic English proficiency. Even where ESOL programmes and/or specialist ESOL support is available in New Zealand schools, it is not provided over such a long time period. Thus mainstream teachers need to take responsibility for supporting language learning over the long period needed to develop proficiency in using English in academic situations.

Fa'afetai

At the time of the study, Fa'afetai was five years old. His family had immigrated to New Zealand from Samoa. At least three languages were in use in his home among members of his extended family: Samoan, Niuean and English. Fa'afetai had been attending a mainstream class at school for about six weeks. English was the main medium of instruction at school, and Fa'afetai was in the early stages of learning English.

The Case Study

This study investigates opportunities for learning available to Fa'afetai in a mainstream class. Following the ideas of Vygotsky (1978) and others such as Lave and Wenger (1991), Rogoff (1990, 1995), Wells (1999) and Wertsch (1991), learning is viewed as a sociocultural process that is constructed between and among people, and occurs through joint activity.

Language is seen as the main tool that mediates learning. Thus, this study focuses on interactions in the classroom as possible opportunities for learning.

The study has drawn on the work of the Santa Barbara Classroom Discourse Group (see, for example, Santa Barbara Classroom Discourse Group, 1992a, 1992b; Green & Dixon, 1993; Tuyay *et al.*, 1995; Crawford *et al.*, 1997). This takes an ethnographic perspective on understanding:

> ... how everyday life in classrooms is constructed by members through their interactions, verbal and other, and how these constructions influence what students have opportunities to access, accomplish, and thus 'learn' in schools. (Green & Dixon, 1993: 231)

I examine how Fa'afetai and his teacher constructed opportunities for learning the languaculture (Agar, 1994) of the class. Agar coined the term 'languaculture' to encapsulate what he sees as the necessary link between language and culture. Furthermore, I situate Fa'afetai's case study within the context of a social studies curriculum unit in a mainstream class at Roadrunner School, a primary school in New Zealand, taking account of the view that in order to understand what is going on in a classroom, we also need to look at the institutional context (Gebhard, 1999).

The data come from a collaborative research programme, called Educational Research Underpinning Development in Teacher Education (ERUDITE) (Alton-Lee, 1999; Alton-Lee *et al.*, 2001). ERUDITE used a microethnographic data collection process developed by Alton-Lee and Nuthall (1992) in their classroom research methodology. This study follows very closely the events and discourse of one curriculum unit of study in a class. Multiple video, audio, and observational records of classroom life during the unit allow for a close analysis of the experiences of the children and the teacher, and their use of language during the unit. Information beyond the classroom comes primarily from interviews with the class teacher and with other members of the school staff.

Roadrunner School

Roadrunner School (a pseudonym) is a state primary school on the outskirts of a metropolitan area adjoining the capital city, Wellington. Roadrunner's mission statement from its school charter is 'To provide a learning environment that will develop positive self-esteem and guide children towards attaining their full potential.'

At the time of this study, Roadrunner catered for five to eleven year olds and had six classes, six full-time teachers, a non-teaching principal, and two teacher aides. There were 125 children enrolled at the school, of whom

64% were Pakeha (New Zealanders of European descent), 26% Māori, 6% Samoan, 2% Tokelauan and 2% Rarotongan. The ethnicities reported here are those entered by the children's parents in the school's enrolment records.

The Ministry of Education had assessed Roadrunner School as a decile 3 school on its socio-economic indicator for schools (a 1–10 scale on which a decile 1 school is judged to draw on a community of the lowest socio-economic mix). Deciles 1–3 are classified in the low socio-economic band.

Ms Nikora's class

The data reported here were collected during a social studies curriculum unit in Fa'afetai's Year 0/1 class of five-year-old school beginners. There were 18 children in the class, eight girls and ten boys. The class teacher was Ms Nikora, who was Māori and spoke Māori but not Samoan. Almost half the children in the class were Māori; some of them spoke Māori, but others spoke little or none. There was one Samoan child in the class other than Fa'afetai; she spoke English but not Samoan. The rest of the children were English-speaking European New Zealanders. The names of all participants are pseudonyms.

For Ms Nikora and all the children except Fa'afetai, English was their main language of use. English was the main medium of instruction at school, and Māori was also used in the class.

Having a new class member was not unusual, because New Zealand has a policy of continuous entry to school. Children begin school at any time during the year, as they turn five. At the time of the study, Fa'afetai was the most recent entrant in the class, but three other children had entered in the month before him, and two in the month before that. What was unusual for the class was that Fa'afetai was a beginner at learning English. This was also new for Ms Nikora. She was an experienced teacher and the Deputy Principal of the school, but she had never before had an English beginner join her class. It was also unusual for this school, and the school had no ESOL policy or programme.

Ms Nikora's classroom had a large mat on the floor in a very central position right in front of the board. Almost all whole-class activities took place on the mat, and a lot of pair and small group work took place there as well. The children were grouped together, the teacher explained what was to happen, and then they worked together in pairs or small groups on the mat. There were also some small tables and chairs in the classroom and other designated zones for activities such as painting and library work.

The social studies curriculum unit

The study focused on a social studies curriculum unit entitled 'Christmas in Hospital'. This was designed by Ms Nikora, who wanted to focus on what Christmas means to different people and the different ways that people experience it in the diverse community she was working in. She also wanted to address physical disability, which was relevant and real to the children because they all knew Zack, an older boy at the school who had spina bifida and used a wheelchair. Ms Nikora found a teaching resource that connected the two issues: a set of pictures and accompanying story about Tyler, a boy who had spina bifida and had to spend a Christmas in hospital (Smythe, 1996). Through the unit of study, Ms Nikora connected Tyler's story, Zack's experience, the children's experiences with Zack, the experience of classroom visitors from community health institutions, the children's personal experiences of hospitals, and the children's personal experiences of Christmas (Alton-Lee *et al.*, 2000; Alton-Lee *et al.*, 2001; Vine *et al.*, 2000).

Ms Nikora chose to work intensively on the 'Christmas in Hospital' unit with her class over three school days in one week towards the end of the school year, which in New Zealand is December. The class worked on the unit for three sessions of about an hour each on each of the three days, for a total of nine hours and eighteen minutes of class time. The first session each day was in the first half of the morning, about 9.30 am to 10.30 am, followed by a morning tea break. The second session was in the second half of the morning, about 11.00 am to noon. The third session was after the lunch break, about 1.30pm to 2.30pm.

Interactions between Fa'afetai and Ms Nikora

I have chosen to explore one-to-one spoken interactions between Fa'afetai and Ms Nikora during the social studies unit as a site for learning. New Zealand teachers who work with NESB students believe that one-to-one interaction is important in fostering their learning (Kennedy & Dewar, 1997: 221–224). I define 'one-to-one' not by who is present, but by who is addressing whom. Other children, or indeed the whole class, may have been immediately present but, if Ms Nikora directly addressed Fa'afetai, or if Fa'afetai directly addressed Ms Nikora, I have included the interaction as 'one-to-one'. I have examined the opportunities those interactions provided for Fa'afetai's learning of English, social studies content, and the practices he needed to participate in the curriculum unit. I explore how they jointly searched for shared contextual understanding to underpin their sense-making processes (Mercer, 2000).

I focus on interactions in which Fa'afetai and Ms Nikora were addressing aspects of the social studies content of the curriculum unit. Wells (1996) identifies two levels, macro and micro, at which teachers realise in practice their responsibilities to their students:

> At the macro level, the teacher is the chief initiator and is responsible, among other things, for selecting the themes for curricular units and the activities through which they are to be addressed ...
>
> At the micro level, by contrast, teaching can be characterised much more in terms of response. Having created the setting and provided the challenge, the teacher observes how students take it up, both individually and collectively, and acts to assist them in whatever way seems most appropriate to enable them to achieve the goals that have been negotiated. (Wells, 1996: 83)

The focus in this study is at the micro level of one-to-one spoken interactions between Fa'afetai and Ms Nikora. These were the times when Fa'afetai and Ms Nikora were orienting specifically to each other, so they were likely to be attending to the languaculture of the class (since Fa'afetai was a beginner at learning English and Ms Nikora did not speak Samoan).

While the focus is at the micro level, this account also situates interactions at the macro level. Clearly these were not all the opportunities for learning available to Fa'afetai. However, my concern in this instance is to explore how their interactions might have mediated Fa'afetai's learning through examining what opportunities Ms Nikora and Fa'afetai constructed for learning aspects of the languaculture of the class, and how they constructed the opportunities.

Transcripts as Representations of Interactions

The research team transcribed video and audio data from the three days of the curriculum unit. Research assistants transcribed all of the data, and researchers transcribed some sections in parallel with the research assistants and checked other sections of their transcriptions.

When transcribing, we tried to represent what we could see and hear from the audio and videotapes, that is, the participants' utterances and acts. In this process, we attempted to minimise interpretation, while recognising that it is impossible to avoid it entirely (Ochs, 1979; Green *et al.*, 1997; Baker, 1997). We took this approach for two reasons. Erickson (1986) calls qualitative research 'interpretive', because interpretation is at the centre of the research process. It is important to make the nature of that interpretation as evident as possible. The second reason is that the whole project was a collaborative one, with different members of the research team drawing on the data to follow their own research questions. We found that the approach we took allowed us to recognise explicitly that interpretations are contestable, and helped to ensure that we held each other accountable for supporting our interpretations from the available evidence.

Transcript conventions

In the transcripts included in this chapter, the first column shows real time (in hour, minutes and 15 second intervals, e.g. 09:33:45). The second column shows speaker and addressee, e.g. MsN/F indicates that Ms Nikora is speaking and she appears to be addressing Fa'afetai. The third column shows the speakers' utterances.

?	rising intonation
underline	part of an utterance that occurred at the same time as another utterance
(softly)	brief description of how the utterance was said
[F smiles]	brief description of what participants were doing, on the same line if utterance and action were simultaneous, on a new line if theywere sequential
{MsN continues}	brief description of interruptions to or continuations of transcribed interactions

The transcripts have allowed us to search for and identify key events relating to participants in the ongoing life of the classroom. Identification of key events has then been checked by reference to the actual data, the videotapes and audiotapes. Description, analysis and discussion of the data draw not only on the transcripts but also on the videotapes and audiotapes on which the transcripts are based.

Managing Fa'afetai's access to the floor in whole class situations

In early work on classroom interaction, Sinclair and Coulthard (1975) in the UK and Mehan (1979) in the USA showed how teachers control the floor in their classrooms. Recently, Martin-Jones and Saxena (2001) have shown how class teachers even control the access of other teachers and teaching assistants to the floor in their classrooms. Control of access to the floor is thus an important aspect of classroom life. Let us consider how Ms Nikora and Fa'afetai managed his access to the floor in class, thus affording opportunities for them to talk about curriculum content-related material.

Ms Nikora began the social studies curriculum unit with an activity in which the children worked in pairs to solve and talk about a Father Christmas jigsaw puzzle. After the puzzle activity, and packing up and putting away the puzzles, Ms Nikora began a whole class activity. She had the class sit in a circle and she said to them, 'We're going to go round in a circle and I'm going to ask you what you think our study might be about from the jigsaw puzzle.' Huhana was sitting next to Fa'afetai in the circle. Ms Nikora called on Huhana first to ask what she thought it (the study) might be about. Huhana said 'Father Christmas'. Ms Nikora then went around the circle away from Fa'afetai, which meant that she called on him last. Other responses were: puzzles, sleigh, presents, parrot, Christmas 'contation', Christmas tree, Christmas decorations, hospitals. For all this time, Fa'afetai had been looking at Ms Nikora or at the large sheet of paper on a display easel on which she was writing the children's responses, or briefly from time to time, at Huhana who was sitting next to him. Finally, Ms Nikora called on Fa'afetai:

Example 1: Interaction 1.4 – Talking about the study

09:40:30		[F is watching MsN]
	MsN/F:	Fa'afetai what do you think it's going to be about?
	F/MsN:	Christmas tree
		[F smiles and rocks back]
	MsN/F:	a Christmas tree
		that's great
	MsN/class:	ok stand up please
		[F stands up]

Ms Nikora allowed Fa'afetai access to the floor in this whole class activity by allocating him a turn by nominating him. Furthermore, Ms Nikora had already noted some shared contextual understanding with Fa'afetai in her interaction with him during the previous jigsaw activity in pairs. She heard him say the words 'Christmas' and 'Christmas tree', although she acknowledged only one of his utterances at that time.

By leaving Fa'afetai till last in this circle activity, Ms Nikora gave him many opportunities to see and hear other children responding. She was establishing further shared contextual understanding here of what the activity was and how to participate in it appropriately. Fa'afetai was supported by the predictable (taking turns around the circle) and repetitive (asking and answering the same question) nature of the activity.

When it was his turn, Fa'afetai responded appropriately, both in terms of curriculum content and in terms of English, thus demonstrating to himself and others that he was a legitimate participant in this particular class activity. Ms Nikora gave Fa'afetai access to the floor by nominating him, drawing on their shared contextual understanding to create an opportunity for him. Fa'afetai drew on this understanding to take up that opportunity.

A little later in Session 1, Ms Nikora had asked the children to talk with a partner about 'what you think is happening in this picture'. The picture was a close-up of a sleeping face, Tyler sleeping with his head on a pillow and the bed covers up to his shoulders. After the partner activity, Ms Nikora gained the attention of the class by clapping, and as she spoke the children moved closer to her to form a class group.

Example 2: Interaction 1.8 – Tyler might die

09:46:00 **MsN/class:** hands up if you can tell me what you think is happening in the picture [F and William are sitting outside the class group]

MsN/F: um Fa'afetai what do you think is happening in there [F turns his head to MsN when he hears his name]

M/MsN: he might die

MsN/F: pardon Fa'afetai

F/MsN: might die (very softly)
he might die (very softly)

MsN/F: he's going to sleep

09:46:15 yes that's right you told me that he was going to sleep [F is looking at MsN, he leans away from William
and sits up straight]

MsN/Ba: what do you think Barry

This time in the class group, Ms Nikora called on Fa'afetai first. When she nominated him, he transferred his attention from William to her. He had just given her an appropriate response to this question in a one-to-one interaction during the previous partner activity. Monique usurped Fa'afetai's turn with her unsolicited response. But Ms Nikora did not acknowledge Monique's turn. Instead, she re-established Fa'afetai's turn by nominating him again. Fa'afetai responded by copying Monique's unsolicited response but he did this so quietly that Ms Nikora could not hear him. She responded to him as if he had given the same response as in their previous interaction and she used the same sentence in confirming his contribution, linking it explicitly to the shared understanding they had arrived at then: 'you told me that he was going to sleep' (09:46:15).

In both these interactions with Fa'afetai, 1.4 (Example 1) and 1.8 (Example 2), Ms Nikora drew directly on the previous partner activities as a basis for class discussion. In the previous interactions she noticed or established a shared contextual understanding with him, and she drew on that to include him as a legitimate participant in the subsequent whole class activity. Furthermore, in 1.8, she included Fa'afetai in the class activity by keeping the floor open for him, in spite of Monique's unsolicited response to her question.

There are differences, though, between 1.4 and 1.8. In 1.4, Ms Nikora used a 'round the circle' format to allocate turns. This meant that she could provide repeated opportunities for Fa'afetai to observe others answering the same question within a predictable turn allocation process. At the beginning of this process and throughout it, Fa'afetai focused his attention on Ms Nikora and on the paper she was recording the children's responses on. However, in 1.8, Ms Nikora opted for a 'hands up' process of bidding for a turn. At the beginning of this process, Fa'afetai was sitting outside the class group, and his attention was not focused on Ms Nikora. In this case, she called on him first, even though he had not made a bid for a turn, perhaps to draw him into the class group.

Fa'afetai also played his part in gaining access to the floor in whole class situations. At the beginning of Session 4, the children were sitting in a group on the mat in front of Ms Nikora. Ms Nikora had asked the class to remember what they had learned on the previous day. William, who was sitting next to Fa'afetai, had contributed 'spina bifida':

Example 3: Interaction 4.1 – Spina bifida

09:30:45 **MsN/class:** can we all say that
class/MsN: spina bifida
MsN/class: can anyone <u>remember</u>
F/MsN <u>spina bifida</u> (loudly)
MsN/class: anyone remember what spina bifida is [F covers his mouth with his hands, rocks slightly and smiles]
can anyone remember [W puts his hand up]
ok William [F puts his hand straight up in the air]
09:31:00 would you like to explain [W puts his hand down, F looks at W and puts his hand down]
F/?: oh (softly)
W/MsN: you have a bend in your backbone
MsN/W: mmhm
MsN/class: is there anything else that anyone else would like to add [F looks at the board, then MsN, he puts his hand up]
MsN/F: Fa'afetai [F puts his hand down to his mouth]
F/MsN: uh [F smiles]
MsN/class: ok [F shakes his head]

{Ms Nikora goes on to take contributions from other children}

Fa'afetai used a strategy here of copying what other children were doing. He was searching for an understanding of how to participate effectively in this context. The other children all said 'spina bifida' out loud (09:30:45) and Fa'afetai did too, but just after the others so he overlapped with Ms Nikora's next turn. Covering his mouth with his hand, rocking and smiling, all suggest that he realised that he had got the timing wrong.

When Ms Nikora asked her question, William put his hand up, the only child to do so (09:30:45). Fa'afetai then put his hand up too, just as Ms Nikora was nominating William. Fa'afetai showed his understanding of the nominating practice by putting his hand down when William was nominated. Evidence that he understood the practice, and was not simply copying William again is that Fa'afetai said 'oh' softly.

When Ms Nikora solicited bids again by saying 'is there anything else that anyone else would like to add?' (09:31:00), Fa'afetai put his hand up again. This time he was not copying anyone else because he was the only one to put his hand up. Ms Nikora nominated him. He had made a successful bid for the floor this time, but then he did not take his turn, though he showed that he understood he was supposed to by putting his hand down to his mouth, saying 'uh' and smiling. As Ms Nikora moved to go on with the lesson, saying 'ok', Fa'afetai shook his head, again signalling that he realised he had not yet got his participation in this practice quite right. Mehan (1979: 139) claims that 'effective participation in classroom lessons involves the integration of interactional skills and academic knowledge', and he describes what Fa'afetai did here as 'form without content' (Mehan, 1979: 137). In this instance, Fa'afetai showed that he knew how to gain access to the floor, but he did not know what to do with it once he had it.

Throughout this interaction, Ms Nikora was focusing on the content of the social studies curriculum unit, while Fa'afetai was focusing on how to participate in the ongoing activity. Fa'afetai was searching for understanding of the choral-response practice and the turn-bidding practice as ways of gaining access to the floor, while Ms Nikora and the other children were treating these as taken-for-granted aspects of their shared contextual understanding.

Managing Fa'afetai's access to the floor in small group situations

In Session 7, Ms Nikora had a discussion with the class about pictures in the Tyler series. Then she spread the pictures around on the floor and asked the children to walk around and talk about the pictures with a partner. She bent down beside Fa'afetai, who was looking at a picture. The picture showed Tyler sitting up in a hospital bed, a tray of toys on the bed, and Tyler's mother standing beside the bed holding a helicopter bubble machine for Tyler to make bubbles. Ms Nikora initiated an interaction with Fa'afetai:

Example 4: Interaction 7.13 – Blowing bubbles

09:56:15	**MsN/F:**	Fa'afetai what's happening in this picture? what's Tyler doing in this picture?
	F/MsN:	uuhh
09:56:30	**Ba/MsN:**	blowing bubbles
	MsN/F:	have we blown bubbles before? [F is looking at the picture]
	F/MsN:	blow bubbles
	MsN/F:	blow bubbles
	F/MsN:	ooh nooo [F points to helicopter bubble machine in picture]
	MsN/F:	yes that's a special one that makes bubbles how did we blow the bubbles
	F/MsN:	weeee [shakes head]
	MsN/F:	how did we blow the bubbles [F looks up at MsN]
09:56:45		we went [MsN makes a circle with thumb and forefinger and blows, puts her arm up then shakes her fingers down] [F makes a circle with his thumb and forefinger and blows through it] [MsN blows twice] yes that's right and they went up in the air didn't they? they went right up right up to the roof and right down [F blows hard]

Ms Nikora gave Fa'afetai access to the floor by nominating him and asking a question, 'what's happening in the picture?' In this first question to Fa'afetai, she focused him on the activity (responding to the picture) and the curriculum content (what is happening in the picture). Wertsch (1985) calls this 'introducing a referential perspective'. When people refer to things, they have a choice of ways to do so. These range from using expressions that involve strategy-based referential perspectives, where their communicative partner needs to understand the purpose of the task they are engaged in to understand the expressions, to using deictic expressions (such as non-verbal or verbal pointing) that allow their communicative partner to understand what they are talking about without necessarily understanding the nature or purpose of the task. In order to understand what Ms Nikora means by 'what do you think is happening in the picture?', Fa'afetai needs to understand the purpose of the task they are engaged in and be aware of appropriate strategies for completing the task.

Ms Nikora then held the floor open for him by rephrasing her question, using a specific reference that related more closely to the picture, 'what's Tyler doing in this picture?' (09:56:15). When a child appears not to understand, an adult often responds by referring to other shared knowledge, in this case, identifying Tyler in the picture. Ms Nikora was attempting to build a shared contextual frame of reference with Fa'afetai, drawing on their shared 'common knowledge' (Edwards & Mercer, 1987) that the boy in the picture was Tyler.

After her second question, Fa'afetai signalled that he understood that it was his turn to speak by saying 'uuhh'. Barry usurped Fa'afetai's turn and answered Ms Nikora's question. Ms Nikora drew on Barry's answer, but continued speaking to Fa'afetai. She made a link with their previous shared experience when they had blown bubbles in class: 'have we blown bubbles before?' (09:56:30). Fa'afetai's response named the action, 'blow bubbles'. He repeated words from her turn, but in this case, he was not just repeating the last words she said, as he did on other occasions (e.g. in Interaction 6.8, see Example 8 below), so it seems that the words 'blow bubbles' had particular salience for him.

Ms Nikora confirmed Fa'afetai's 'blow bubbles' response by repeating it. Fa'afetai then noticed the helicopter bubble machine in the picture. Ms Nikora again made a link with their previous shared experience through her question, 'how did we blow the bubbles?' Fa'afetai looked at Ms Nikora, but did not respond. She then answered her own question, demonstrating their previous shared experience non-verbally for Fa'afetai, then commenting on it verbally (09:56:45). Ms Nikora often used gesture and actions to support the development of shared understanding with Fa'afetai. He copied her non-verbal demonstration.

Ms Nikora kept the floor open for Fa'afetai in spite of Barry's response to her question. She focused their joint attention both verbally and non-verbally on curriculum-relevant concepts.

A little later, Fa'afetai, Barry and Ms Nikora were looking at a picture that showed Tyler in his wheelchair with a Christmas tree nearby. Ms Nikora initiated an interaction with Fa'afetai:

Example 5: Interaction 7.14 – Wheelchair

Time	Speaker	Utterance
09:58:00	**MsN/F:**	what's this?
		can you remember what this was called? [F leans over and wipes his hand over the picture]
	F/MsN:	Christmas tree
	MsN/F:	there's the Christmas tree in the back
		but what's this?
09:58:15	**F/MsN:**	car [F is obscured]
	Ba/MsN:	wheelchair
	MsN/F:	it's like a car
		it's a wheelchair [F is looking at picture]
		that's right
	F/MsN:	wheelchair
	MsN/F:	yes
		who's got a wheelchair at school [F picks up picture]
	?/MsN:	Zack
	MsN/?:	Zack
09:58:30	**Si/MsN:**	I saw a big one
	MsN/Si:	you saw?
	Si/MsN:	a big one

Ms Nikora gave Fa'afetai the floor by asking him to name the wheelchair. Fa'afetai had been more interested in Christmas trees than almost anything else during the three days – he kept coming back to them, and in this case named the Christmas tree that was in the picture. Ms Nikora acknowledged his response by reformulating it, relating it in a more specific way to the picture: the Christmas tree is 'in the back' (09:58:00). She then drew his attention to the wheelchair and he named it 'car'.

In Session 2, the class watched a video, *Curious George goes to hospital*, in which George (a monkey) got into a wheelchair and ran amok crashing into things. The narrator and a character in the video both referred to the wheelchair as a 'go-cart'. Fa'afetai watched the video intently. When the character referred to the wheelchair as a go-cart, Fa'afetai said 'go car' to himself. It is possible that in his response to Ms Nikora's question here in Session 7, Fa'afetai drew on his previous experience of watching the video when he called the wheelchair 'car'.

Barry corrected Fa'afetai's response by saying 'wheelchair'. Ms Nikora took up Fa'afetai's response 'car', even though it seemed not to answer her question. She searched for shared contextual understanding by reformulating his response as 'like a car', and only then confirmed Barry's naming of it as 'wheelchair'. Again, in this interaction, she kept the floor open for Fa'afetai in spite of another child contributing to the interaction.

Wheelchairs were a curriculum focus, and she extended that to Zack, another curriculum focus, holding the floor open for Fa'afetai by asking him another question, 'who's got a wheelchair at school?' (09:58:15). As she asked the question, Fa'afetai picked up the picture, and by doing so indicated to Ms Nikora that they no longer shared joint attention. At that point, Ms Nikora no longer kept the floor open for Fa'afetai. She allowed other children the floor to contribute curriculum content-related comments.

Fa'afetai takes his turn

As we have seen, there were occasions when Fa'afetai did not take the floor when Ms Nikora offered it to him. However, on other occasions he showed that he did know when it was his turn to speak, and took his turn in responding to Ms Nikora by using single words or short phrases. On yet other occasions he used other strategies in order to take up his turn.

Near the end of Session 2, after a brief class discussion, Ms Nikora asked the children to 'draw what would make you feel happier if you went into hospital or what if you went to visit someone you might take them to make them feel happier'. She then handed out their thinking books – blank books that she had given the children in Session 1. Several times during the unit, she asked the children to think about some aspect of the curriculum content and draw about it in their thinking books. She adapted the thinking book concept for young children from Swan and White's (1990, 1994) work with older children which requires students to record what they have learnt, to make links with their prior experiences and knowledge, and to generate questions.

After she had handed out the thinking books, Ms Nikora initiated an interaction with Fa'afetai:

Example 6: Interaction 2.27 – Feel happy in hospital

12:01:15		[F is looking at MsN handing out thinking books]
	MsN/F:	Fa'afetai
	F/MsN:	oo
	MsN/F:	on this page Fa'afetai
		what would make you feel happy in hospital
	F/MsN:	umm
		[F stands up, moves and touches TV]

	MsN/F:	yes watching TV
		[F takes thinking book and begins to move away]
12:01:30	**F/MsN:**	watching TV
		bye bye

Ms Nikora gave Fa'afetai access to the floor by asking him a question. Fa'afetai responded first with 'umm', a filler that allowed him to signal that he knew it was his turn to speak. He then used a non-verbal gesture, touching the TV. Ms Nikora took that as a response and reformulated Fa'afetai's gesture as a verbal utterance to acknowledge and confirm it: 'yes watching TV'. In her confirming response, Ms Nikora modelled for Fa'afetai how he could have responded verbally. What Fa'afetai's gesture did was move the interaction on, because Ms Nikora then had the opportunity to accommodate to his response.

In an interview, Ms Nikora commented on the importance of non-verbal acts and shared experience as a basis for participating in class discussion activities. She gave the example of a class trip to the swimming pool that occurred after the 'Christmas in Hospital' unit:

> Fa'afetai enjoyed the trip, and he found ways of joining in class discussion afterwards. The class was brainstorming, 'We went to the pool and what did we do?' Fa'afetai couldn't say 'hydroslide', but he acted it out with a 'whomph!'

In Session 9, Fa'afetai was drawing. Ms Nikora asked him a question, then reformulated it in more specific terms:

Example 7: Interaction 9.6 – Skipping rope

13:54:00	**MsN/F:**	what's this one Fa'afetai?
		can you do the skipping rope?
		[F glances at MsN]
	F/MsN:	mm?
	MsN/F:	can you do the skipping rope [makes a circling motion with her hand]
	F/MsN:	yip [F jumps out of his chair and pretends to skip]
	MsN/F:	can you draw the skipping rope? [makes a drawing motion with her hand]
		[F moves back to his picture]
13:54:15		[F begins drawing a big semi-circle]
	MsN/F:	ohh that's good
		[MsN points to the part F has just drawn]
		skipping rope

		[F nods]
		yes
		[F changes crayons]
13:54:30		[MsN points to F's picture]
	MsN/F:	where's the handles?
		what colour are the handles?
	F/MsN:	(unclear)
	MsN/F:	they're green aren't they
		[F draws]
		the green bits
		{F changes crayons, MsN speaks to another child}

Fa'afetai took up his turn by responding 'mm?', seeking clarification. When she repeated her question, Ms Nikora used gesture to support Fa'afetai's understanding. Fa'afetai interpreted Ms Nikora's question as being about skipping rather than about drawing. He responded verbally 'yip' and nonverbally by showing her that he knew how to skip. Ms Nikora asked her question again, this time substituting the more specific verb 'draw' for the general verb 'do' and using a drawing gesture to support Fa'afetai's understanding.

Fa'afetai responded nonverbally by beginning to draw, and Ms Nikora named what he was drawing 'skipping rope'. Fa'afetai took his turn by acknowledging her comment nonverbally with a nod. Ms Nikora then went on to ask about the handles. Again, Fa'afetai's nonverbal responses served to move the interaction on. He also showed his understanding of the turn-taking process when he did not take a turn when Ms Nikora asked 'they're green aren't they' (13:54:30). Ms Nikora showed that she interpreted this as indicating that he did not wish to continue with the interaction by initiating an interaction with another child.

In Session 6, Ms Nikora was reading to the class from a picture book, *Rita Goes to Hospital.* The picture showed Rita in a hospital bed breathing into a mask and the doctor breathing into a mask:

Example 8: Interaction 6.8 – Doctor

13:46:30	**MsN/class:**	then the doctor came in [reading aloud, F is touching E's leg]
		hi Rita [reading aloud, F runs his fingers along E's leg]
		let's put on our masks and do a little breathing he said [reading aloud]

	MsN/F:	Fa'afetai
		[F looks at E then at MsN, he is smiling]
13:46:45		can you see the doctor [points to the picture in the book]
	F/MsN:	doctor [looks at the book]
		{MsN continues reading from the picture book, F continues looking at the book for a few seconds, then looks at E and touches his leg again}

Fa'afetai was making playful physical contact with a classmate, rather than paying attention to the class activity (see Vine, 2003, regarding Fa'afetai reconstructing teacher-assigned activities as joint physical play activities). Ms Nikora got his attention by saying his name, and then reminded him that he should be engaged in listening to the story by asking him a question about it. Fa'afetai signalled that he shared her understanding of the 'listen to a story' practice, by looking at the book, responding to her question (repeating 'doctor') and continuing to look at the book, at least for a short while, when Ms Nikora started reading aloud again.

A strategy that Fa'afetai used to take up his turn in interactions with Ms Nikora was to repeat the last word in her preceding turn. Their interaction is 'dialogic' (Bakhtin, 1981, 1986; Maybin, 1994: 132), not just in the sense that they are taking turns in a conversation, but in the sense that their meanings, intentions and responses are closely interwoven and interdependent. Bakhtin argues that:

> We know our native language – its lexical composition and grammatical structure – not from dictionaries and grammars but from concrete utterances that we hear and that we ourselves reproduce in live speech communication with people around us. (Bakhtin, 1986: 78)

We can see Fa'afetai here reproducing part of Ms Nikora's utterance as he endeavoured to participate in speech communication in a second language. As Bakhtin also wrote:

> When we select words in the process of constructing an utterance ... We usually take them from *other utterances*'. (Bakhtin, 1986: 87)

Fa'afetai has taken his word very directly from Ms Nikora's utterance, but he has not simply taken her meaning. Bakhtin further claims that:

> The word in language is half someone else's. It becomes 'one's own' only when the speaker populates it with his own intention, his own accent, when he appropriates the word, adapting it to his own semantic and expressive intention. (Bakhtin, 1981: 293)

Fa'afetai adapted Ms Nikora's word to his own intention. His strategy meant that he did not actually answer her question. He may not even have intended to say anything about the doctor, but we can see from his word and his associated actions (looking at the book and continuing to look at it as Ms Nikora continued to read from it) that he indicated that he was paying attention and making an effort to participate appropriately in the turn-taking process.

Fa'afetai took his words from other children, as well as from Ms Nikora. In Interaction 1.8 (Example 2 above), he used this strategy of repeating someone else's words to take his turn when he copied Monique's unsolicited response 'he might die' in his response to Ms Nikora's question.

It was usually Ms Nikora who initiated one-to-one interactions with Fa'afetai, but Fa'afetai did initiate on a few occasions when he had come across something that interested him.

In Session 8, Ms Nikora was explaining the next activity to the class. They were going to make cards for the children that have to spend their Christmas in hospital. Ms Nikora had some old Christmas cards for them to look at to get ideas. Fa'afetai leaned across the table and picked up a Christmas card:

Example 9: Interaction 8.16 – Santa

11:17:30	**F/MsN:**	look the kismas tree [holds card up to MsN]
	MsN/F:	yes
		that is santa [points at the card F is holding]
	MsN/class:	ok [F looks around the table at the cards]
		{MsN continues giving instructions to the class}

Although he had interrupted her explanation to the class, Ms Nikora acknowledged and accepted Fa'afetai's comment. She then expanded on it by identifying Santa on the card. She acknowledged Fa'afetai as a legitimate participant, and built on their shared contextual understanding of 'Christmas' by adding the identification of 'Santa'.

How Ms Nikora and Fa'afetai worked together to further his learning

Ms Nikora's way of organising her class facilitated one-to-one interactions. She planned a range of activities for the children to do either individually, with a partner, or in small groups. She explained a task to the class, then the children worked on it and she moved around the room talking to individuals or small groups about what they were doing. The one-to-one interactions between Fa'afetai and Ms Nikora that I have analysed here occurred either as part of class discussions or as she moved among the children in this way.

Ms Nikora gave Fa'afetai access to the floor, both in whole class and in small group situations, often drawing on their shared contextual understanding to create opportunities for him. He drew on this shared understanding to take up such opportunities. Once Ms Nikora and Fa'afetai had begun an interaction, she kept the floor open for him in spite of incursions by other children. She allowed another child the floor during an interaction with Fa'afetai only if that child asked a legitimate question about the activity they were engaged in, or if Fa'afetai indicated that they no longer shared joint attention.

Ms Nikora observed what Fa'afetai said and did in classroom activities, so that she extended her understanding of what he knew. She then drew on that shared contextual understanding from previous classroom activities to create opportunities for Fa'afetai to participate in classroom activities. She linked past activities to present ones and thus emphasised the value of past experience.

She provided opportunities for Fa'afetai to observe other children participating in activities. Fa'afetai's participation in activities and his demonstration of knowledge of relevant curriculum content were thus supported by predictability and repetition. For his part, Fa'afetai observed other children as a basis for having a go at participating himself.

At times Fa'afetai was searching for understanding of classroom practices that were taken for granted by Ms Nikora and other children in the class as they focused on curriculum content. Ms Nikora accepted and confirmed his efforts to participate in the classroom practices, even when he did not quite 'get it right' in terms of either the practice or the curriculum content.

Fa'afetai and Ms Nikora shared an understanding of some of what Mercer (2000: 28) calls the 'conversational ground rules'. Fa'afetai knew when it was his turn to speak in their interactions. He contributed to the interactions by answering questions with one or two words, or using a 'filler' that could be interpreted as indicating that he was paying attention and knew it was his turn to speak, but he was thinking or was not sure how to respond. Sometimes Fa'afetai used a non-verbal response to take his turn in an interaction. By doing so, he continued the interaction, demonstrated his understanding, and made it possible for Ms Nikora to reformulate his response verbally, thus modelling curriculum-related use of English. He also kept the interaction going on occasions by repeating a word or words from Ms Nikora's previous turn (or from another child's turn). These were not always the final words in Ms Nikora's turns, so it seems that Fa'afetai was constructing them as in some way salient for him. Fa'afetai also drew on his previous experience to take his turn in interactions. Ms Nikora then searched for a basis for shared contextual understanding so that she could take up his contribution and relate it to relevant curriculum content. Sometimes Fa'afetai's response was inappropriate. For her part, Ms Nikora incorporated his responses into the ongoing interaction as best she could. Thus they were co-constructing meaning, both through interactional procedures and through engaging with curriculum content.

Ms Nikora usually initiated their interactions on curriculum-related matters, but Fa'afetai initiated at times, when something particularly interested him. Thus, both took responsibility for initiating interactions, as well as for keeping them going.

A focus on naming was common in Ms Nikora and Fa'afetai's interactions on a range of topics related to the content of the curriculum unit. Hajer (2000) has shown the importance of directly addressing vocabulary in secondary school mainstream classrooms with advanced second language learners. It is equally important for Fa'afetai in his early experiences at school. We could construct a very narrow interpretation of what Ms Nikora and Fa'afetai were doing in these interactions. However, constructing this as 'just naming', or as in some way limiting Fa'afetai's opportunities for learning, does not take account of the following.

Ms Nikora made it clear in her interviews with us that she believed that what Fa'afetai knew was likely to be more than what he could say in English, and indeed more than he could understand in English. So she facilitated the establishment of shared contextual understanding by ensuring that non-verbal resources (such as people, pictures, picture story books and Fa'afetai's drawings) and shared experiences with them mediated her one-to-one interactions with Fa'afetai.

Fa'afetai and other members of the class had opportunities to construct concepts in many ways, mediated by these non-verbal resources as well as by spoken and written texts. Thus in the languaculture of this classroom, words and phrases such as 'Christmas', 'blow bubbles' and 'wheelchair' were not just names, they had the potential to connect with complex jointly-constructed meanings. Fa'afetai may have been limited in the use he could make of verbal aspects of the languaculture, but this did not mean that he was excluded from all the jointly-constructed meanings.

In secondary school mainstream classrooms, Hajer (2000) has shown that, to support language and content learning for advanced second language learners, it is important for the structure of the lesson activities and the frameworks for student participation to be clear and recognisable. At the beginning of his school experience, Fa'afetai had to learn the structures and practices of his classroom. When Ms Nikora constructed experiences of using English with Fa'afetai to mediate their joint understanding of curriculum concepts, she was not just helping him to learn relevant English, she was also helping him to understand part of what 'doing school' is about – showing what you know by saying it. Bloome *et al.* (1989: 272) use the term 'procedural display' for the 'interactional and academic procedures that count as doing a lesson and the cultural meanings and values associated with doing a lesson'. They showed how teacher–student interactions could be oriented towards completing lessons rather than academic aims. However, Bloome notes that:

> procedural display and substantive engagement in academic knowledge are not mutually exclusive, nor are they necessarily opposite ends of a continuum of cultural action. (Bloome, 1990:72)

As Gallego *et al.* point out:

> Although some cultural knowledge is acquired through explicit instruction, a great deal is acquired implicitly and often occurs outside of participants' conscious awareness. Whether cultural knowledge is conscious or not, the data are clear: Children learn to behave in terms of their local classroom cultures. (Gallego *et al.*, 2001: 970)

Throughout their interactions, Ms Nikora was scaffolding (Bruner, 1975; Wood *et al.*, 1976) Fa'afetai towards an understanding of what were appropriate academic responses in this classroom situation, both in substance and procedurally.

Ms Nikora introduced a referential perspective in many of her utterances, assuming and/or working towards a shared understanding of the purpose of the activity they were engaged in. She used verbal and non-verbal deictic expressions, and other gestures and actions, to support Fa'afetai's understanding of what she said, often supporting links with previous shared experience. When he did not share her referential perspective, she sometimes drew on knowledge of curriculum content that they did share to provide a more specific reference that he understood. They could then build from that shared understanding.

Ms Nikora addressed social studies curriculum content in one-to-one spoken interactions with Fa'afetai in every session of the unit, constructing with him repeated opportunities for engaging with the languaculture of the class with respect to aspects of curriculum content. Platt and Troudi (1997) expressed concern that the teacher in their case study of a child in a Florida third grade mainstream class was not providing the sort of support the child needed to learn the academic content and language aspects of the curriculum. This case study of interactions between Fa'afetai and Ms Nikora during a social studies curriculum unit shows that a mainstream class teacher can provide appropriate support. Fa'afetai may have been a very young child, and a beginner at learning English but Ms Nikora had many one-to-one interactions with him during this three-day unit. Together they worked on his learning of English, his learning of curriculum content, and his learning of school procedures that accompany the curriculum content.

Closing Comment

Ms Nikora had no previous experience of working with English beginners, nor had she had any training that was directed towards dealing with immigrant children. She made it clear in interviews during the study that she felt inadequately prepared to deal with the situation she was faced with, and that she did not feel at all confident about handling the situation.

I believe the analysis presented here shows that, as an experienced and reflective teacher, Ms Nikora was in fact able to provide Fa'afetai with effective opportunities for learning. This does not, however, obviate the need for all New Zealand teachers to have access to appropriate teacher education opportunities that would enable them to deal not just effectively but also confidently with immigrant children in their classes (Kennedy & Dewar, 1997: 181–187).

Members of the ERUDITE (Educational Research Underpinning Development In Teacher Education) programme have shown elsewhere (Alton-Lee *et al.*, 2001; Vine *et al.*, 2000) how classroom-based research such as that described here can be drawn on to provide teacher education experiences. We believe there is a need for more research like this, and for much more use of the sort of micro-analysis it allows for in teacher education. Such material has the potential to take pre- and in-service teachers 'inside' the processes and interactions that occur daily in classrooms so that they can analyse and understand how they can best participate in teaching and learning.

Acknowledgements

The Educational Research Underpinning Development in Teacher Education (ERUDITE) programme was funded by Pub Charity, Wellington, New Zealand, and directed by Adrienne Alton-Lee. I would like to thank Adrienne Alton-Lee for welcoming my collaboration in the programme and for her generosity in supporting and contributing her insights to my work within the programme. I also wish to thank Pub Charity, and members of the collaborative research team: Lena Klenner, Catherine Diggins, Ngaio Dalton, Maureen West, Karen Trass, Everdina Fuli, Sue Delport, and Adam Craig.

Some of the groundwork for this article was undertaken during the period March–April 1999 when the I was a Visiting Scholar with the School of Education, University of Massachusetts, Amherst, USA. Some of the writing was done in February to May 2002 when I was a Visiting Researcher at the Utrechts instituut voor Linguīstiek OTS, Universiteit Utrecht, The Netherlands.

Elaine Vine can be contacted at the School of Linguistics and Applied Language Studies, Victoria University of Wellington, PO Box 600, Wellington, New Zealand (email: elaine.vine@vuw.ac.nz).

References

Agar, M. (1994) *Language Shock: Understanding the Culture of Conversation.* New York: Quill, William Morrow.

Alton-Lee, A. (1999) Rethinking the relationship between classroom research and educational practice: The ERUDITE research case studies in teaching, learning and inclusion. *Teachers and Curriculum* 3, 81–86.

Alton-Lee, A. and Nuthall, G. (1992) A generative methodology for classroom research. *Educational Philosophy and Theory* 24 (2), 29–55.

Alton-Lee, A., Diggins, C., Klenner, L., Vine, E. and Dalton, N. (2001) Teacher management of the learning environment during a social studies discussion in a new-entrant classroom in New Zealand. *Elementary School Journal* 101 (5), 549–566.

Alton-Lee, A., Rietveld, C., Klenner, L., Dalton, N., Diggins, C. and Town, S. (2000) Inclusive practice within the lived cultures of school communities: Research case studies in teaching, learning and inclusion. *International Journal of Inclusive Education* 4 (3), 179–210.

Baker, C.D. (1997) Transcription and representation in literacy research. In J. Flood, S.B. Heath and D. Lapp (eds) *Handbook of Research on Teaching Literacy through the Communicative and Visual Arts* (pp. 110–120). New York: Macmillan.

Bakhtin, M.M. (1981) *The Dialogic Imagination: Four Essays* (M. Holquist, ed.; C. Emerson and M. Holquist, trans.). Austin, TX: University of Texas Press.

Bakhtin, M.M. (1986) *Speech Genres and Other Late Essays* (C. Emerson and M. Holquist, eds; V.W. McGee, trans.). Austin, TX: University of Texas Press.

Bloome, D. (1990) Toward a more delicate elaboration of procedural display: A rejoinder to Atkinson and Delamont. *Curriculum Inquiry* 20 (1), 71–73.

Bloome, D., Puro, P. and Theodorou, E. (1989) Procedural display and classroom lessons. *Curriculum Inquiry* 19 (3), 265–291.

Bruner, J.S. (1975) The ontogenesis of speech acts. *Journal of Child Language* 2, 1–19.

Carrasquillo, A.L. and Rodriguez, V. (2002) *Language Minority Students in the Mainstream Classroom* (2nd edn). Clevedon: Multilingual Matters.

Clegg, J. (ed.) (1996) *Mainstreaming ESL: Case Studies in Integrating ESL Students into the Mainstream Curriculum.* Clevedon: Multilingual Matters.

Collier, V.P. (1987) Age and rate of acquisition of second language for academic purposes. *TESOL Quarterly* 21, 617–641.
Collier, V.P. (1989) How long? A synthesis of research on academic achievement in a second language. *TESOL Quarterly* 23, 509–531.
Crawford, T., Chen, C. and Kelly, G.J. (1997) Creating authentic opportunities for presenting science: The influence of audience on student talk. *Journal of Classroom Interaction* 32 (2), 1–13.
Creese, A. (2000) The role of the language specialist in disciplinary teaching: In search of a subject? *Journal of Multilingual and Multicultural Development* 21 (6), 451–470.
Cummins, J. (1981) Age on arrival and immigrant second language learning in Canada: A reassessment. *Applied Linguistics* 2, 132–149.
Cummins, J. (1994) The acquisition of English as a second language. In K. Spangenberg-Urbschat and R. Pritchard (eds) *Kids Come in All Languages: Reading Instruction for ESL Students* (pp. 36–62). Newark, Delaware: International Reading Association.
Edwards, D. and Mercer, N. (1987) *Common Knowledge: The Development of Understanding in the Classroom.* London: Methuen/Routledge.
Erickson, F. (1986) Qualitative methods in research on teaching. In M. Wittrock (ed.) *Handbook of Research on Teaching* (3rd edn, pp.119–161). New York: Macmillan.
Forman, E.A., McCormick, D.E. and Donato, R. (1997) Learning what counts as a mathematical explanation. *Linguistics and Education* 9 (4), 313–339.
Gallego, M.A., Cole, M. and The Laboratory of Comparative Human Cognition (2001) Classroom cultures and cultures in the classroom. In V. Richardson (ed.) *Handbook of Research on Teaching* (4th edn, pp. 951–997). Washington, DC: American Educational Research Association.
Gebhard, M. (1999) Debates in SLA studies: Redefining classroom SLA as an institutional phenomenon. *TESOL Quarterly* 33 (3), 544–556.
Gillham, B. (ed.) (1986) *The Language of School Subjects.* London: Heinemann.
Green, J.L. and Dixon, C.N. (1993) Talking knowledge into being: Discursive and social practices in classrooms. *Linguistics and Education* 5 (3/4) (Special issue: Santa Barbara Classroom Discourse Group) 231–239.
Green, J., Franquiz, M. and Dixon, C. (1997) The myth of the objective transcript: Transcribing as a situated act. *TESOL Quarterly* 31 (1), 172–176.
Hajer, M. (2000) Creating a language-promoting classroom: Content-area teachers at work. In J.K. Hall and L.S. Verplaetse (eds) *Second and Foreign Language Learning through Classroom Interaction* (pp. 265–285). Mahwah, NJ: Lawrence Erlbaum.
Kennedy, S. and Dewar, S. (1997) *Non-English-Speaking Background Students: A Study of Programmes and Support in New Zealand Schools.* Wellington: Ministry of Education, Research and International Section, Research Unit.
Lave, J. and Wenger, E. (1991) *Situated Learning: Legitimate Peripheral Participation.* Cambridge: Cambridge University Press.
Lemke, J. (1990) *Talking Science: Language, Learning, and Values.* Norwood, NJ: Ablex.
Levine, J. (ed.) (1990) *Bilingual Learners and the Mainstream Curriculum: Integrated Approaches to Learning and the Teaching and Learning of English as a Second Language in Mainstream Classrooms.* London: Falmer Press.

Martin-Jones, M. and Saxena, M. (2001) Turn-taking and the positioning of bilingual participants in classroom discourse: Insights from primary schools in England. In M. Heller and M. Martin-Jones (eds) *Voices of Authority: Education and Linguistic Difference* (pp. 117–138). Westport, CT: Ablex.

Maybin, J. (1994) Children's voices: Talk, knowledge and identity. In D. Graddol, J. Maybin and B. Stierer (eds) *Researching Language and Literacy in Social Context* (pp. 131–150). Clevedon: Multilingual Matters in association with The Open University.

McCloskey, M.L. (2002) President's message: No child left behind? *TESOL Matters* 12 (4), 3.

Mehan, H. (1979) *Learning Lessons: Social Organisation in the Classroom*. Cambridge, MA and London: Harvard University Press.

Mercer, N. (2000) *Words and Minds: How We Use Language to Think Together*. London and New York: Routledge.

Ministry of Education (1993) *The New Zealand Curriculum Framework*. Wellington: Learning Media.

Mohan, B. (1986) *Language and Content*. Reading, MA: Addison-Wesley.

Mohan, B., Leung, C. and Davison, C. (eds) (2001) *English as a Second Language in the Mainstream: Teaching, Learning and Identity*. Harlow, Essex: Longman.

Ochs, E. (1979) Transcription as theory. In E. Ochs and B.B. Schieffelin (eds) *Developmental Pragmatics* (pp. 43–72). New York: Academic Press.

Penton, R. (1996) Analysis of the language content and perspectives in the national curriculum statements. *Many Voices: A Journal of New Settlers and Multicultural Education Issues* 9, 4–10.

Platt, E. and Troudi, S. (1997) Mary and her teachers: A Grebo-speaking child's place in the mainstream classroom. *Modern Language Journal* 81 (1), 28–49.

Rogoff, B. (1990) *Apprenticeship in Thinking: Cognitive Development in Social Context*. New York and Oxford: Oxford University Press.

Rogoff, B. (1995) Observing sociocultural activity on three planes: Participatory appropriation, guided participation, and apprenticeship. In J.V. Wertsch, P. del Rio and A. Alvarez (eds) *Sociocultural Studies of Mind* (pp. 139–164). Cambridge: Cambridge University Press.

Santa Barbara Classroom Discourse Group (1992a) Constructing literacy in classrooms: Literate action as social accomplishment. In H.H. Marshall (ed.) *Redefining Student Learning: Roots of Educational Change* (pp. 119–150). Norwood, NJ: Ablex.

Santa Barbara Classroom Discourse Group (1992b) Do you see what we see? The referential and intertextual nature of classroom life. *Journal of Classroom Interaction* 27 (2), 29–36.

Sinclair, J.McH. and Coulthard, R.M. (1975) *Towards an Analysis of Discourse: The English Used by Teachers and Pupils*. Oxford: Oxford University Press.

Smythe, K. (1996) *Christmas in Hospital: A Social Studies Unit for Junior and Middle Levels*. Hamilton, New Zealand: Developmental Publications Ltd.

Swan, S. and White, R. (1990) Increasing meta-learning, Part 2: Thinking books. *Set: Research Information for Teachers* 2, item 11.

Swan, S. and White, R. (1994) *The Thinking Books*. London: Falmer Press.

Tuyay, S., Floriani, A., Yeager, B., Dixon, C. and Green, J. (1995) Constructing an integrated, inquiry-oriented approach in classrooms: A cross case analysis of social, literate and academic practices. *Journal of Classroom Interaction* 30 (2), 1–15.

Vine, E.W. (1984) When does more mean 'less'? A study of language use in arithmetic problems. *Australian Review of Applied Linguistics* 7 (1), 157–168.
Vine, E.W. (1985) Comprehending the language of primary school mathematics. In *Language Studies: Reading Curriculum. Reader* (pp. 226–232). Victoria: Deakin University.
Vine, E.W. (1997) *Language across the Curriculum: The Language Learning Potential in a Science Text.* Wellington; Melbourne: New Zealand Council for Educational Research; Australian Council for Educational Research (originally issued as article 14 in *Set: Special 1997: Language and literacy.*)
Vine, E.W. (2003) 'My partner': A five-year-old Samoan boy learns how to participate in class through interactions with his English-speaking peers. *Linguistics and Education* 14 (1), 99–121.
Vine, E.W., Alton-Lee, A. and Klenner, L. (2000) Supporting curriculum learning and language learning with an ESOL learner in a mainstream class. *Set: Research Information for Teachers* 3, 4–8.
Vygotsky, L S. (1978) *Mind in Society: The Development of Higher Psychological Processes.* Cambridge, MA: Harvard University Press.
Wells, G. (1996) Using the tool-kit of discourse in the activity of teaching and learning. *Mind, Culture, and Activity* 3 (2), 74–101. (Reprinted in G. Wells (1999) *Dialogic Inquiry: Towards a Sociocultural Practice and Theory of Education* (pp. 231–266). Cambridge: Cambridge University Press.)
Wells, G. (1999) *Dialogic Inquiry: Towards a Sociocultural Practice and Theory of Education.* Cambridge: Cambridge University Press.
Wertsch, J.V. (1985) Adult–child interaction as a source of self-regulation in children. In S.R. Yussen (ed.) *The Growth of Reflection in Children* (pp. 69–97). Orlando, FL: Academic Press.
Wertsch, J.V. (1991) *Voices of the Mind: A Sociocultural Approach to Mediated Action.* London: Harvester Wheatsheaf.
Wood, D., Bruner, J. S. and Ross, G. (1976) The role of tutoring in problem solving. *Journal of Child Psychology and Psychiatry* 17, 89–100.

Chapter 6

Students from Diverse Language Backgrounds in the Primary Classroom

PENNY HAWORTH

Introduction

In recent years, New Zealand schools have faced rapid increases in the numbers of students from diverse language and cultural backgrounds (Ministry of Education, 1999). The Ministry of Education refers to these students as non-English speaking background (NESB) students and this is the term used within this chapter to ensure consistency with other chapters in the book. However, I personally prefer to use the more positive term of *students from diverse language backgrounds,* as this promotes the idea that these students have already acquired a first language and culture. NESB students do not have a first-language deficit; nonetheless, many of them struggle to stay afloat in the English medium of the school, in what Cummins (1984) refers to as submersion rather than immersion classrooms. Rapid changes in school demographic characteristics may also result in teachers feeling as though they are continually swimming against the currents of change, or even being swept along out of control (Hargreaves, 1994). On the other hand, change may positively stimulate the growth of sound policies, useful resources, and effective classroom practices, and contribute to the enhancement of NESB students' bilingual development and curriculum competency. The realities could, of course, be expected to fall somewhere along this continuum.

The study described in this chapter looks at two teachers and the NESB students in their classroom, which could be best described as a *regular classroom*. This term has its origins in Penfield's (1987) work, and has also been used in other recent New Zealand studies (Barnard *et al.*, 2001; Johnston, 1999). Penfield (1987: 21) defines a *regular classroom* as 'a setting in which the subject matter and literacy skills are taught entirely in English and the majority of the students are native speakers of English.' She also notes that, in most cases, the teachers in regular classrooms have had no training in how to deal with NESB students. The term *regular* is preferred to the term *mainstream*, as the latter is often associated with learners in a classroom setting with special learning or behavioural difficulties, and may therefore have negative connotations for NESB students. In this chapter, however, I have chosen to simply use the terms *classroom* and *classroom teachers*, as these are more straightforward and generic.

The need for more research into the planning and evaluation of programmes for NESB students in schools has been recognised for some time (Barnard, 1998: 108; Richards & Hurley, 1988:52). However, much of the literature so far has focused on the intensive English teaching situation, or the English for Speakers of Other Languages (ESOL) Programme. Only a few studies, either internationally or in New Zealand, have focused on the classroom setting, although this is where NESB students spend most of their school day and week.

NESB students have been in New Zealand schools for many years now, but recently there has been increased research interest in this area. In 1997, the Ministry of Education funded a national investigation into the provisions for NESB students in schools (Kennedy & Dewar, 1997). This resulted in identifying a range of effective policies and practices. Funding and resources have also been surveyed in Hamilton primary schools (Barnard & Rauf, 1999). Of late, however, research attention seems to have shifted to classroom teachers and their responses to the NESB students in their classrooms. For example, studies have looked at the classroom interactions of NESB learners and the influences on their cognitive and language development (Barnard, 2000, 2002; Haworth & Haddock, 1999; Vine, 1998). These studies generally build on the work of Gibbons (1991) in Australia. The attitudes of teachers to the NESB students in their classrooms have been surveyed (Penfield, 1987) in the United States, and a study has been carried out in the UK to investigate the attitudes and feelings of a small number of teachers who had NESB students in their classrooms (Franson, 1999). In New Zealand too, the attitudes of secondary school teachers to the NESB students in their classrooms have also been surveyed (Johnston, 1999) and, more recently, Barnard *et al.* (2001) surveyed secondary school teachers' perceptions of NESB students and the role of the ESOL support teachers in their school. The latter study was carried out in the city of Hamilton and was followed by a comparative study in Auckland (Cameron & Simpson, 2002) that looked at secondary school teachers' perceptions of what would help them most with the NESB students in their classrooms (such as more planning time, better resources, more assistance in class, or more professional development).

It needs to be recognised that, not only are studies like those noted above relatively scarce, but researchers who have ventured inside the classroom have tended to take a unilateral perspective on the situation, examining *either* the children's interactions, *or* the teachers' reactions. This chapter describes a broader exploratory study that aimed to find out more about the daily realities in two primary school classrooms. In addition to individual semi-structured interviews with the classroom and ESOL support teachers in the school, the study included about fifteen hours of in-class observation time in each of the two participating classes. The findings from this preliminary study provide some useful insights into the classroom teachers' perceptions of the NESB students in their classes, their perceptions of their roles in relation to these students, and how they and their students coped in everyday learning and teaching situations. Before going on to describe this study, however, I will briefly describe the three critical professional tensions that impacted on teachers at the time of the study (November 2000). These tensions are commonly reported in both the New Zealand and the international literature, and relate to the amount of relevant professional knowledge that classroom teachers have about teaching, assessing, and organising programmes for NESB learners.

The first critical tension that can be identified in the literature is the paucity of relevant professional training for classroom teachers of NESB students. Classroom teachers are often described as professionally ill equipped to meet the needs of NESB students, both overseas (Andrews, 1999; Brumfit, 1991; Scollon & Scollon, 1995) and in New Zealand (Cameron & Simpson, 2002; Haworth & Haddock, 1999; Kennedy & Dewar, 1997). Interestingly, Cameron and Simpson (2002) found that, although teachers in both Hamilton and Auckland felt under pressure from the influx of NESB students, those in Auckland, where numbers of NESB students are greater, seemed to be coping better. They put this down to the greater opportunities for professional development that were provided for the classroom teachers in Auckland (Cameron & Simpson, 2002: 22–23).

In a large-scale study of teachers of NESB students in New Zealand, Kennedy and Dewar (1997) found that classroom teachers generally learn how to cope with NESB students through 'trial and error'. As this takes time, it may offer a plausible explanation for why the descriptor *frustrated* is often associated with these teachers' feelings. For example, Franson (1999: 63), who interviewed three such teachers just outside London, found that they reported feeling 'frustrated' and 'overwhelmed'. Similarly, Penfield (1987), in her New Jersey survey of 179 classroom teachers, noted that many teachers said that they were frustrated. She found that this resulted in them being unwilling to deal with the additional burden of NESB students in their classrooms. Johnston (1999), who surveyed 59 classroom teachers in New Zealand, also found that teachers felt frustrated, and connected this to their inability to effectively teach and communicate with the NESB students in their classes. Further to this, Barnard *et al.* (2001: 24) found that classroom teachers were frustrated by the 'amount of time the NESB students demanded due to problems with the English language'. From these reports, it seems that, while classroom teachers' frustrations may arise from professional inadequacy, this may in turn lead to negative feelings being generated about the presence of NESB students in their classes.

The literature also reveals that teachers lack knowledge about assessing NESB students. Teachers in Franson's (1999) London-based study reported having difficulty in assessing their NESB students. In New Zealand, too, teachers have reported struggling to assess NESB students accurately. For example, Haworth and Haddock (1999) found that limited teacher knowledge could contribute to the English proficiency of NESB students being over-rated, resulting in schools missing out on crucial funding. Haworth and Haddock suggest that teachers may over-rate the English proficiency of NESB students because they may observe only the children's general ability to converse socially, rather than examining their specific ability to cope with the language demands of the curriculum. Further support for this interpretation is found in the work of Cummins (1984) and Baker (1996), who note the differentiation between BICS (basic interpersonal communication skills) and CALP (cognitive academic language proficiency). BICS has been described as 'surface fluency' (Baker, 1996: 151), while CALP relates to more abstract, context-reduced language, such as that required in the school context. Language utilising CALP lacks the contextual support and the familiarity of shared topics usually found in everyday conversation.

A third tension centres on how teachers define and organise the programme for NESB students. Mohan, Leung and Davison (2001) note that the content of the programme for NESB students has been a source of dispute in many countries. In New Zealand, this discussion has centred around three key dilemmas:

(1) whether to establish a *separate* curriculum for ESOL (Lawson, 2001; Syme, 1999), or to use the *existing* English curriculum with a supporting set of teacher strategies/guidelines (Bedford, 2001; Middleton, 1999);

(2) whether to focus on classroom *curriculum* areas and provide *cultural* connections (Barnard, 1998), or to emphasise issues of English *language* such as vocabulary, grammar and text structure (Davison, 2001);

(3) whether to *withdraw* NESB students for intensive ESOL classes, or to cater for these students in their *classroom* programme (e.g. Millett & Vine, 2000; Syme, 1995).

Related to the issue of teacher knowledge is the that of teacher professionalism. This is a matter that has recently been debated internationally. For example, Johnston (1997) and Scollon and Scollon (1995) both refer to the traditionally haphazard career pathways for teachers of NESB students. In New Zealand too, there has been interest in trying to develop professional standards in the field (White, 1997). However, in New Zealand schools it is even more complex, as the vast majority of support teachers of NESB students are teacher aides or part-time teachers with limited tenure (Cameron & Simpson, 2002; Barnard & Rauf, 1999; Haworth & Haddock, 1999; Haddock, 1998). Furthermore, regular teachers – particularly if there are just small numbers of NESB students in a school or class – do not always prioritise professional development in this area. Becoming more expert in teaching NESB students is often not seen as enhancing the career pathways of these teachers, as they are usually more interested in professional courses that focus on teaching in specific curriculum areas.

In the United States of America, legal civil rights cases have been won on the grounds of inequitable educational support for minority students (Zephir, 1999). Although in New Zealand there have as yet been no such legal cases documented, the fact remains that NESB children are in the classroom for most of their day. While many of them cope and cope well, a large number have insufficient English language to cope with the curriculum optimally and independently, and many of their teachers are ill-equipped to adequately meet their needs. So, the context for teaching NESB students in New Zealand schools is one with many professional uncertainties. The study that I am about to describe aimed at finding out more about how teachers and the NESB students in their classes go about coping in this situation, in the hope that the findings would enhance the effectiveness of teacher education programmes in this area.

The Setting and the Participants

The primary school where this study was carried out was decile 3 (at the lower end of a 10-point scale related to the socio-economic status of the parent community), and is located in the centre of a medium-sized city in the North Island of New Zealand. It is typical of a number of schools in this broad geographic area, in that it has small numbers of NESB students (around 10% of the total population), from a mix of backgrounds. In this case, the NESB children were mainly from Asian and Pacific Island origins.

Two classes were involved in the study: a Year 3–4 class of 31 students about 7–8 years old, including four NESB students (from China, Samoa, Tonga and Korea); and a Year 5–6 class of 25 students about 9–10 years old, including three NESB students (from Cambodia, China and Tonga).

The school employed two support teachers (a teacher and a teacher aide) who were interviewed at the start of the study to provide some background to the programme. Both support teachers were employed part-time in a number of different roles in the school. The lead NESB students' support teacher had had experience as a classroom teacher, and had also completed an advanced level undergraduate Certificate in Teaching English to Speakers of Other Languages (TESOL). The teacher aide had partially completed the same certificate programme at the time of the study. The support teachers worked mainly in a withdrawal situation; however, the teacher aide reported that at times she also worked in the classroom. In withdrawal times, the teacher aide generally used word games and activities to build basic English vocabulary and initial sight words with younger learners in the school. The lead support teacher worked with those NESB students in the upper part of the primary school who had been identified as having the highest level of English-language needs. She acknowledged that other NESB students in the school also needed additional help, but that her programme was necessarily constrained by time and budget limitations.

The two classroom teachers who participated in the study, Alice and Brenda (both pseudonyms) could both be described as 'experienced'. Alice, the teacher in the Year 3–4 class, had more than 20 years of teaching experience. Brenda, the teacher in the Year 5–6 class, was in her tenth year of teaching. Both had taught NESB students in previous classes, and Alice had also had a short stint working as a support teacher for NESB students some years back, although she was quick to point out that she had never undertaken any professional development relevant to this area. The school had recently participated in a Ministry of Education professional development contract aimed at teachers of NESB students. The support teachers had been involved with this, but neither of the classroom teachers in the study had participated in the programme.

The Case Study

This is an initial exploratory study. As the focus is on just one school, the findings are by no means exhaustive and may indeed be later reinterpreted in the light of findings from the main phase of the study, which examines a larger sample of schools and classroom teachers. However, the preliminary findings do provide a number of stepping-off points for future research.

The case study approach, as a qualitative approach, follows a tradition of being essentially evolutionary in nature, with the focus on gathering rich insights from multiple perspectives rather than relying entirely on quantitative data and statistical analysis (Strauss & Corbin, 1998).

As noted earlier, the literature to date has provided little in-depth insight into the everyday realities for primary teachers with NESB students in their classrooms. It was therefore decided, for the preliminary phase of this study, to take a number of 'snapshots' of the classroom situation from the different perspectives of the researcher, the ESOL teachers, the classroom teachers, and the students. Collegial interactions between the support teachers and the classroom teachers were also examined. In the interests of providing a coherent chapter within the present volume, however, only the perspectives of the researcher and the teachers are covered here. The names of all participants – teachers and students – are pseudonyms.

The study began with individual interviews with the support teachers. This provided background information about the programme for the NESB students in the school and the role the support teachers and the classroom teachers played in this. Next, three continuous days of classroom observation were carried out in each of the two classrooms participating in the study. Observations of classroom interactions involving NESB students were recorded using a narrative-style of report (similar to the naturalistic reports of children at play compiled by Cullen and Allsop, 1999). In our study, the researcher was an 'engaged spectator' or an interested non-participant (Brown & Canter, 1985: 225). The observation period in each classroom was followed by an hour-long semi-structured individual interview with the classroom teacher. This interview was divided into two main parts. In the first section of the interview, the focus was on gathering background information about each teacher's professional experiences and her self-perceived roles in relation to the NESB students. In the second part of the interview, we reflected on specific mini-episodes from the preceding observation period. The value of such *critical incidents* in provoking effective teacher reflection is well recognised in studies that investigate teachers' practices and explore how teachers' theories and beliefs are inherent in these practices (e.g. Richards & Lockhart, 1994; Wragg, 1994).

The NESB Student Support Programme

In their interviews, the support teachers identified issues related to assessment of NESB students, the employment of teacher aides, and the balancing of roles between the support teachers and the regular classroom teachers.

In her interview, the lead support teacher, who was also responsible for the assessment of NESB students for funding purposes, raised a number of concerns about the validity of the national assessment process used to determine funding levels for NESB students. She stated, for example, that it was not realistic to place a 5-year-old NESB student in the 'below cohort level' for written language, since others at that age were also non-writers. However, she felt that to describe the child as being 'at cohort level' might deprive the child of much-needed funding and learning support. She also noted that the reading level tests used with native speakers often did not give accurate results, as some NESB children had very good 'technical skills' in reading while their overall comprehension levels could be quite low.

The lead support teacher also expressed some concerns regarding teacher aides in ESOL support positions being responsible for assessing NESB students:

> It really worries me when I find that, in other schools, teacher aides are totally responsible for all this stuff. How can they possibly assess kids against cohorts in classrooms when they don't exactly know – haven't got the experience of what should or shouldn't be happening – what benchmarks are for written [or] oral. All they see is the children who are with them. They don't see the bigger picture and they're expected to put assessment labels on them.

Both support teachers said that they tried to include class topics and the individual interests of the students in their programmes. This was seen as crucial to the ultimate effectiveness of the programme, and appeared to contribute to overall teacher satisfaction. However, when interviewed later, the classroom teachers saw this as less than ideal. They expressed concerns over how to ensure that their programme was linked to the support programme.

If knowledge is power, the school setting is no exception. In the interviews, differences of opinion surfaced between the support teachers and the classroom teachers regarding the location of the files on the NESB students in the school. These files were kept in the teaching space used by the lead support teacher who commented:

> because it's cross school, you have to have systems in place to make it actually easier for yourself, because if I've got all my paper work here safely in my room, when I want something I don't have to go all over the school to find it. I copy things; I keep things. And classroom teachers will also know that – ESOL paperwork – they know I have it. They don't actually need it. I need to have it here. They don't need it.

While this sounded very practical and straightforward at the time, the later interview with Alice, the classroom teacher in the Year 3–4 class, revealed some conflicting views about this. She related an incident in which a student teacher in the classroom asked her how long the NESB children had been in New Zealand. She reported that she was unable to give that information, as she did not have it on her records for the children:

Alice: ... but that data, how long the children have been in the country, is often not given to us

Penny:[1] I think that's held with [the lead Support Teacher], isn't it?"

Alice: [The Lead Support Teacher] may have it, I don't know, but I would not be able to tell you if [a particular NESB child] was born in the country [New Zealand] ... I have to go back to their enrolment slip to see what [language] was spoken at home.

The classroom teachers were not always clear about what the support teacher could, or did, do with the NESB students. For example, although the lead support teacher ran a programme focused on reading skills, with one day for writing in first language, Alice thought that the senior school support programme dealt with only writing. She also felt there was insufficient reading or maths support for NESB students. In addition, while Alice was able to see the potential benefits of greater collaboration with the support teachers, she was unsure about who should action this:

Alice: It would be good for the children to be writing about the experiences they are having [in the regular classroom] ... supermarket ... we've been to the Science Centre ... what we're studying in class ... it would be good to, but umm, I don't know if I should initiate that or not.

Some of these gaps in communication between the support teachers and the classroom teachers were later addressed by the school – perhaps as a result of feedback from the study.

The NESB Students in the Classroom

In line with the qualitative nature of the study, no prior categories were established before undertaking the observations of the NESB students in their classrooms. Of course, it has to be acknowledged that the researcher's focus and insights will inevitably be influenced by her background knowledge as a teacher educator and a researcher in this field. Saville-Troike (1989) notes that, although the world is filled with many things, we actually *see* only those that have meaning for us.

Although a qualified teacher, I had not worked as a classroom teacher for many years, so the aim of the classroom observations was initially to gain familiarity with the context, and then subsequently to identify interesting scenarios for later discussion. After collection and analysis, data were found to fit into three major categories related to the NESB students' interaction zones, their participation in directed teaching sessions, and their actions in independent learning situations.

NESB students' interaction zones

The NESB students' interactions with other students in the classroom tended to be relatively stable over the time of the study, and could also be described as being somewhat limited in range. Larger groups that these students were part of (usually up to four students in total) often included another NESB student; but pairing with a non-NESB student was more often the norm. The latter finding appears to contrast with the findings of earlier studies by Barnard *et al.* (2001), Johnson (1999) and Penfield (1987), which identify NESB students as socially isolated in the classroom. Penfield notes that this isolation may be due to classroom teachers' lack of expertise in creating dynamic in-class interaction for these students. It may be that the two classes in the current study were particularly successful in integrating NESB students with others as part of their learning programme. It may also be significant that both Penfield and Barnard *et al.* looked at secondary school classrooms – perhaps primary school classrooms are more interactive learning environments. However, Cameron and Simpson (2002) report the efforts of secondary school teachers to encourage interaction between NESB students and others. In the light of such disparities, it is worth considering that the concept of 'socially isolated' could be interpreted on many levels. Does it follow, for instance, that NESB students are socially isolated if their interactions are restricted to the same few children? The work of Barnard (2002) suggests that the level of the students' English proficiency and the presence or absence of peers from the same first language background may be key influences on the nature of the interaction in a class. This may be relevant in the school where the current study was located, as parents there often asked for their children to be placed in classrooms apart from their own linguistic group so they would be obliged to use English. Although this was sometimes not possible, in classes where there were two or more NESB children from the same linguistic background they tended not to talk with each other during learning tasks, and were often seated in different parts of the classroom.

Although the NESB children in the classes observed did not appear to interact extensively with each other, the seating position that these children took up on the mat area (where direct teaching was generally carried out) was suggestive of a closer association. The NESB students in the Year 5–6 class tended to seat themselves *within touching zone* of other NESB students, towards the front of the mat area. In the Year 3–4 class, most of the NESB students also sat within touching zone of each other, but more towards the centre of the mat. However, one NESB student in this class would regularly sit close to the teacher's chair. She was constantly out of the touching zone of other NESB students, but maintained visual and verbal contact with a non-NESB peer whom she often worked with in the class. Although the NESB children, it seemed, often said little, their close proximity in the mat area appeared to perform a positive supportive function. It is possible that having other NESB students nearby provides reliable reference points where individuals can check on their interpretations of events (such as teacher instructions). Barnard's (2000) study also reinforces the value of the support group in enhancing understanding. The importance of such a reference group, within an environment that constantly offers uncertainty and challenge for these students, should certainly not be underestimated.

In each class, one NESB student appeared to be more extroverted and seemed to be regarded as a sort of 'social leader' by others at their group table. This student would often be seen engaging in mischievous interactions with one or more non-NESB students at their table (e.g. repeatedly engaging in playful kicking games under the table) while the teacher was not looking. At the time when the social leader NESB student was off task and distracting other students, all the other NESB students in the class were usually found to be quietly working away on the set task. It is interesting to note that such mischievous interactions were never observed to involve two or more NESB students. Nonetheless, the social leader NESB student was always the initiator. Such behaviour raises the question of whether these particular NESB students perceived their actions as socially acceptable, or whether this sort of behaviour was perceived as necessary for initiating positive social interaction with their non-NESB peers. Then again, it may be that these children were just naturally more boisterous than some of their NESB peers.

Over the time of the study, one NESB student in the Year 5–6 class was never observed to interact with anyone else at her group table (which happened to contain the social leader NESB student for that class). These two NESB students were from different ethnic backgrounds and were different genders. However, the quieter student did appear to be part of a very stable pair with a non-NESB student, and sometimes interacted with another NESB/non-NESB pair of students at another table. In her interview Brenda later remarked that she had consciously tried to add more diversity to this child's interaction patterns by seating her at a different table. She felt that in the new grouping this child would encounter greater language extension and more cognitive stimulation. However, the seating change did not appear to have motivated this child to extend her interactions. It is not known, of course, whether the child was in fact gaining maximal input, but was not yet feeling competent or confident enough to interact in this setting. On the other hand, it is possible that the other children in the new group discouraged the interaction. For example, in an earlier study (Haworth & Haddock, 1999) Year 5–6 students, working in groups, were observed to be actively avoiding interaction with the NESB students in the group when the teacher was not nearby. This effect disappeared however, when the teacher changed to pairing the NESB children with native speakers. It is likely that mixed pair work (NESB students with native-speaking students) may reduce the pressure of negative peer expectations placed on native-speaking children of this age level when working in larger groups.

NESB students in directed teaching sessions

In directed teaching sessions on the mat, the NESB students were never seen to *ask* direct questions. They were on several occasions, however, observed raising their hands and *answering* questions put by the teacher, as well as interacting freely with their nearby peers. During these teaching sessions, the NESB students were observed to respond only to questions that required *recall* and *specific knowledge*. They were not seen to raise their hands in response to questions about *word meanings*, or more *global* questions such as (during reading by the teacher): 'What's happened so far?' These questions may have been too challenging to those students with limited English proficiency.

Although the NESB children generally appeared attentive while on the mat, their attention was sometimes observed to wander, but the classroom teacher either did not notice this or decided not to draw attention to it. One such occasion is illustrated below. The incident involved a Samoan girl and a Chinese boy in the Year 3–4 class, both of whom could be described as being below cohort level in English language proficiency. The teacher had been introducing the idea of *temperature* to the class, who were all sitting in the mat area at the front of the class. The teacher had held up a copy of a book entitled *Temperature,* asked the children how to say the word, and discussed what the word temperature could mean. A number of children (including some NESB children) had reported their experiences with thermometers and temperatures when they had been sick. However, they did not seem to have had experience with recording the temperature in different physical zones (which the teacher planned to do later). They were now going to work in pairs with the teacher's help to read the small book about temperature. The example below begins at 11.20 am and lasts about five minutes. All names used are pseudonyms.

Example 1

11.20 Jon (a Chinese child) and his partner don't get a book. Jon says, 'Mrs Woods, me,' and holds out his hand. This interaction with the teacher, although not strictly accurate or complete, is successful in obtaining the required book.

11.21 The teacher asks the children to look in the back of the book for the word 'temperature' in the index, then in the contents at the front of the book. Jon takes a while to do this, but his partner helps him. While this is happening, Rebecca (a Samoan child) reads a different page from the one being discussed by the teacher. She holds her book up so that the teacher can't see what she is doing and flicks through the pages ahead, apparently looking at the pictures.

11.24 The teacher asks the children to put their hands up if they can see that the temperature on the thermometer diagram in the book goes up in 5s. Rebecca puts up her hand with all the others although she is still not looking at the right page. After this, however, she turns back to the correct page and continues the lesson, sharing her book with her partner.

On the occasion illustrated above, Rebecca may have been previewing the book in order to gain a better understanding of the topic being discussed and read about. In fact, this may not have been 'attention wandering', but a positive strategy to cope with a complex new concept being introduced by the teacher. Occasions when NESB children show off-task behaviour in class may perhaps be cues to teachers that the students do not understand, or need more time or help to process an idea. However, the teacher stated in her later interview that she had not noticed the incident on this occasion. This reflects the difficulty that regular teachers may have in picking up such cues when they are working to meet the needs of many diverse learners in a large teaching situation. Even if she correctly identifies the cues, the teacher still has to weigh the benefits of changing her planned course of action for just one or two children in a class group.

Another episode when an NESB child was observed off-task was recorded during a ten-minute long story-reading session in the library. As the teacher, Brenda, read to her Year 5–6 class, two of the NESB students moved off to one side near the front of the group. There, unseen by the teacher, they quietly read an easier reading book while Brenda continued reading to her class. When Brenda and I reflected on this incident later, we realised that her book needed to be read at a fast colloquial pace to capture the mood of the story. It may be that, when the class activities become too fast or too complex to follow, the NESB students find alternative activities to occupy themselves quietly. Lack of focus on the task could, however, also be related to interest and motivation levels of the student in relation to the topic. The book that the two NESB students were observed reading on the occasion above was in fact one they had begun to read before the teacher commenced reading to the class.

NESB students with lower English levels were often observed looking down when the teacher was talking to the class. However, this changed in response to certain teaching actions, as seen below in the introduction to a writing session in the Year 5–6 class. The child involved is Somai, a Cambodian girl with English proficiency at about cohort level.

Example 2

9.44 As usual the NESB students are sitting within touching zone on the mat. You could draw a diagonal line across the front grouping and join all four of them together.

9.45 Somai is looking down at her feet as the teacher introduces the writing task. The teacher begins to write what to do on the board. Immediately Somai looks up and watches.

9.46 Somai looks back down again while the teacher talks to the class about what they could include in their writing.

9.47 Somai looks up again as the teacher asks a question.

The NESB students in both classes were often observed to look up, and seemed to attend more closely if the teacher wrote on the board. Both classroom teachers did this regularly. For instance, in the Year 5–6 class, Brenda usually outlined the steps in the writing task and wrote these on the board. In the Year 3–4 class, Alice always put key words on the board when introducing a new writing topic. When sitting on the mat while the teacher was teaching the class, the NESB children were observed to look up and seemed to attend more closely at the following times:

- if the teacher wrote on the board (as seen in the example above);
- if a pointer was used (as in Year 3–4 shared reading);
- if a question was asked by the teacher (as seen in the example above);
- if a peer answered a teacher-initiated question;
- if concrete objects or physical actions were used as part of the explana-

tions (e.g. Alice introduced the idea of contrasting colours in a Year 3–4 art class by asking various children to stand side by side and then drawing attention to the colours in their clothes).

While looking down may be a mark of respect for superiors in some cultures, the change in physical stance of NESB students at particular points in the lesson would seem to have important implications for the selection of teaching strategies when there are NESB students in the class. It is likely that the NESB children looked up and attended when the teaching strategy used was helpful in conveying meaning.

NESB students in independent learning situations

NESB students were often observed to make use of prior learning experiences to support their independent learning. For example, on one occasion the Year 5–6 class was set a task to select a newspaper article, research facts in the article on *who, what, when* and *where,* and write about this. Somai and her non-NESB peer, decided to look through the newspapers for an article on 'Children's Day' that the teacher had used with them in a recent lesson. This took some time, but they pursued their mission in the apparent belief that the task would be made easier if they selected an article that they had already read and understood. Their search was eventually rewarded, and they subsequently completed the set task successfully.

Despite the presence of a more socially interactive NESB student in each class, the NESB students generally appeared to be quiet and compliant in the classroom, as their teachers later observed when interviewed. The selection of non-confrontational responses may enable NESB students to maintain their image as quiet cooperative students. This is in keeping with non-Western philosophies that reinforce the importance of maintaining harmonious relationships and saving face for the teacher (Gudykunst & Kim, 1997; Haworth 1996; Haworth, 1998). However, this 'model' behaviour may have other causes. It is possible that NESB students may simply be endeavouring to behave like everyone else, even when not able to fully participate in classroom learning. I refer to this as *imitating learning*. For example, Rebecca from Samoa was observed during free reading time one afternoon. She was turning the pages of a book but, on closer observation, the pages were being turned in a haphazard order, and her eyes did not appear to be focused on the print. She also frequently tried to draw others at her table into conversation with her, when the teacher was not looking. The event is captured in the following example during silent reading in the Year 3–4 class at 1.45 pm, when Alice the teacher was involved in sorting out an incident that had upset another child during lunchtime.

Example 3

1.45 It's silent reading time. The children need to select books from the pile on the table in front of them. Rebecca's group has already settled to read quietly, but Rebecca is late. She arrives, sits down, places a book in front of her and opens it, then starts to put on her socks. Once this is done, she looks at others at her table and talks to a child alongside, interrupting her reading.

1.48 Rebecca flicks the pages of her book, sometimes forwards and sometimes backwards in no apparent order. She stops and interrupts her neighbour again. She persists although her neighbour ignores her.

1.50 Rebecca reads for a brief moment, then she watches the child across from her. She stretches out across the table, and the non-NESB child beside her says, 'Stop it. Shsh!' with a finger to her lips. Rebecca yawns and lolls across her desk briefly before she goes back to aimlessly flicking pages in her book.

It is interesting that Rebecca, the NESB student described in the above incident, was the same student who was observed to be looking at a different page during a reading group session with the teacher on temperature (Example 1). The classroom teacher, Alice, also later mentioned this child as a concern, saying that she had made less-than-average progress in reading this year. As NESB children with low English proficiency need to make faster-than-average progress so they can catch up with their cohort's English language development, this was even more concerning.

In contrast to the *imitating learning* strategy illustrated above, the NESB children sometimes used imitation in a positive way, *as a strategy for learning*. For example, when Year 5–6 students were working on computers or with calculators, two NESB students with low English levels were observed to be watching and shadowing the actions of a non-NESB student peer. This apparently helped them to keep up with the class and to complete the set tasks. A further example occurred when children in the Year 3–4 class were set the task of writing a summary of the latest part of a continuing story that the teacher had been reading to the class. Jon, an NESB student with low English proficiency, returned to his desk but did not immediately begin to work. From time to time he would surreptitiously take a peek at the writing of two non-NESB children at his table, Alan and Tracey. The following is an excerpt from the observation notes for the first 12 minutes of the writing time.

Example 4

9.23	The children return to their tables. Jon (a Chinese student) puts his name on his work, then looks across at Tracey, the girl who sits opposite him.
9.24	Jon plays with his pen then watches Tracey intently for a few moments. I wonder what use this will be. Since Tracey sits on the other side of the table her work will upside down to Jon.
9.25	Jon shuffles his body across to the left and watches Alan, the boy on the other side of him. Jon fiddles with his pen again and keeps looking around.
9.26	Alan sits back to think and Jon copies from Alan's paper.
9.27	Jon keeps leaning over his paper as though he is writing, but nothing is being written.
9.28	Jon twiddles with his pen and writes a couple of letters.
9.29	The teacher comes to answer a question from Rebecca (a Samoan student at the far end of the table). As she passes she looks over at Jon who appears to be writing. She pauses briefly beside him and says, 'Good', then goes to work with children at other nearby tables.
9.35	Jon is now writing independently, and has been doing so for 5–6 minutes. He has produced about eight lines of text on his page.

After the teacher came to Jon's group table and praised what he had done, Jon continued working independently on his writing, apparently reassured that he was on the right track. Overhearing the teacher's comments to other children in the vicinity of his table may have further supported this. It is worth considering that newly arrived NESB students in the regular classroom may need constant reassurance related to their understanding of set tasks. Barnard (2000) also identifies this need.

On the whole, classroom peers did seem to be helpful in providing support to NESB students in the learning situation. However, it was sometimes difficult to confirm this without being able to hear extended stretches of verbal interaction. For example, a native-speaking student was observed to overtly correct Somai in the Year 5–6 computing class; but it was not possible to determine whether this was a grammatical correction or a reflection on the fact that the NESB student had received help to complete the task:

Somai: We done it!
Ruth: No, I did it!

Although NESB students did, at times, rely on others to help them to cope with class learning tasks, some with greater English proficiency were also observed on a number of occasions to stand up for themselves and to hold their own point of view. For instance, a Year 5–6 NESB child was seen to walk away and leave her partner (with whom she normally did everything) during a problem-solving session. This occurred after her partner (who was a native English speaker) stated that she wanted to do a task that the NESB student had previously completed. In the Year 3–4 class an able NESB child was overheard reprimanding another child: 'Stop making fun of her name'. On another occasion, concerning where to record a question from the reading worksheet, the child said: 'No, it has to be in here'. Such incidents suggest that NESB students, as they increase in confidence, are capable of exerting their own personalities, making their own decisions, and being more than followers of their more fluent English-speaking peers.

Perceptions and Practices of the Regular Classroom Teachers

The interviews with the two participating classroom teachers provided insights into their experiential knowledge, their perceptions of the NESB students, and their perceived roles and confidence in teaching these students.

Teacher experiential knowledge

The two classroom teachers in the study drew extensively on their individual professional knowledge and experiences to devise ways of dealing with the NESB students in their classes. Each teacher had therefore developed her own practices to meet the challenge of teaching these students in her class. Interestingly, Barnard and his colleagues (Barnard *et al.*, 2001) found that social science teachers in secondary schools were more aware of the cultural contributions that students bring to their classes, and inferred that the background experiences and knowledge of these teachers contributed to their practice.

When asked how she went about teaching the NESB students in her Year 5–6 class, Brenda (the teacher with the lesser prior experience with NESB students) linked the needs of these students to those of students with special learning needs – a student category for which she had already developed effective and explicit teaching strategies:

Brenda: It was pretty much like a special needs person who had that level for reading.

Failure to distinguish the specific needs of NESB students from the needs of those students with limited learning abilities devalues the abilities and knowledge that bilingual children bring with them to the learning situation. NESB children who are literate in their first language have learnt useful skills that they can transfer to the reading of subsequent languages.

In contrast with Brenda, Alice (the more experienced classroom teacher) was able to describe specific pre-planned teaching strategies that she used with NESB students. For instance, she regularly included use of headphones with audio-taped reading texts, and shared books and poems. She also enhanced the learning of these children in her classroom by acknowledging their children's linguistic and cultural backgrounds. She was able to give several examples of this in her interview, such as using a variety of languages for the greetings at the start of the day, and using various languages to count the claps given to children on their birthdays. This class had also prepared a Chinese meal when a Chinese-speaking student teacher was in the class. It is worth acknowledging that, for more challenging cultural activities, teachers from a monocultural background will almost certainly require the support of an informed resource person – at least for the first time.

During the interviews, both classroom teachers reported that they drew on professional intuitions, derived from their years of teaching experience, to enable them to respond on the spot to the perceived needs of their learners. They reported that they usually did not consider these actions as part of their written planning for particular lessons. A good example of this occurred in an art lesson in the Year 3–4 class. Alice had already demonstrated the concept of *contrast* by using examples of children's clothing in the introduction to the lesson. However, as the children began their work, she realised that some students needed more help. She then brought around a box of coloured crayons to each group table and helped the children to select objects with contrasting colours. Alice reflected about this episode in the interview after the lesson:

Alice: ... going around with the contrasting colours was not something that I, when I did the planning at home, I had actually written down. But once I was actually in that situation and saw, [I] just thought that was the necessary thing to do and picked up on it ... it was reinforcing the verbal with the visual.

It is interesting, however, that Alice did not specifically consider the

NESB students' needs when her in-action reflections caused her to take steps to clarify the concept of contrast. Alice explained her actions more as a global response to the perceived needs of a number of children in the class who had learning needs.

In contrast to this type of global strategy, Brenda consciously chose to work alongside some NESB students who she thought might have difficulty with the problem-solving concepts that were central to a particular lesson. These students were often attended to earliest. It is possible, of course, that Brenda was more consciously aware of these students in the class because of the research that was taking place. In her later interview, when talking about her efforts to meet the needs of the NESB children in the course of a lesson, Brenda explained:

Brenda: It's probably more luck and off the cuff than pre-planned.

Some teaching strategies do however appear to be pre-planned as an integrated part of the regular teaching routine. For instance, the classroom teachers in this study were aware that learning presented difficulties for a large number of students in the class. They therefore both made conscious use of the whiteboard to record key words, to provide structures for writing, and to clarify instructions during teaching sessions. Brenda noted that these were strategies that benefited a number of students who needed to be 'kept on track', not only the NESB students. In the quote that follows, Brenda also reveals some anomalies in her perceptions about the level of English that the NESB children in her regular class will have. Furthermore, her final statement raises the possibility that she may have been reacting defensively to any possible perceptions of her having low expectations for these children.

Penny: In terms of your planning, do you consciously think of teaching strategies that you put in place for those children?

Brenda: I, no, I don't suppose I do, umm, I suppose I'm assuming they've got enough of the language to actually get them through that stage.

Penny: You actually wrote the steps on the board [in the problem-solving lesson].

Brenda: Again that's not for some of those kids with language difficulties. It's not purely for them, it's sort of the ones who are ...

The knowledge of both classroom teachers, with regard to teaching NESB students, frequently appeared to be more implicit than explicit, and was therefore not always easy to articulate. For example, when describing how she tells student teachers about what to do with NESB children in the class, Alice referred to these children as part of a wider category of children who require *special attention* in the class. On further probing on whether a special *type* of attention might be required for the NESB children, Alice still could not give any specific advice that would help student teachers to teach these students in the class. Alice could, however, easily see that including first language and culture may benefit the NESB students, although neither teacher had previously been confident that many the teaching strategies they regularly used might benefit these students in their classes. As both teachers work regularly with student teachers in their classes, a more conscious awareness of explicit teaching knowledge would seem to be vitally important.

Teachers' perceptions of NESB students

As also found by Barnard *et al.* (2001), the classroom teachers in this study generally identified NESB students as quiet and cooperative. This was interesting in the light of some of the examples illustrated and discussed above, such as inattention and the behaviour of a 'social leader' NESB child in each class. Therefore, the teachers' attitudes may have been based on positive stereotypes. Despite the tendency by Brenda to try to deal with NESB children by including them in the more familiar grouping of 'special needs', both classroom teachers seemed to have some awareness of the different needs of NESB children. For instance, when talking about the use of Burt word recognition tests (which are designed for native English speakers) with students, Alice understood there could be some discrepancies in the interpretation of the results:

Alice: This is only a measure of vocabulary of course, it's not a measure of comprehension.

Brenda also talked about the social leader NESB child in her class. She mentioned his excellent intellectual abilities and the need to keep him challenged. Interestingly, Brenda saw his more social attributes in terms of 'popularity':

Brenda: They flock to him because he's got the answers – [he's] very sure of himself and he knows what he's doing.

Brenda also noticed that, while one NESB child regularly came up close and seemed to need physical contact with the teacher, another kept her distance from the teacher:

Brenda: She seldom talks to me.

Brenda noted that this child's reluctance to interact with her was like the behaviour of a number of other NESB students she had worked with. It was positive, too, that she had considered that personality as well as culture could be involved in the student's silence:

Brenda: I'm not sure if it's a shy thing or a cultural thing.

Teachers' perceived roles and confidence with NESB students

As these teachers had not received any explicit professional input on how to teach NESB students, it is not surprising that they were often found to have low self-efficacy in this task. Bandura (1997: 3) says: 'Perceived self efficacy refers to belief in one's capabilities to organise and execute the courses of action required to produce given attainments.'

It is possible that the classroom teachers in this study may have been hesitant to assert their knowledge in the face of the perceived expertise of the researcher.

When asked about what would most help these students in her class, Brenda (the less experienced teacher), identified that more *teacher aide time* would be useful. She revealed her lack of self-efficacy when subsequently asked whether the teacher aide could be used for other tasks, allowing her to work more with these students. She responded that the teacher aide in the school would be better for this job because she undertaken some professional development in this area. Brenda also overtly expressed doubts about how effective she herself could be, faced with her perception of the enormity of the task:

Brenda: The biggest issue is am I doing as much as I can to get this child to be able to live and survive in our society.

Of the two teachers, Alice had greater self-efficacy in relation to teaching the NESB students in her class. In response to being asked what would help her most with these students, Alice said that she wanted to have fewer students in the class so that she could spend more time meeting the needs of the NESB students. However, even Alice, who had previously worked in an ESOL support position, when asked about providing input into this programme in the school, was unsure about the value of her contribution:

Alice: I wouldn't know what sorts of things to do with the children.

Alice's comments also reflect the burden of responsibility that she felt as the classroom teacher. The NESB children were in *her* classroom, therefore *she* was ultimately responsible for their learning:

Alice: I still think the classroom teacher's very important – for you to build up the relationship with that child. And they need you to do the teaching when they don't have specialist help. And when it comes down to the nitty gritty, let's face it, I'm the one who writes the report. I'm the one who is accountable for the learning objectives. I'm the one who's accountable to the boss [the Principal] and to ERO [the Education Review Office]. Not the teacher aides and not the, not the, not the, well [names the lead support teacher] to a certain extent. Ultimately I'm the one who writes the report, because when I write these children's reports I don't get any input from [the lead support teacher].

The low levels of teacher self-efficacy may relate to the ambivalence that these teachers expressed about whether the classroom teacher or the support teacher held the major responsibility for the NESB students. This ambivalence is also reported in Barnard *et al.* (2001: 24). Clarifying the separate yet interdependent roles of classroom and support teachers, and finding ways to share the responsibility for planning the programme for NESB students, would seem to be important on-going tasks for schools to undertake.

The current study shows that it may be possible that teachers build more self-efficacy with the NESB students by simply spending more time teaching them. Although lacking in formal training in the teaching of these students, Alice may have acquired higher self-efficacy through the time she had spent as an ESOL support teacher. She also had more teaching experience overall, as well as more experience with students from diverse cultural and linguistic backgrounds. If we expect teachers to build skills on the job with NESB students, then *time* in that job becomes a vital factor.

Balancing various needs

When there are many students with many different needs, the NESB students' needs have to be balanced against other priorities in the classroom. The following comments from the interviews with classroom teachers reveal some of the stresses that these teachers were under in trying to meet all of the needs presented by learners in their classroom:

Alice: ... there's one child with an IEP (individualised educational programme – for children with identified learning difficulties), two with quite severe behaviour problems, emotional problems, umm, and you just have little time to actually focus on the needs of the NESB children.

Brenda: In my class this year I had eight reading below their chronological age.

Alice: It's so difficult to monitor thirty one children on three different learning objectives – I try to put them in clusters.

Alice: It's very hard to divide yourself into 31 pieces each day and provide the specific learning needs that every child needs.

Similar time and workload issues were also mentioned in studies of the perceptions of secondary school teachers (Barnard *et al.*, 2001; Cameron & Simpson, 2002; Penfield, 1987).

The classroom teachers in the present study were aware that the needs of the NESB students could be easily overlooked. They reported that this was most likely to happen when other needs, such as those of learners with challenging behaviours, were visibly present in the class:

Alice: ... a lot of the time its those who are making the most noise and then its those who I sort of try to think about – certain ones like you don't hear anything from and think, 'I haven't seen anything you've done ... I haven't actually talked to you'.

Brenda: It's sad in a way, they're not so demanding or disruptive, so they get less of your time ... If you're being honest they are usually quiet and most are willing to learn.

Conclusions

This final section summarises the key findings from the study, notes some possible avenues for future research, looks at possible implications for teachers and teacher educators, and offers suggestions for ways forward.

This study has provided some initial insights into what it's like for two teachers and the NESB learners in their classes. If nothing else, the study highlights the enormous complexity of the teaching task. Classroom teachers are constantly challenged to try to meet the many diverse needs of learners in their classes. As it was not possible to meet all the students' needs all of the time, teachers in this study had developed whole-class strategies that were feasible within the class programme. These strategies included the use of diverse greetings in roll checks; class themes related to students' home cultures; writing up key vocabulary on the board; providing writing outlines; and the use of technology, such as tapes with headphones. These strategies were described as 'not just benefiting the

NESB students' and were thus more easily implemented within the classroom.

Although there was constant pressure on teachers to control the whole class, both teachers in the study saw that they had a responsibility to meet individual learning needs as part of their teaching role. However, the study shows that when classroom teachers are faced with multiple demands on their attention, and lack prior knowledge about teaching NESB students, they may be unable to isolate and productively discuss strategies geared specifically for this one small group of students. These difficulties may be further exaggerated when the NESB students are not homogeneous in terms of ethnicity, culture, first language, intellectual ability, or English proficiency. The teachers in the present study therefore found it necessary to simplify the situation by classifying students in ways that related to their own prior professional knowledge. In this study, at least one of the classroom teachers perceived the NESB students in the same category as those students with special learning needs. Both teachers had already received professional input and generated explicit strategies on how to teach these students. Categorising students in this way appeared to simplify the in-action processing of the teachers so that the class learning and teaching could proceed smoothly. Despite there being some teaching strategies common to both groups, inappropriate grouping with students who are native speakers of English may result in some of the NESB students' specific needs being overlooked. Further training on how to meet the needs of NESB students would expand teachers' skills and enhance their explicit knowledge in this area. Cameron and Simpson (2002: 21) note an increase in the number of regular teachers in Auckland secondary schools gaining qualifications in ESOL. However, this change may take longer to impact on primary school teachers – especially those in provincial areas – as there are fewer NESB students in many of these schools. However, it does provide a reason to be optimistic about the future.

Scollon and Scollon (1995) note that most classroom teachers are part of the dominant English-speaking culture; so, crossing into unfamiliar cultural and linguistic territories is likely to be a challenge for these teachers. The classroom teachers' tendency to place a low priority on professional input related to teaching NESB students may reflect the surrounding sociopolitical context. It is possible that seeing differences is somehow uncomfortable when people purport to belong to an egalitarian society in which difference is de-emphasised. Rajen Prasad, a former Race Relations Conciliator has suggested that there is an atmosphere of timidity regarding discussing and addressing racial matters in New Zealand (cited in Panny, 1997). This creates a dilemma for teachers. On one hand, teachers may not want to be seen to focus on the NESB students' English language limitations, wishing instead to focus on the children's other positive attributes. On the other hand, if teachers do not take account of the English language needs of these learners, they may fail to convey knowledge in a way that is comprehensible to the child, or to extend the child's language in constructive ways. As Gibbons (1991: 119) puts it: 'The limits of my language are the limits of my life'.

An initial exploratory study is perhaps a bit like a bus tour. As we travel along the main route, we get a glimpse of many interesting side routes that we don't have time to go down, but which might yield constructive outcomes. One such side route is the interaction between teachers' strategies and learners' responses. It would be interesting, for instance, to know more about the physical positioning and non-verbal responses of students, and to explore how this relates to the learners' understanding and to particular teaching strategies. Once teachers become more adept at interpreting NESB students' responses in their classes they may feel more confident about generating teaching strategies to meet their needs. Research that extends the list of strategies for teaching these students, with a particular focus on those that teachers can implement easily in a whole class situation, would also be helpful

Another interesting avenue for more in-depth investigation is the way in which NESB learners' social interactions with others in the classroom combine with more academically-oriented interactions to promote learning. Are BICS and CALP really as separate as Cummins would have us believe, or are these aspects mutually supportive in building generic language proficiency for the NESB students in the regular classroom? Effective group dynamics undoubtedly play a part in this. The social leaders identified in each classroom in this study were certainly also the more able NESB scholars.

The findings of this study may imply that the odds are stacked against teachers being able to implement effective classroom programmes that include rather than exclude NESB students. However, the literature on teacher reflection in this field (Richards & Lockhart, 1994; Richards & Nunan, 1990), and more recent studies on teacher autonomy (Sinclair *et al.*, 2000), would suggest that this is not the case. Although teachers in many cases have had to learn by trial and error, it seems that they are extremely resourceful, and do indeed cope with all sorts of challenges. This is further supported in Haworth and Haddock (1999). Kennedy and Dewar (1997) also found that classroom teachers did improve their skills with NESB students – but after some time. The case of Alice, in this study, illustrates the advantages of longer time and reflection on the needs of NESB students.

However, the amount of time required to develop effective teaching strategies without professional input may be impracticable. After substantial teaching experience (10 and 20 years respectively) and having had NESB students in their classes all year, neither teacher in this study was found to have high levels of self-efficacy with these students. Nonetheless, Alice, while not having high self-efficacy with these students, did appear to have more than Brenda (the less experienced teacher). Alice, it may be remembered, had worked for a short time as a support teacher of NESB students. Although Alice had not received any formal training in this area, the opportunity for focused practice may have been useful. It is worth considering that, while classroom teachers are sometimes given time out of the class for professional development, few have had the opportunity to work intensively with NESB students. Professional input can be expected to provide teachers with more confidence, but the addition of focused practical experience with NESB students may also be helpful in accelerating the generation of effective teaching strategies that can later be selectively transferred to classroom situations.

In the primary school classroom, while teachers are expected to teach classes or groups *en masse*, they are also expected to respond to the needs of *individuals* in their classes. One outcome of this dichotomy is that particular needs of individual NESB children may constantly linger at the periphery of a teacher's awareness, giving rise to on-going reflection on unresolved issues. However, if the numbers of these students in a class are small, and the students are generally regarded as cooperative, it is likely that their needs will not naturally float into the foreground of teachers' reflections on their practices. It is therefore vital that teacher educators find effective ways to direct and increase teachers' conscious attention to the challenge of the NESB students in their classrooms.

Acknowledgements

I wish to warmly acknowledge the input of my supervisors Dr Alison St George and Dr Cynthia White. Their unfailing and expert support continues to move me constructively forward in this evolving research process. I would also like to thank Massey University for the research grants that have enabled this study to become a reality. Finally, and most especially, thanks to the school, teachers and children who participated in this study.

Notes

1. Throughout the chapter, the interviewer was the author, Penny Haworth.

References

Andrews, S. (1999) Why do L2 teachers need to 'know about language'? Teacher metalinguistic awareness and input for learning. *Language and Education* 13 (3), 161–177.

Baker, C. (1996) *Foundations of Bilingual Education and Bilingualism*. Clevedon: Multilingual Matters.

Bandura, A. (1997) *Self-efficacy: The Exercise of Control*. New York: W.H. Freeman.

Barnard, R.C.G. (1998) Non-English speaking background students in New Zealand schools. *New Zealand Journal of Educational Studies* 33 (1), 107–114.

Barnard, R.C.G. (2000) NESB students in Hamilton primary schools. *Many Voices* 15, 15–19.

Barnard, R.C.G. (2002) Peer tutoring in the primary classroom: A sociocultural interpretation of classroom interaction. *New Zealand Journal of Educational Studies* 37 (1), 57–72.

Barnard, R., Campbell, L., Campbell, N., Smithson, D. and Vicker, K. (2001) Survey of the regular classroom teacher's perspective of DLE students in Hamilton Secondary Schools. *Many Voices* 17, 21–25.

Barnard, R. and Rauf, P.J. (1999) Non-English speaking background pupils in Hamilton primary schools: A survey of learners, teachers and ESOL provision. *The TESOLANZ Journal* 7, 36–47.

Bedford, J. (2001) Report from Auckland secondary sector meeting. *The TESOLANZ Newsletter* 10 (3),15.

Brown, J. and Canter, D. (1985) The uses of explanation in the research interview. In M. Brenner, J. Brown and D. Canter, D. *The Research Interview: Uses and Approaches* (pp. 217–245). London: Academic Press.

Brumfit, C. (1991) Language awareness in teacher education. In C. James and P. Garrett (eds) *Language Awareness in the Classroom* (pp. 24–39). Harlow: Longman.

Cameron, S. and Simpson, J. (2002) ESOL Teachers' perspectives on the provision for DLE students in Hamilton and Auckland secondary schools. *Many Voices* 19, 16–23.

Cullen, J. and Allsop, G. (1999) Enriching the knowledge base of children's play. A paper presented at the Seventh Early Childhood Convention, Nelson, New Zealand.

Cummins, J. (1984) Wanted: A theoretical framework of relating language proficiency to academic achievement among bilingual students. In C. Rivers (ed.) *Language Proficiency in Academic Achievement*. Clevedon: Multilingual Matters.

Davison, C. (2001) Identity and ideology: The problem of defining and defending ESL-ness. In B. Mohan, C. Leung and C. Davison. (eds) *English as a Second Language in the Mainstream: Teaching, Learning and Identity* (pp. 71–90). London, New York: Longman.

Franson, C. (1999) Mainstreaming learners of English as an additional language: The class teacher's perspective. *Language, Culture and Curriculum* 12 (1), 59–71.

Gibbons, P. (1991) *Learning to Learn in a Second Language*. Newton, NSW: Primary English Teaching Association.

Gudykunst, W.B. and Kim, Y.Y. (1997) *Communicating with Strangers: An Approach to Intercultural Communication*. Boston: McGraw-Hill.

Haddock, D. (1998) TESOLANZ commissioned report on the TESOL tutor profile and competencies. *The TESOLANZ Journal* 6, 89–99.

Hargreaves, A. (1994) *Changing Teachers, Changing Times. Teachers' Work and Culture in a Postmodern Age*. London: Cassell.

Haworth, P. A. (1996) Cultural perceptions of learning situations: Overseas syudents in their first year of teacher education in New Zealand. Unpublished MA thesis, Massey University.

Haworth, P. (1998) Good teaching and learning: A matter of perception? *Set: Research information for teachers* 2, article 13.

Haworth, P. and Haddock, D. (1999) Seeing DLE students with new eyes: Adjusting the teaching focus. *Many Voices* 14, 7–15.

Johnston, B. (1997) Do EFL teachers have careers? *TESOL Quarterly* 31 (4), 681–710.

Johnston, M. (1999) The regular teacher's perspective of non-English speaking background students in secondary schools. *Many Voices* 14, 19–24.

Kennedy, S. and Dewar, S. (1997) *Non-English-Speaking Background Students. A Study of Programmes and Support in New Zealand Schools*. Wellington: Research and International Section, Ministry of Education.

Lawson, O. (2001) Secondary sector issues: Is ESOL a subject? Do we need an ESOL curriculum? If not an ESOL curriculum then do we need ESOL guidelines? What about ESOL and the NCEA framework? *The TESOLANZ Newsletter* 10 (3), 6.

Middleton, S. (1999) Looking forward to the past: Curriculum issues for EAL students. *English in Aotearoa*,3B (ESOL focus issue), 68–70.

Millett, S. and Vine, E. (2000) ESOL withdrawal classes: making links through Social Studies. *The TESOLANZ Journal* 8, 67–78.

Ministry of Education (1999) *Non-English Speaking Background Students in New Zealand Schools: A Handbook for Schools*. Wellington: Learning Media.

Mohan, B. Leung, C. and Davison, C. (eds) (2001) *English as a Second Language in the Mainstream: Teaching, Learning and Identity*. London, New York: Longman.

Panny, R. (ed.) (1997) *People, People, People*. Proceedings, comments and essays from the Third National Conference of the New Zealand Federation of Ethnic Councils. Christchurch: New Zealand Federation of Ethnic Councils (Inc).

Penfield, J. (1987) ESL: The regular classroom teacher's perspective. *TESOL Quarterly* 21(1), 21–39.

Richards, J.C. and Hurley, D. (1988) Getting into the mainstream: Approaches to ESL instruction for students of limited English proficiency. *New Settlers and Multicultural Education Issues* 5 (3) 44–53.

Richards, J.C. and Lockhart, C. (1994) *Reflective Teaching in Second Language Classrooms*. Cambridge: Cambridge University Press.

Richards, J.C. and Nunan, D. (1990) (eds) *Second Language Teacher Education*. Melbourne: Cambridge University Press.

Saville-Troike, M. (1989) *The Ethnography of Communication: An Introduction*. Oxford: Blackwell.

Scollon, R. and Scollon, S.W. (1995) *Intercultural Communication: A Discourse Approach*. Oxford: Blackwell.

Sinclair, B., McGrath, I. and Lamb, T. (eds) (2000) *Learner Autonomy, Teacher Autonomy: Future Directions*. Harlow: Longman in Association with the British Council.

Strauss, A. and Corbin, J. (1998) *Basics of Qualitative Research: Techniques and Procedures for Developing Grounded Theory*. Thousand Oaks, London: Sage Publications.

Syme, P. (1995) Intensive English or mainstream? What is the best provision to make for new learners of English in New Zealand secondary schools? *Research Report* 95 (1). Christchurch: Education Dept, University of Canterbury.

Syme, P. (1999) The English curriculum and DLE students. *English in Aotearoa* 3B (ESOL focus issue), 65–68.

Vine, E.W. (1998) Opportunities for learning ESL through interactions with peers in a new entrants class. *The TESOLANZ Journal* 6, 59–73.

White, C.J. (1997). TESOLANZ draft philosophy of professional standards. *TESOLANZ Newsletter* 6, 15.

Wragg, E.C. (1994) *An Introduction to Classroom Observation.* London: Routledge.

Zephir, F. (1999) Challenges for multicultural education: Sociolinguistic parallels between African American English and Haitian Creole. *Journal of Multilingual and Multicultural Development* 20 (2), 134–154.

Chapter 7

Private Speech in the Primary Classroom: Jack, A Korean Learner

ROGER BARNARD

Introduction

As a result of the significant change in immigration policy in 1987 (noted by Peddie in Chapter 1), the number of NESB (non-English-speaking background) learners in New Zealand schools has rapidly increased. Many have limited proficiency in English language and, when they arrive in their new country, they are placed in regular classrooms where they often find themselves isolated from other children who speak the same first language. Typically, except for a few hours a week in withdrawal English language classrooms (Barnard & Rauf, 1998), they are immersed in a learning environment which, although perhaps superficially similar to classrooms in their home country, is founded upon very different educational beliefs, attitudes and practices. Thus, these children have to come to terms, not merely with issues relating to second language acquisition, but also to the challenge of an alien learning culture in their new schools and classrooms. This is especially true in the less formal primary classrooms in New Zealand, where there is great emphasis on the socialisation of young children and the development of appropriate learning and communication skills rather than on the transmission of information. Immigrant learners have to re-recreate themselves as individuals by participating in the activities of those around them – their peers and their teachers. Their ability to fully participate, and be valorised as members of the learning community, is constrained by their limited proficiency in English and by their cultural unfamiliarity.

A number of studies have been carried out into immigrant learners in primary schools in North America (Poole, 1992; Willett, 1995), the UK (Bourne, 1992; Fisher, 1993) and Australia (Gibbons, 1998), as well as in New Zealand (Barnard, 2002; Haworth, this volume; McNaughton, 1995; Vine, this volume). Many of these studies have focused on the social speech of these learners in interaction with their teachers and peers. There have, however, been relatively few studies carried out into the area of the private speech of young second-language learners in immersion situations. As Ellis (1999: 238) has said, 'researchers have focused almost entirely on social interaction, paying little attention to the interactions that learners engage in inside their heads'. It is felt that an examination of private speech can serve to illuminate aspects of the cognitive, cultural and affective development of young immigrant learners in a new culture of learning. This chapter discusses this issue with specific reference to an eleven-year old Asian immigrant learner in his first year at a primary classroom in a provincial town in New Zealand. It will do so from a sociocultural perspective.

Appropriation by Inner and Private Speech

A sociocultural perspective is based on Vygotsky's general genetic law of cultural development (Vygotsky, 1978: 57). This posits that, while innate biological factors play an important part in development, any learning of cognitive and cultural concepts is primarily stimulated by, and realised through, the interactive use of cultural tools, chief among which is language. There is, therefore, an inextricable causal relationship in Vygotsky's thinking between cognitive and cultural development and interpersonal language. The process that transmutes meaning co-constructed on the social plane to a more personal understanding on the intrapsychological plane has been termed 'appropriation' (Bakhtin, 1981: 293). How this occurs has been explained by Ushakova, a Russian researcher working in the Vygotskian tradition:

> Speech as a means of communication is a two-way process. Two partners speak at the same time, except that one speaks aloud and the other speaks to the self ... Thought, along with internal and external speech, develops simultaneously. (Ushakova, 1994: 140)

Understanding is appropriated when the meaning and use of the concept shifts from the external (social) plane to the internal (personal). Thus, in social interaction three conversations occur at the same time: one between the two social partners, and the other two within each of the interlocutors. It has been suggested (Lantolf, 2002, private communication) that private speech is, in essence, a form of social speech, in which 'I' is conversing with 'me', and the dialogue that occurs is a form of self-regulation.

The silent conversation with the self suggested by Ushakova was called 'inner speech' by Vygotsky (1986/1934), who developed his thinking about inner speech from Piaget's (1926) discussion of egocentric speech in young children. Although Vygotsky shared some of Piaget's assumptions in this area, there were important differences. Piaget considered that egocentric speech had no communicative or cognitive function, but was merely an accompaniment to action and would wither away with increasing maturation. By contrast, Vygotsky considered that inner speech, far from being a mere accompaniment to thought, serves a crucial role in cognitive development, and functions at all levels of maturation, serving as a 'transitional mechanism' (Vygotsky, 1986: 218), through which thought can be formed, developed and expressed before emerging on the social plane. But inner speech does not merely *transmit* data from the external to the internal plane: it *re-creates* meaning. By turning the speech data inward, and applying it to the individual's own mental frame of reference and value system, the appropriated meaning is bound to be, to a greater or lesser degree, different from that reached on the social plane.

Neurological evidence of inner speech has been established by experimental research. For example, Ushakova (1994) reported various laboratory studies conducted in the Soviet Union, and in particular referred to the work of Sokolov (1968), who managed to identify concrete relationships between inner speech and thinking processes. During a series of experiments, Sokolov detected hidden movements of the articulatory organs; this suggests that under cognitive stress the speech organs are articulated – even though there may be no audible representation. Based on such work, Ushakova herself (1994: 145) developed a general 'mechanismic' description of inner speech, which comprises a hierarchy of functional levels, each of which comprises separate linguistic components working in harmony. Ushakova and her colleagues (Ushakova, 1994: 148) proceeded to test the model in a range of experiments that focused on the mechanics of inner speech in both first and second languages. The lowest level is that of self-stimulating language use (such as singing or repeating words), followed by commentary and descriptive language (accompanying or describing one's own activity, or describing objects and others in the immediate environment). The highest level is self-guiding language, which is intended to gain control over the mental processes (Saville-Troike, 1988: 569).

However, while such experimental research is helpful in identifying the basic mechanisms of inner speech, the artificiality of laboratory conditions does not permit a clear understanding of the circumstances in which private speech might occur in natural settings. A problem that arises in investigating inner speech is that, by its nature, it is inaccessible to anybody but the most introspective thinker – and even then, once inner speech is consciously formulated, it loses its pristine quality and ceases to be pure thought. Sometimes, however, the inner conversation between 'I' and 'me' emerges onto the audible plane as private speech. The relationship between inner and private speech has been described thus:

> Inner speech functions to organise and make sense of a person's experience of the world. Just as social speech mediates the individual's relationship to the world of others and objects, private speech, its derivative, mediates the relationship between the person and his or her inner mental order, or what Vygotsky called consciousness. (Pavlenko & Lantolf, 2000: 165)

When self-directed private speech does surface on the audible plane, it often retains some of the same truncated syntactic and phonological characteristics that Vygotsky (1986: 234) posited for inner speech. Inner speech has an abbreviated syntax, where predicativity predominates. The simple explanation for this phenomenon is that the individual has a clear mental idea of the topic, or theme, of what s/he is thinking about, but might need to articulate the new information contained in the predicate as a way of processing, or appropriating, new ideas. With regard to the sound system, in the individual's mind words and their meanings are inextricably bound together; thus separate words often undergo phonological abbreviation, and then become agglutinated. What emerges on the external and audible surface, therefore, is entirely meaningful to the speaker – indeed is *saturated* with meaning – but often, and as a direct consequence, is far from comprehensible to the listener. Lantolf & Appel (1994: 15) argue that, the more difficult the task, the more fully structured (social-like) private speech becomes. Even here, private speech is usually quieter than speech intended for social communication. Therefore, until audio technology was sufficiently sensitive – and unobtrusive – to capture private speech in naturally-occurring situations, research into this area was thwarted.

Private Speech in Second Language Learning

Various studies have investigated the use of private speech by adult second-language learners to facilitate the process of learning (De Guerrerro 1987, 1994, 1999; Lantolf 1997; Lantolf & Frawley, 1984; Ohta, 1995). Frawley and Lantolf (1985) provided confirmation for Sokolov's (1968) experiments: when put in challenging situations, the language learners they studied relied a great deal on private speech to maintain control of the task. More than 90% of the adult learners in De Guerrerro's 1994 study reported that inner or private speech helped them to clarify thoughts, assisted them to store and retrieve language items, imitate pronunciation, and ask and answer self-directed questions. These studies indicate that private speech 'is of utmost importance for the long-term retention of L2 input and consequently for the permanent and successful learning of the L2' (De Guerrerro, 1994: 102). In his 1997 study of adult learners of Spanish, Lantolf reported the use of playful private language as:

> Talking out loud to yourself in Spanish; repeating phrases to yourself silently; making up sentences or words in Spanish; imitating to yourself sounds in Spanish; having random snatches of Spanish pop into your head. (Lantolf, 1997: 11)

Working from his view that 'for Vygotsky, play is not a means for the child to have fun', Lantolf (1997: 4) argued that, although there is some sense of satisfaction in engaging in this sort of language play, the need for it diminishes or is eliminated altogether as the learner becomes more proficient (Lantolf, 1997: 17). In contrast, Cook (1997) took another view of language play: that it *is* fun, and he refers to it as 'ludic' language play. Taking his cue from Bakhtin's (1981) notion of 'carnivality', Cook distinguished two sorts of ludic language play. There is playing with the *form* of the language (rhyme, rhythm, alliteration, punning, etc.) and playing with the *meaning* of language (using semantic units to create a fictional world against which to match, perhaps parody, the real world). In contrast to Lantolf, Cook argued that such second language play, far from diminishing, actually becomes richer and more complex with cognitive and cultural maturation.

Early work on the private speech of younger, school-aged second language learners was conducted in the United States by Saville-Troike (1988), who used radio microphones to collect the private speech of nine young Asian children (aged between 3 and 8 years) in nursery and elementary classrooms. Saville-Troike reported that the children in her study used both English and their first language in their private speech. English tended to be used when the learners were focusing on the language or language-related activities, and the first language was used to describe or refer to objects or events in the environment rather than language itself. Saville-Troike suggested that her data 'offer support for the qualitative hierarchy of self-stimulating, commentative, and self-regulatory speech functions which have been posited by Vygotsky (1962) and others' (Saville-Troike, 1988: 586). Anticipating Cook's argument, she found that, when the children were focusing on the *form* of the second language, they used private speech for rehearsal, experimentation or creativity. By contrast, when the children were focusing on the *sound* of the second language, their private speech was used mostly for play and 'the apparent kinaesthetic pleasure of repeating words and phrases' (Saville-Troike, 1988: 587). Interestingly, it did not appear to matter to these children whether they understood what they were saying in second-language private speech, whether as rehearsal or as play.

Later research by Broner and Tarone (2001) found that young children in Spanish immersion classes, like Saville-Troike's Asian learners, used playful private speech for rehearsal purposes (Lantolf, 1997) as well as for amusement (Cook, 1997). Both types of language serve the process of language acquisition, but in somewhat different ways. The rehearsal function facilitates language learning as the speaker seeks to memorise lexical, phonological and syntactic structures in order to approximate to these norms. Ludic language play, on the other hand, may facilitate language learning in two ways. First, raising the emotional engagement with the discourse may make it more noticeable, and thus more memorable. Second, playing with meaning allows the learner to appropriate the language to his or her own semantic frame of reference. Broner & Tarone (2001: 376) distinguished the two types by referring to the following five cues:

- whether laughter is present or absent;
- whether the private speech was marked by shifts in voice quality and pitch rather than shifts in volume;
- whether the language items that used were well known or new;
- whether or not there is a fictional world of reference; and
- whether there is an audience other than the self.

The authors point out that the two forms of language play intermingle within any stretch of discourse. They also point to the importance of individual differences: some learners are less playful than others.

Functions of Private Speech: A Summary

The research into this area suggests that private speech may serve at least three distinct functions: metacognitive, rehearsal and creative amusement.

(1) *Metacognitive* – as indicated above by Sokolov's experiments, private speech may occur when a learner talks him/herself through a task of enhanced difficulty in an attempt to retain control over the situation. This may be termed the metacognitive function, and may be realised by instructions, or questions, or evaluatory comments directed to the self (Lantolf, 2000) in order to promote understanding.

(2) *Rehearsal* – the inner preparation for subsequent verbal activity on the social plane. Some of that rehearsal may be considered simply as imitation: privately repeating another person's lexical, syntactic and

prosodic patterns may allow the learner time and opportunity to reflect internally on the meanings ascribed by that person. Alternatively, the learner may recast the ideas and opinions of more 'expert' interlocutors into slightly different lexical, syntactic or phonological patterns. Much more clearly than mere parroting, such reformulation reveals the process of appropriation in action.

(3) *Language play*, in which the form or meaning of the language is used primarily for self-amusement and fun. This sort of private speech can also assist in the development of manipulative and creative use of the second language.

Thus, there have been several studies into the positive use of private speech by second language learners. However, there has been little research that indicates how private speech may reveal negative feelings associated with the process of language and cultural acquisition. In the case study that follows, this issue will be explored by the presentation and discussion of transcript data.

The Case Study

The setting for the study was an intermediate (upper primary school, Years 7 and 8) in New Zealand with some 450 eleven- to thirteen-year old students in the school. A Ministry of Education audit report carried out the previous year indicated that the ethnic composition of the school was as follows:

Pakeha*	54%	Māori	22%	Pacific Islands	4%
Asian	14%	Somali	2%	Other	4%

* *Pakeha* refers to New Zealanders of European descent

The Ministry of Education provides funding to schools to support the English language development of some of the NESB learners. In order to apply for funding, a school is required to assess the language competence of every NESB student both on arrival and periodically afterwards. If a child is unable to understand or communicate more than a few words of English, he or she is deemed 'minimally competent'. According to the school's records, 47 students were identified as needing English language support: 31 of these had been at school in the previous year; 16 arrived at various times during the year in which the research was conducted. The major provision of English support to NESB learners in the school was by withdrawing them from their regular classes for language lessons in the ESOL (English to Speakers of Other Languages) unit. This unit was run by an ESOL-trained teacher, supported by two part-time teaching assistants.

For those students deemed to have 'minimal English', this tuition amounted to some four or five hours a week; for those above that level, the withdrawal provision was rather less, perhaps one and a half hours a week.

Over the course of a school year, from January to December, I was a participant observer in a Year 7 classroom – 'Room 7'. Most of the 30 or so students were Pakeha, with four Māori and two of mixed Māori and Pakeha descent. There were also eight NESB students, and five others subsequently joined the class at various times during the year. Particular attention was paid to interactions between these new learners and their classmates. These interactions were recorded by lapel microphones attached to small cassette recorders that the students kept in pockets or pencil cases. At the beginning of the year, the broad aims of the project were explained to the students in the class and this was followed by a letter of information and a consent form, which was signed by each child and a parent or caregiver.

The immigrant children who were the focus of the main study (Barnard, 2000) arrived in the country at various times during the year. As each one was enrolled in school, the mother and child were interviewed together by myself and a research assistant who was a native speaker of their first language; they were then given a letter and consent form in their first language to sign. By this time, the mainstream teacher had inducted the class into the 'ground rules' for classroom interaction. These conventions included matters such as bidding for turn, individual deskwork, modes of group work, and criteria for good performance – standards for written work, 'research' projects, self-evaluation, etc.

When these new students joined the class, the use of the cassette recorders to capture students' interactions was a well-established practice in the classroom. Like their classmates, they very soon ignored the presence of the microphones, and the interactions that were recorded were natural and spontaneous. Sometimes as many as four cassette recorders were in operation in a class at any one time, and many thousands of interactions were thus recorded over the year. These interactions were transcribed verbatim and, through a process of constant comparative analysis, patterns emerged that indicated ways in which students interacted.

However, there were many occasions when private speech was audible, and a key issue that arose was the way that the private speech of the NESB learners reflected the extent of their understanding of, and ability to integrate into, the culture of learning of the New Zealand primary classroom. In contrast to the reports reviewed earlier (Broner & Tarone, 2001; Saville-Troike, 1988), the present study investigated the occurrence of private speech over a longer time frame – a period of months. Much of the recorded data indicated that the private speech of the students, both NESB and otherwise, was used for the metacognitive, rehearsal and ludic functions suggested by the earlier research.

One of the difficulties identified in the published research is how to distinguish clearly between private speech and speech intended for social interaction (Wells, 1999). The criteria provided by Broner and Tarone (2001) have proved very useful in making reasonable inferences about the occurrence of private speech in the present study, but nevertheless some ambiguities arose. Elaine Vine (2002, private communication) has suggested that the tape recorder might itself function as a 'hearer' – that is, the apparently private speech that is recorded might in some sense be (intentionally?) addressed to the eventual listener of the tape. I felt that, initially at least, there was an element of this among some of the students in Room 7. However, Jack – the subject of this chapter – was the only Korean speaker in the class, and he was not aware that a Korean speaker would eventually listen to the tape. It is, therefore, reasonable to assume that any utterance he made in Korean was directed at himself, rather than intentionally for an external audience.

Jack

Jack (a pseudonym) was an 11-year-old Korean boy who arrived in Hamilton in the middle of March with his mother and younger sister; his father continued to work in Korea. Jack joined his new school and class on his third day in New Zealand – six weeks after the start of the school year.

Jack was enrolled at school along with another Korean boy who had arrived in Hamilton with him. The other boy, a 12-year-old, was staying with Jack's uncle, who had been resident in Hamilton for a few weeks. The uncle spoke a little English, but his sister (Jack's mother) knew none. On account of their age, the boys were placed in different year forms.

On entry to the school, Jack was interviewed by the ESOL teacher, who judged that his English was 'minimal': he knew the alphabet and some basic words, and could count up to 20 (after 16, only with some prompting). Jack was provided with about four hours a week of withdrawal ESOL tuition, but for the other thirty or so classroom hours each week, he was in a context largely of incomprehensible input.

In the mainstream, Jack was allocated a place right at the back of Room 7, where he stayed for the rest of the year. For several weeks, his immediate neighbours included three very pleasant boys who were considered by the teacher to be below average in terms of academic achievement, and tended in various ways (for example, by two of them constantly drumming their fingers on their desks) to be somewhat disruptive. Jack's verbal participation with both the teacher and his classmates remained minimal – the main reason being his lack of communicative competence in English. He was, however, usually attentive during the teacher's instructions and dialogues, and closely observant of his classmates' actions – in an effort to understand, and perhaps imitate, what was required. While his attention sometimes wavered, and he gazed around the room, he seemed to do so much less frequently than some of the other NESB learners. He tried to participate to the best of his ability in many of the classroom activities – most successfully in the written computation tasks in maths lessons, for which he was working well within his cognitive competence.

It is very significant that a few days after Jack's arrival, the class attended a three-day annual camp in the bush with other classes. The school placed considerable emphasis on this event as a way of social bonding among the students, and between students and teachers. Jack was unable to attend the camp owing to his late enrolment; instead, while his peers were at camp he was given a few extra ESOL lessons in the mornings, and he went home in the afternoons. The two-week Easter vacation occurred a few days after the class returned from camp. The implications of Jack's being unable to develop his social relationships at this critical moment after his arrival, while incalculable, were probably considerable.

Transcript conventions

NB the names of all participants are pseudonyms.

01, 02, 03, etc.	the sequence of utterances in an exchange
Ro, Ja, Pe, etc.	first letters of a student's name (e.g. Ja = Jack)
T	the teacher ('Mrs Martin')
[in square brackets]	comments from field notes
word underlined	given emphasis by the speaker
xxxxx	inaudible/unintelligible utterances
...	short pauses
>	speech overlapping with next utterance
utterances in # ... #	private speech in English
utterances in # *italic* #	private speech in the first language (Korean)
(utterances in round brackets)	English version of previous Korean utterance

Note: In spoken Korean, it is very common to omit subject pronouns, and even object pronouns, where the context makes the meaning unambiguous. There are no impersonal pronouns corresponding to 'it' and 'they', and possessive pronouns are not used where the context makes it clear to whom something belongs. In the transcriptions of private speech which follow, personal pronouns are given in the English versions (especially 'I' me, 'it', etc.) so as to make the meaning clear.

Jack's Private Speech

After the Easter recess, Jack would typically enter Room 7 before the due time and eventually learned to respond to casual greetings with 'Fine, thank you', usually spoken very quietly. He might smile a greeting, but rarely initiated a spoken interaction, even briefly. At his desk, before a lesson commenced, he might riffle through a Korean magazine or a dictionary; often, he would wait pensively for the lesson to begin. Like other children, he was not always enthusiastic when the teacher called the class to order. For example,

Example A: 12 May 8.59 – Exploring language

01 **T:** Is Abdul here? Right. You and xxxxx Good morning everyone

02 **Ps:** Good morning Mrs Martin>

03 **Ja:** Good morning Mrs Mart ... [mutters in a low, complaining tone] # *Igo kajigo ochuliogo krae*? (What are you going to do with this?) #

Jack had been told to bring a bilingual dictionary to class, and he had done so. His self-questioning is similar to that reported in other studies (Broner & Tarone, 2001; De Guerrerro, 1994; Lantolf, 2000). As well as indicating a metacognitive function in process, the interrogative form of the utterance suggests very strongly the social nature of private speech – a conversation, or at least the start of one, between 'I' and 'me'.

Example B: 8 May 9.44 – Spelling

01 **T:** Right. In five minutes time we're going to share those sentences

02 **Ja:** (sighs wearily) # *ah, nado igol heyaman tuena* (Oh, do I have to do this?) *kwerobta kwerobta kwerobta!* ... (I'm suffering! suffering, suffering!) *ahh ... haaa* # [fidgets with exasperation]

Here, too, Jack's self-questioning shows both a metacognitive function and a social aspect. Many of his classmates had a similar reaction at the start of a lesson or new activity, although others showed a more positive attitude. At other times, his private speech was more laconic.

Example C: 15 May 9.22 – Spelling

01 **T:** I'd like you to get ready for your spelling tests – draft books
02 **Ja:** [drawing in breath] # *ah, itta!* (Whew, I've got it!) #

This suggests that Jack was learning to understand some routine classroom instructions, and his private speech (02) may be seen as indicating his readiness to participate in the lesson. Some of the captured private speech of his classmates in Room 7 revealed the children playing with language not only for rehearsal purposes but also for amusement, in the same way as the children studied by Saville-Troike (1988) and Broner and Tarone (2001). However, it may be noted that Jack did not seem to use private speech for ludic purposes. The following interaction, which occurred a few minutes later in the same lesson, is significant

Example D: 15 May 9.30 – Spelling

01 **T:** Right. Tongues are away. Carlin xxx>
02 **Ri:** What's this? >
03 **Ja:** xxx children ... pencil case ... Walkman xxx [mutters unintelligibly]
04 **T:** Jack. Here's a gold card for you. Right. [gives it to him] Gold card. Really good. No, that's all right. What you've got to do, and one of the boys will go with you, is to go to Room 1 at some stage and get it filled in – all right – from Mrs Smith
05 **Na:** Mrs, Mrs?
06 **T:** Mrs Smith – yes>
07 **Ri:** It's got a line in it, bu>
08 **T:** [to Jack] That's OK. Yeah, but you still need that filled in, OK. So that. It can go into his clear file, cos at the moment all it's got is, Jack Room 7. All right? It's good that he knows why he's got it. All right? And then he can go and work it out [walks away]
09 **Ja:** [silence]

Despite the teacher's instruction (01) for the class to be quiet, Richard took the opportunity, while Mrs Martin was talking to another student, to initiate an informal interaction with Jack. The point of his question (02) is obscure; he may have been eliciting some language practice from Jack, as the latter recited (03) a number of words in English. While he was doing so, the teacher approached and gave him a gold card for some previous excellent work. It is very unlikely that Jack understood much of what the teacher said (04, 08), but the physical presence of a gold card might have indicated that he had done something praiseworthy. Mrs Martin did not explain precisely what, and Jack did not enquire: presumably, he lacked confidence in his ability to ask for, or understand, information of this nature – either from the teacher or from his classmates. The significant point is that, after the teacher left, Jack made no comment to himself indicating either puzzlement or pleasure at this honour. It would be surprising if questions did not arise in his mind, but he did not verbalise them. In itself, this underlines the tentativeness of making any assumptions from audible private speech. Nevertheless, it is also interesting that Jack was never heard to express in his private speech any sort of pleasure or enthusiasm.

The following extract occurred during a lesson in late June – several weeks after Jack's arrival. The teacher told the class that they had two minutes to finish their work, an instruction that Jack appeared to understand. He sighed, perhaps with exasperation, and continued checking in his dictionary, muttering occasionally and unintelligibly in Korean, and humming to himself. He then turned to his neighbour Michael and wrote with his finger on the desk.

Example E: 26 June 10.32 – Language arts

01 **Ja:** [writing with his finger on desk] Today?
02 **Mi:** Tell?
03 **Ja:** Today
04 **Mi:** Today. Do you want me to spell it?
05 **Ja:** Er – yes. Uhh
06 **Mi:** OK, erm. Here [writes 'today' for Jack]
07 **Ja:** Wah?
08 **Mi:** What do you want?
09 **Ja:** want? What xxx
10 **Mi:** Yeah
11 **Ja:** Waa
12 **Mi:** What – do – you – want, from me? Do you want me to tell you something?
13 **Ja:** xxx
14 **Mi:** Tell
15 **Ja:** Aaa
16 **Mi:** Tell.
17 **Ja:** [sighs, apparently in exasperation] # *itaekaji* (Up to now / so far) # ... [starts to write with his finger]
18 **Mi:** When ... Tell ... How>
19 **Ja:** # *ah, ahu.* (Ah) # [as he writes with his finger on the desk]
20 **Mi:** Ah, get it finished! Get it – You've got to get it finished

today, or you've probably got to go home and do it for homework

21 **Ja:** xxx [appears to understand]

This was the first time that Jack had been recorded as having initiated a verbal task-related interaction with a classmate, and illustrates his lack of communicative competence (or confidence) even after several weeks in the class. At first, Michael did not understand what Jack wanted, nor did he clearly see what he was writing on the desk. Through such miscomprehension, Jack's need for clarification about when the task had to be completed was in danger of being sidetracked into a matter of spelling. Jack, however, persisted in using all linguistic and non-linguistic resources he could muster and Michael (showing great patience) eventually understood (20) what Jack wanted. It is difficult to interpret Jack's Korean utterance (17): it may have been an impatient indication of the time it had taken to get his message across, but it also seems to be the climax of the interaction between the boys: thereafter, comprehension appeared to come more easily.

The following examples (Fa, Fb and Fc) occurred in a lesson in mid-October. The class had been given sets of vocabulary tasks, the level of which varied according to their performance in a pre-test. Jack was in the lowest group. The first task he had to do was to put a set of words in alphabetical order

Example Fa: 16 October 9.50 – Vocabulary

01 **Ja:** [vocalising the rubric] # Write out ... Write out, er ... twelvu worduz ... al,pha,betical order ... 'ask' ... What? # [touching Peter, pointing, rising volume] What?

02 **Pe:** Yeah – Alphabetical order

03 **Ja:** Order? [flicking through dictionary]

04 **Pe:** Yeah – ABCDEFG [singing ditty] Alphabetical, order

05 **Ja:** Order? [Ja checks in dictionary] # Order? Order #

06 **Pe:** Order

07 **Ja:** [saying quickly to himself] # A B C D E F G #

08 **Pe:** OK – 'ask' [putting his finger on a word on the list]

09 **Ja:** A K S

10 **Pe:** Yeah [points to Jack's worksheet] and 'ask', is first >

11 **T:** Put up your hand if you have <u>not</u> received your worksheet>

12 **Pe:** And then, B C D E >

13 **Ja:** Ah! I know. [looks through dictionary, muttering] # *eoryoukutkatundae* (This seems difficult) Order ... Order? ... G ... H I J # [finds the entry] # *aah, yogitta!* (Ah – here it is!) #

This extract, like the one above, shows the interface between social and private speech, and also the continuing limits of Jack's communicative competence. Jack externalised his metacognitive processing while reading through the task rubric (01): verbalising (in English) only the key elements. It may be inferred that the repetition aloud of parts of the task rubric was a form of self-regulation, focusing his attention so as to appropriate the task requirements; he appeared not to understand the meaning of 'order', and his first 'What?' (01) appears to be private speech addressed to himself, even possibly a rehearsal for his intended interaction with Peter. The second, slightly louder and accompanied by tugging Peter's sleeve and pointing to the worksheet, was sufficient to enable the other boy to recognise his need. Peter's laconic response (02) was inadequate: Jack echoed Peter's response, with a rising intonation (03), which suggests that he had received the correct word, but could not attribute meaning. Noting Jack riffling through his bilingual dictionary, Peter expanded his explanation by quietly chanting an alphabet song. The following five brief exchanges (03 to 07) occurred while Jack was looking through his dictionary, and it is clear that he was beginning to appropriate some elements of meaning, evidenced by repeating 'order' and saying (not singing) the ditty that Peter had just chanted. (Here the interface between private and social speech is far from clearly demarcated.) Peter built on this evidence of Jack's burgeoning understanding by indicating the first word on the list; Jack again showed (09) some understanding, which Peter confirmed (10) by telling and showing Jack what to do, and then elaborating (12). Jack (13) explicitly – and in English – marked his understanding of what he had to do – which he sought to consolidate by further reference to his dictionary. Although he now understood what to do, he found the task difficult – as he said to himself in Korean (13). His private speech indicated his developing mental activity: he kept the English word at the forefront of his mind while using Korean to comment on his activity, culminating in his final utterance – further indication of appropriation having occurred. He then got on with the task with no apparent need for further assistance, writing the words in alphabetical order and repeating in private speech key lexical elements of the task.

The following exchanges followed shortly after the previous one. By now Jack had completed the first task, and was about to start the second task, the rubric of which was:

Identify which words in the list are nouns. There should be eight of them.

Example Fb: 16 October 9.58 – Vocabulary

14 **T:** [approaching] How're ye going Jack?

15 **Ja:** [checking his dictionary] Yeah ... # *hal-gut-ee-da ... hal-gut-ee-da, hal-gut-ee-da* (Going to ... going to, going to) #
16 **T:** [looking at Ja's work] Good. Yes [T leaves]
17 **Ja:** [reads through the rubric for the task, and identifying a key word, then] # shouldn't should, shouldn't, should # [looking though dictionary, then mutters] # *ige muoya?* (What is it?) #

The teacher's enquiry received a very short response, Jack keeping his eyes on his work. His following utterance in Korean (15) suggests a self-direction to get on with the work; it is also possible to suggest that he had appropriated the sense of the teacher's 'going' (14). It is interesting that he did not seek help from the teacher at this point, but tried to work out (17) the task instructions for himself, repeating the word 'should' as he consulted the dictionary. His question in Korean, clearly addressed to himself, is a typical form of metacognitive self-regulation, similar to those reported by Lantolf (2000: 88). Jack soon became stuck and sought help from Peter, who was working on another set of tasks:

Example Fc 16 October 10.01 – Vocabulary

18 **Ja:** # What ... what ... what? # [tugs Peter's shirt to catch his attention, pointing to his worksheet]. What?
19 **Pe:** Well, I'm not sure
20 **Ja:** Not sure?
21 **Pe:** Well, I don't know
22 **Ja:** # *ahh, huehanhada iguh!* (Ah, this is so strange!) # [checks through his dictionary for each word in the rubric] # *nun iguh aruh?* (Do you know what this is?) ... *aruh?* (Do you?) ... *naega igul uttuke aruh?* (How can I know all this?) ... *jae-gil!* (Bloody hell!) # [searches for the meaning of words he finds, reciting the alphabet] # A B C D E G H I K ... *ahu, jae-gil ahh duh-rub-da jeongmal!* (Ah, really, bloody hell!) ... naming word, er na-ming word, naa-ming wor-oh, naam-ing word # [finds 'naming' in dictionary and reads the entry] #*Eerumul bootchida?* (To name?) *jimyunghada?* (To name?) *myungsa ... myungsa* (Noun, noun) ... *jaegil, jaegil erun!* (Bloody, bloody hell!) ... *ahniya* (Not sensible) ... Name the ... *igae moounji ahseyo?* (Do you know what this is?) #

After checking his dictionary, Jack waited for an opportunity (18) to interrupt his classmate, which he did with a typically minimal verbal cue, and pointing at his worksheet. Peter read the instructions, but – to Jack's evident disappointment – said he was not sure (19). Perhaps Peter did not want to engage with Jack, preferring to get on with his own work. Jack echoed his response (20), the rising terminal tone suggesting that he wanted to continue the exchange. After a brief rejoinder (21), Peter returned to his own work. Jack spent the next four minutes (22) carefully checking the words of the task rubric in his dictionary, repeating the key words in English to himself, together with a running commentary in Korean. This self-directed talk may have assisted Jack to monitor his control over the task by keeping the key words in the forefront of his mind. Unlike the private speech reported by Villamil and de Guerrerro (1996: 63), he was evaluating less his own performance than the difficulty or obtuseness of the task. As he did so, his annoyance palpably grew – giving rise to expletives and other expressions of anger. It is worth remarking at this point that Jack's outward demeanour gave no indication of his inner feelings; he sat quietly, and his mutterings did not attract the attention of his classmates or his teacher.

His private speech is realised in full sentences (apart from the omission of pronouns, typical of spoken Korean) and – with few exceptions – phonologically complete. What is interesting here is his register: the utterances 'Do you know what this is? ... Do you?) and 'How can I know all this?' are in an informal register, as indicated by the (repeated) use of '*aruh*'. This marker would suggest an addressee who is Jack's peer, or – more likely – Jack himself. However, his final utterance 'Do you know what this is?' appears as if spoken to an adult or to the teacher, indicated by his use of '*ahseyo*' a marker of social respect. In both cases, a possible interpretation is that this private speech might be intended as a rehearsal for social speech – except, or course, that no one else in the room spoke Korean. Alternatively, it could be an example of the sort of 'double voicing' suggested by Broner and Tarone (2001: 375). It may be speculated that, having received no satisfactory answer from himself-as-peer, addressing the latter question as if to a teacher was an attempt at self-regulation through a subtle sort of private role-play.

The extracts below (example G) occurred during a mathematics lesson one hot and sunny day in November. In class, the students had been identifying patterns in a series of triangles. The teacher then took the class outside to sit on the grass while she went over the work they had done. As the class settled down, Jack muttered to himself, showing some resentment at having to sit on the grass in the afternoon heat:

Example G 6 November 11.49 – Mathematics Lesson

01 **Ja:** # *aah ... salgishiiruh* (I don't want to live) aah ... *yogisuh kkomjirak daemyun suh itt-uh-ya hana!* (I can't believe I have to

be here! They are so slow – stupid!) # [mockingly, about the other students] # *ahh ... moouh chojiraleeya iguh ... igun chojirraleeya iguh ... igun chojiraleeda* (F***! ... F***!) # [taking pens etc out of his pencil case] ... # *salgishiiruh ... ahu* (I don't want to live ... aah) ... *jon-na salgishiltta!* (I bloody well don't want to live!) #

The above monologue occurred over a two-minute period, while the teacher got the class settled. Jack's private speech, especially his use of strong swear swords, indicates a surprising degree of vented frustration, which increased as the lesson proceeded. The teacher then started the first of a series of assisted performances by asking some students to go through the task sheet with her for the benefit of the class as a whole.

02 **T:** OK, if I said to you one, three, five, seven, nine – what's the next number. Can you tell me what's the pattern?
03 **P:** Erm, in twos. It's going up in twos
04 **T:** Good, going up in twos. OK. Now, listen to these ones. Two, four, eight, sixteen. Jack, What's happening there? What's that pattern?
05 **Ja:** [promptly] Time two [more slowly] Times two?
06 **T:** Good. Times two. Well done! Who can give me another word that means the same as times two?
07 **P:** Doubling.

Despite his dissatisfaction with the setting, Jack was ready and able to respond (05) to the teacher's (rare) elicitation. A few moments later, while the teacher was interacting with others, Jack's private speech again revealed his intense boredom and annoyance:

08 **St:** I don't understand the next part.
09 **T:** [to class] ... Well, think about it [tells students to read through their worksheets
10 **St:** Mrs Martin, could you xxx...
11 **Ja:** # *jaegil* (Bloody hell) ... *jon-na jaemitda!* (Bloody interesting!) ... *jon-na jaemituhsuh jookgetuh* (This is so bloody interesting that I wanna die) # ... [ironically] # *sal gi shiltta* (I don't wanna live) ... *jon-na jaemituhsuh jookgetuh* (This is so bloody interesting that I wanna die) ... *jookgoshipda!* (F***! I wanna kill myself) ... *jookjimothae saruh*!! (F***! If only I could die) ... *jon-na salgishiltta* (This is bloody killing me) ... *mooseon jaemiga it-uh-ya-ji* (This is so bloody far from being fun) ... *moonjaegatjido anun gul* (It's so easy that it doesn't seem to be a question at all) ... *jon-na jaemitda* (Bloody interesting) ...

> *jaemmieetuhsuh duejigetta* (This is so bloody interesting I might as well kill myself) ... *mak michyu jookgetdah* (It's driving me mad) ... *hankukeesuh eettangun mak ttaryu jookeenunde* (If I were in Korea, I'd beat all these up) # [referring to a group of students who are off task] ... # *naega jyeneboda mul mothae* (It's not like I'm heaps worse than them) ... *ahu, jangnanhanya aedul jikum jangnanhanda* (Ah – it's not playtime – these kiddies are mucking around) *aedul jangnanhanda, jangnanhae!* (They're mucking around, just mucking around!) ... *ah, jotta jaemitda* (Bloody interesting) ... *jugido jaemitgae hane* (They're enjoying themselves over there) ... *mak joogul jiyungeeda* (I'm nearly dying) ... *ahh, mak jaemituhsuh duejigetdah* (I'm bloody dying here) ... *aah, jon-na jaemitdah* (It's just too interesting) ... *jaemituhsuh mak oolgetuh* (So bloody interesting that I'm almost about to cry) ... *jon-na chajeungna – ah, XX*! (Bloody annoying – ah, F***!) #

This stream of consciousness over a period of five and a half minutes – crude, ironic, impatient, and accompanied by constant clicking of his ballpoint pen – was most probably provoked by the uncomfortable setting and by the simplicity of the tasks the teacher was reviewing. After the teacher had called upon another student to work on an assisted performance, she asked Jack to come to her side:

12 **T:** OK. I've had a little chat with Areal, and she's got it all correct ... Jack>
13 **Ja:** Yes>
14 **T:** come and stand here and tell me about it. [Jack moves to her; then she addresses the class] Listen to Jack, please>
15 **Ja:** [looking at his paper with triangles] # *iruke hanunko gatundae* (I think it might work like this) #
16. **T:** OK. We're looking at our first triangle. How many sides?
17 **Ja:** Three side
18 **T:** Good. Two triangles – how many sides?
19 **Ja:** Four side
20 **T:** Check. One >
21 **Ja:** One, tw>
22 **T:** two three, four>
23 **Ja:** # *eegutman hanungo aani yeyo?* (Is this all we're going to do?) #
24 **T:** five. Yeah, one, two, three, four, five – OK?
25 **Ja:** Yeah
26 **T:** Yeah. Three triangles?

27 **Ja:** # *hana, dul set net dasut* (one, two three four five) # six ...

This was the start of the second longest recorded interaction between the teacher and Jack in the seven months he had been in the class. The required task information was simple – too simple, according to Jack's ironic private utterance (23) – and although his understanding of the required information is evident, it seemed necessary or helpful for him to count first in Korean (27) before providing the correct answer in English. The interaction continued:

28 **T:** Good. So – are you listening there, Yorin? Jack's just told us that the first one's got three sides, the second one has got five sides, the third one's got seven sides. If we put a fourth one in Jack, how many sides would it have?
29 **Ja:** # *jamkanmanyo* (Just a moment please) # [looking at the teacher, then to self, lower pitch and volume] ... # *sam, sa, eelgop* (three, four, seven) #
30 **T:** You wanna write it for me? >
31 **Ja:** mm>
32 **T:** if you can't say the word, the number?
33 **Ja:** # *jamkanmanyo* (Just a moment, please) # [draws the triangles on a piece of paper]
34 **T:** That's the idea. Good. Yes
35 **Ja:** # *xxx* # [counting in Korean?] Eleven?
36 **T:** Good man. So each time, it's going up by how many numbers? ...

Jack's reaction (30) to the teacher's question is interesting. Asking her in Korean to wait a moment, he used a polite tone, as he would do to a Korean teacher – although, of course, Mrs Martin would not have understood. Again (as in Example Fc), this might be an example of a private role-play. His private speech alerted the teacher to his presumed inability to express his understanding in English, and he readily followed her suggestion (31), once again making use of respectful private speech (33) to regulate his activity. He then showed his appropriation of the concept, first visually (33) and then verbally (35), which was confirmed by the teacher. The interaction continued:

37 **T:** ... it's going up by how many numbers?
38 **Ja:** [3 seconds] Four?
39 **T:** No – one>
40 **Ja:** one, one>
41 **T:** Er – sorry sorry, three, five –

42 **Ja:** [two seconds] Seven

43 **T:** Yes. Next one'd be – ?

44 **Ja:** Eleven

45 **T:** Nine. Then eleven>

46 **Ja:** Oh>

47 **T:** After eleven there'd be – ? Keep drawing your pattern

48 **Ja:** [to himself] # *yogi hana du* (You need to add one here) #

49 **T:** Each time it goes, you see you've made another one. How many sides?

50 **Ja:** # *xxx* #

51 **T:** You've already got that>

52 **Ja:** Two

53 **T:** Two. Good man. So each time it goes up by – ?

54 **Ja:** ... [2 seconds] Two

55 **T:** Yeah. Good. Well done. [addresses class] Now ...

56 **Ja:** Aah! ...

Jack's initial utterances in this exchange (38, 40, 42, 44) indicate perhaps a growing confidence to respond in English, albeit minimally and with some hesitation, without recourse to mental or private verbal activity in Korean. However, he reverted to private speech in Korean (48) – most likely a form of self-regulation – although what he actually said afterwards (50) was unintelligible. The teacher's final questions were intended as a concept check, and Jack's prompt and correct answers in English informed the teacher of his understanding.

Despite his relative success in the assisted performance, Jack expressed annoyance as he resumed his seat, and in fact continued to curse and swear volubly:

57 **Ja:** [sighs as he sits on grass] # *Aah! jon-na salgishiltta!* (F***! I don't want to live!) ... *shiganee jom ppali galsuneun upna!* (I want the time to pass quickly!) ... *jon-na monjiral haneunji* (Bloody hell, I don't understand) ... *ah, gamyun malee andoeji!* (I can't communicate, dammit!) ... *gunyang, dolaburigetne* (Hell, I'm going crazy) ... *sonsangnimhante gamyun aju maleul mothagetne* (I wonder why I can't say anything whenever I stand in front of the teacher) ... *jon-na chajeongnage* (It's bloody pissing me off!) *ahu, ahu, moreumyun byungshiniji igo!* (If you didn't know this you'd be an idiot!) # [addressing himself] ...

58 **T:** Now we're going to stop here and go inside.

Jack's frustration with his inability to communicate even simple concepts in English is poignantly evident, adding to the general frustration he expressed at the start of the alfresco lesson. As in all of his private speech, there was none of the syntactical abbreviation or phonological agglutination normally assumed to be features of private speech. This is perhaps surprising, given the intensely personal feelings he was venting. He continued talking to himself after the teacher told the class to go back inside. So voluble was he that it came to the notice of some of his classmates:

59 **Ja:** # *ah, jookeun moksoomeeda* (Ah, I'm a dead man) ... *hagi shireunguh* (I don't wanna do this) ... *jookeunmoksoomeda* (I'm a dead man) ... *hangido shirutdunghu* (I didn't even wanna do this) ... *salgido shillta* (I don't wanna live) ... *jookgishirusuh hananunguhda* (I don't want to die – that's the only reason I'm doing this) ... *jon-na chajeoungna, haesuh jiral balkwangeeda!!* (This is bloody annoying – F***ing hell!) #

60 **Ca:** What's the matter? Jack, What's the matter?

61 **Ja:** # *jon-na jaemitda – moouhya, kkujuh!* (Bloody interesting – hey, f*** off!) #

62 **St:** Is he swearing?

63 **Ja:** # *youngguhga shillta, younguhga shiruh!* (I hate English, I hate English) # [putting his pens etc into his pencil case]

64 **Ca:** [whispering] Jack's swearing! He's swearing!

Although Jack was unable to express the cause of his annoyance to his classmates, they understood he was upset, and Calvin tried to help him (60). Not understanding, or perhaps not caring about, Calvin's motive in speaking to him, Jack told him to go away (61). Although of course Calvin did not understand Korean, he was left in no doubt about the underlying intention of Jack's utterances. Jack's final comment as the class broke for lunch (63) indicates his utter dejection.

What the above lesson shows is the level of frustration and anger that Jack felt at times, and perhaps increasingly over the year. The precise cause of his mood cannot be stated, although the combination of the weather, the triviality of the task and his communicative incompetence were evidently contributing factors. There may, of course, have been external causes on this particular occasion. It was certainly unusual for Jack to manifest annoyance so vocally.

Conclusion

Jack's competence in English was judged to be still at the level of 'minimal' after seven months in Room 7. There is evidence to suggest that his receptive competence in both listening and reading improved, but his verbal response to elicitations, and his ability to initiate interactions, remained at most monosyllabic. Only very occasionally was he observed bidding for turns by raising his hand, and the teacher rarely nominated him. Although he occasionally sought to interact with his peers, he was never seen to initiate a verbal interaction with the teacher, even when it was apparent that he needed help.

His ability to interact in the classroom was further impaired by ambient social factors. He was seated right at the back of the class for the entire time he was in Room 7. His first neighbours were friendly but not very helpful. In the latter part of the year, he tried very hard to initiate and sustain interactions – mostly non-verbal – with two other boys, Peter and Gene. However, he had absolutely no social contact with these, or any English-speaking friends, outside school. He took no part in social or cultural activities, whether school-related or otherwise, that involved English speakers. For example, his interest in soccer became known in April, and both he and his mother were advised that he should join one of the school's teams. He did not do so; neither did he watch with his classmates the extensively televised FIFA World Cup that year.

Despite the good intentions of Jack's classmates and their sometimes strenuous efforts to help him, they were unable to provide more than very basic help, even towards the end of the year. The official curriculum document states that 'learners from language backgrounds other than English should work towards the same objectives as native speakers' although it adds 'they will approach the objectives differently, and may at times be working at different levels from most of the class' (Ministry of Education, 1994: 15). In fact, Jack was largely unable even to work towards – let alone achieve – the same curricular objectives as his peers. His ability to do arithmetical tasks involving little or no verbal language was evident, but no attempt was made to develop his outstanding ability in this area – for example, by providing calculation tasks more suited to his limited English proficiency. He was also eventually able, sometimes with much effort and great difficulty, to carry out routine tasks, such as handwriting, spelling, and vocabulary. The only time he was engaged in a task-related dialogue with the teacher – which occurred in November (Example G) – he felt the task was utterly trivial and boring.

Unable to communicate any but his most basic needs in English, Jack was certainly unable to demonstrate any significant development in such cognitive areas as reasoning skills or logical thinking. In the absence of Korean classmates, he had no one who could stimulate his higher mental functioning in his first language. Although he often appeared attentive to the ambient discourse of learning, it is evident that most of it was conducted well beyond his level of understanding. Transcriptions of his private speech in English as well as, to a lesser extent, in Korean, show his application of intelligence and perseverance in an attempt to appropriate – often mediated by a bilingual dictionary – the meaning of key terminology. His efforts in this direction were hindered by the fact that many key items of vocabulary were presented to him orally rather than in writing. His own written work – other than copying – remained firmly at the word level, as did his oral communication.

Behaving very much according to Korean classroom conventions, Jack was quiet, attentive and ostensibly polite in class, causing no disturbance or disruption to the discourse of learning in Room 7 – with the one exception illustrated above. Underlying his outward behaviour were aspects of his personality that remained largely inaccessible, although his loneliness, lack of confidence and a sense of helplessness – almost of despair – emerged at times in his private speech. Unlike the children in Broner and Tarone's (2001) study, he was certainly not having fun. In short, without effective assistance, Jack was unable to appropriate key cultural and conceptual aspects of the curriculum.

Implications for Pedagogy

The child's distress illustrated above throws into question the issue of placing NESB learners in unsupported regular classrooms before they are linguistically competent to understand the content and processes of the curriculum. Evidently, Jack needed more than the four or five hours of withdrawal ESOL tuition that the school was able to provide. One possible solution, or addition, would have been to provide a Korean-speaking teaching assistant to guide him in the regular classroom. This would have presented some practical, as well as financial, problems because the Korean community was, and still remains, very small in provincial New Zealand. In any event, to place children in a content of incomprehensible input for most of the school week is to effectively deny them access to the curriculum.

Even had Jack's English competence been higher, he would still have faced cultural and conceptual challenges. It would have been helpful to have ensured that there was a Korean classmate in Room 7. At the very least, Jack would then have had moral support, and perhaps the two might have assisted each other's cultural and conceptual development by sharing their burgeoning understanding, or discussing the possible reasons for the lack of it. As it was, Jack was forced to rely on inner resources alone, and the stress that this occasioned was at times intolerable.

It is not feasible to suggest that regular primary teachers should have linguistic competence in all the various languages that are represented in the school, but some experience of learning another language would help teachers to appreciate the linguistic – and cultural – problems faced by NESB learners. Also, both pre-service and post-experience teaching programmes should focus on the needs of learners from non-English speaking backgrounds rather more than they have done in the past. At the very least, teachers need to be sensitive to the strangeness of New Zealand classrooms to immigrant children, who are unfamiliar with much of the background knowledge assumed of students educated here, and are unaware of the conventions and rationale of classroom discourse. Teachers also need to develop a repertoire of strategies for coping with, rather than avoiding, the challenges presented by NESB learners. Such strategies might involve simplifying the linguistic demands of tasks, or designing tasks specially tailored to meet the resources of the learners – for example, by reducing cultural assumptions. They might also include ways of reformulating oral instructions and explanations in such a way as to be comprehensible to learners with limited English. They could increase the verbal participation of NESB learners by soliciting responses from them after other students had provided models (for further suggestions see Chapters 5 and 6 of this volume).

Another strategy might be to identify train, and monitor suitable students to act as peer tutors. Such mentors might complement the efforts of the teacher – as they are likely to be physically and psychologically more accessible to the newcomers than teachers at times when help is most needed. Being themselves engaged in classroom activities, peer tutors may act as interpreters of the learning context – for example, by explaining the rules and standard of conduct inside and outside the classroom, the rationale and requirements of various learning tasks and also by clarifying areas within the academic/cognitive dimension (Barnard, 2002). They might also be encouraged, both inside and outside the classroom context, to share common interests with their NESB fellows. It is reasonable to suggest that it could be more effective to use the limited ESOL support on training peer tutors rather than on withdrawal tuition.

Implications for Research

One important corollary of the above is the need for action research projects in schools to identify and, if possible, to remedy practical difficulties faced by NESB learners and their teachers. Such projects are already under way in New Zealand in the LTL (*Learning Through Language*) programme promoted by the Ministry of Education and, of course, elsewhere. As Penton (2002) has reported, such schemes need school-wide commitment, and appropriate resources, if they are to be successful.

The illustration of private speech in Korean has raised questions about the formal features of private speech. With regard to syntax, other than the omission of pronouns, Jack's syntax was far from abbreviated. It was fully formed; moreover, it often consisted of complex and even compound-complex sentences. It was also, with very few exceptions, clearly and fully articulated with little of the phonological agglutination and external ambiguity that Vygotsky and others have suggested. Of course, further investigation might reveal whether this is a matter of individual variation, or indeed a language-specific phenomenon.

Ushakova (1994) reported the increased evidence for inner speech under cognitive stress, and Lantolf and Appel (1994) argue that, the more difficult the task, the more fully structured (social-like) private speech becomes. It seems likely that difficulty can be measured not merely in terms of cognitive challenge, but also in terms of emotional response. If this is the case, it strengthens the notion that private speech is a form of dialectic between interior interlocutors – a form of social, rather than inner, speech. This too requires further investigation.

This case study (and other studies investigating private speech), provide a sharp insight into the learning process – 'cognition in flight', as Vygotsky (1978: 68) called it. Thus, future studies of private speech would assist our understanding of the challenges faced by immigrant students and minority language learners, and ways by which they seek to cope with these challenges. Attention might focus on the affective domain, and the extent to which emotional factors facilitate or hinder cultural and conceptual development. In particular, research could attend to private speech revealing negative feelings. Further investigation would also reveal whether the use of private speech for the regulation of affective factors atrophies, maintains or increases with maturation.

Acknowledgements

I should like to thank all the members of Room 7, and especially Jack, for allowing me to share their school life for a year. I am deeply indebted to my research assistant, Mrs Jin Sook Kim, for her diligence in transcribing and interpreting Jack's private speech in Korean. I am also very grateful to Neil Mercer and Elaine Vine for their constructive comments on an earlier draft of this chapter.

References

Bakhtin, M. (1981) *The Dialogic Imagination* [M. Holquist, ed.; M. Holquist and C. Emerson, trans.]. Austin, TX: University of Texas Press.

Barnard, R.C.G. (2000) Non-English speaking background learners in the mainstream classroom: A New Zealand case study. PhD thesis, University of Southampton.

Barnard, R.C.G. (2002) Peer tutoring in the primary classroom: A sociocultural interpretation of classroom interaction. *New Zealand Journal of Educational Studies* 37 (1), 57–72.

Barnard, R. and Rauf, P.L. (1998) Non-English speaking background students in Hamilton primary schools: A survey of learners, teachers and ESOL provision. *The TESOLANZ Journal* 8, 36–47.

Bourne, J. (1992) Inside a multilingual primary classroom: A teacher, children and theories at work. PhD thesis, University of Southampton.

Broner, M.A. and Tarone, E. (2001) Is it fun? Language play in a fifth-grade Spanish immersion classroom. *The Modern Language Journal* 85 (iii), 363–379.

Cook, G. (1997) Language play, language learning. *ELT Journal* 51 (3) 224–231.

De Guerrerro, M.C.M. (1987) The din phenomenon: Mental rehearsal in the second language. *Foreign Language Annals* 20, 537–548.

De Guerrerro, M.C.M. (1994) Form and function of inner speech in adult second language learning. In J.P. Lantolf and G. Appel (eds) *Vygotskian Approaches to Second Language Learning* (pp. 83–116). Norwood, NJ: Ablex.

De Guerrerro, M.C.M. (1999) Inner speech as mental rehearsal: The case of advanced L2 learners. *Issues in Applied Linguistics* 10, 27–55.

Ellis, R. (1999) *Learning a Second Language through Interaction*. Philadelphia and Amsterdam: John Benjamins Publishing Co.

Frawley, W. and Lantolf, J.P. (1985) Second language discourse: A Vygotskian perspective. *Applied Linguistics* 6, 19–44.

Fisher, E. (1993) Distinctive features of student–student classroom talk and their relationship to learning: How discursive exploration might be encouraged. *Language and Education* 7 (4), 239–257.

Gibbons, P. (1998) Classroom talk and the learning of new registers in a second language. *Language and Education* 12 (2), 99–118.

Lantolf, J.P. (1997) The function of L2 play in the acquisition of Spanish. In W.R. Glass and A.T. Perez-Leroux (eds) *Contemporary Perspectives on the Acquisition of Spanish* (pp. 3–24). Somerville, MA: Cascadilla Press.

Lantolf, J.P. (2000) Second language learning as a mediated process. *Language Teaching* 33, 79–96.

Lantolf, J.P. and Appel, G. (eds) (1994) *Vygotskian Approaches to Second Language Research*. Norwood, NJ: Ablex Publishing Co.

Lantolf, J.P. and Frawley. W. (1984) Second language performance and Vygotskian psycholinguistics: Implications for L2 instruction. In A. Manning, P. Martin and K. McCalla (eds) *The Tenth LACUS Forum 1983* (pp. 425–40). Columbia, SC: Hornbeam Press.

McNaughton, S. (1995) *Patterns of Emergent Literacy*. Oxford: Oxford University Press.

Ministry of Education (1994) *English in the New Zealand Curriculum*. Wellington: Learning Media.

Ohta, A.S. (1995) Applying sociocultural theory to an analysis of learner discourse: Learner–learner collaborative interaction in the zone of proximal development. *Issues in Applied Linguistics* 6, 93–122.

Pavlenko, A. and Lantolf, J.P. (2000) Second language learning as participation and the (re) construction of selves. In J.P. Lantolf (ed.) *Sociocultural Theory and Second Language Learning* (pp.155–177). Oxford: Oxford University Press.

Penton, R. (2002) Improving the achievement of secondary NESB and international students in mainstream classes. *Many Voices* 20, 4–7.

Piaget, J. (1926) *Language and Thought of the Child.* London: Routledge and Kegan Paul.

Poole, D. (1992) Language socialization in the second language classroom. *Language Learning* 42 (4), 593–616.

Saville-Troike, M. (1988) Private speech: Evidence for second language learning strategies during the 'silent period'. *Journal of Child Language* 15, 567–590.

Sokolov, A.N. (1968) *Vnutrennjaja Rech i Myshlenie [Inner Speech and Thought].* Moscow.

Ushakova, T.N. (1994) Inner speech and second language acquisition: An experimental-theoretical approach. In J.P. Lantolf and G. Appel (eds) *Vygotskian Approaches to Second Language Research* (pp. 135–156). Norwood, NJ: Ablex Publishing Co.

Villamil, I. and de Guerrero, M.C.M (1996) Peer revision in the L2 classroom: Social cognitive activities, mediating strategies, and aspects of social behavior. *Journal of Second Language Writing* 5, 51–75.

Vygotsky, L.S. (1962) *Thought and Language* (A. Kozulin, ed. and trans.). Cambridge: MA: MIT Press.

Vygotsky, L.S. (1978) *Mind in Society: The Development of Higher Psychological Processes.* Cambridge, MA: Harvard University Press.

Vygotsky, L.S. (1986/1934) *Thought and Language.* Cambridge, MA: MIT Press (originally published in 1934 as *Myshlenie i Rech,* Moscow).

Wells, G. (1999) Using L1 to master L2: A response to Anton and DiCamilla's 'socio-cognitive functions of L1 collaborative interaction in the L2 classroom'. *Modern Language Journal* 83 (2), 248–254.

Willett, J. (1995) Becoming first graders in an L2: An ethnographic study of L2 socialization. *TESOL Quarterly* 29 (3), 273–305.

Chapter 8

The Construction of Learning Contexts for Deaf Bilingual Learners

RACHEL LOCKER MCKEE AND YAEL BIEDERMAN

Introduction

The ability to verbalise experience and to engage in social interaction through language is central to the human processes of thinking and learning. Deaf[1] children face the predicament of acquiring a primary language, forming social relationships, and understanding the world within a communication environment that is largely inaccessible to them, as most of them are raised in families who hear and speak.[2] The small percentage of deaf children born to deaf parents usually acquire sign language as a home language, while most deaf children develop sign language fluency from peers at school or later in life when they establish contact with other deaf people. Signed languages have evolved naturally in deaf communities throughout history in response to the physiological and cultural need for communication that is comprehensible through the eyes. The use of sign language and common social experiences bond deaf people in communities and formal organisations that have distinctive cultural and sociolinguistic characteristics (Baker & Battison, 1980; Higgins, 1980; Lane *et al.*, 1996; McKee, 2001, Monaghan; 1996; Padden & Humphries, 1988; Penman, 1999).

From its inception in 1880 until at least 1980, deaf education in New Zealand centred almost exclusively on the 'problem' of learning to articulate and understand spoken and written English. Sign language transmission was seen as an undesirable by-product of contact between children who attended deaf residential schools (Collins-Ahlgren, 1989; Forman, 2000). This pedagogical approach, known as oralism, produced few deaf people who successfully acquired intelligible speech or achieved academically (Allen, 1986; Dugdale, 2000; Johnson *et al.*, 1989; Paul, 1998; Pritchett, 1998; Townshend, 1993; VandenBerg, 1971).

Since the 1990s in New Zealand (and earlier elsewhere), rhetoric and practice in deaf education have been altered by a paradigm shift from a deficit/curative view of deafness to a recognition of deaf people as a community with an autonomous language, New Zealand Sign Language (NZSL). In response, policy in the two Deaf Education Centres[3] has endorsed a bilingual–bicultural option that utilises NZSL and written English and facilitates children's contact with deaf adults as social role models. Paradoxically, growing acceptance of the pedagogical and cultural value of a bilingual approach is paralleled by the increasing prevalence of mainstream placement of deaf students since the 1970s. Some 85% of deaf and hearing-impaired children are now enrolled in mainstream classes as compared with 8% in a Deaf Education Centre, and 5% in deaf unit classes in regular schools (AC Nielsen, 2000). A proportion of deaf children who are mainstreamed use some form of sign language as their primary language, usually with a teacher aide who signs spoken communication[4] and with some a visiting teacher of the deaf who may or may not be proficient in NZSL. Deaf children in this situation may be either recognised or 'de facto' bilingual learners (Krashen, 1996) – mostly the latter, since in general, mainstream schools do not perceive deaf children's use of sign language in terms of bilingual status.

This chapter focuses on the construction of educational contexts for deaf children by examining how NZSL and English are used to mediate learning and interaction for two children whose primary language is NZSL: one in a bilingual class at a Deaf Education Centre and one in a mainstream school. The research questions we address include:

(1) How do interaction and instruction in the bilingual classroom and the mainstream classroom respectively support the development of first language competence in NZSL, the acquisition of world knowledge, and the linking of NZSL and written English?
(2) How do learning activities in the bilingual classroom and the mainstream classroom respectively enable deaf students to participate in a community of learners and to establish their identity as deaf bilinguals?

In the bilingual class, we identify ways in which participation in a community of signing peers and a signing teacher contributes to the child's ability to develop NZSL and an understanding of written English as a second language and to establish her identity as a deaf bilingual. For the mainstreamed child, who does not share a primary social language with class members, access to comprehensible interaction is examined with respect to how effectively the child can engage with the content and interactional form of learning activities at school. This chapter adds to a growing body of research that investigates linguistic and social dimensions (amongst others) of the inclusion of deaf students in mainstream schools (e.g. Antia 1982; Cawthon, 2001; Cocks 1988; Higgins, 1990; Hopwood & Gallaway, 1999; Kluwin & Stinson 1993; Schein *et al.*, 1991; Stinson & Antia, 1999; Stinson & Lang, 1994; Ramsey, 1997; Winston, 2001).

Our discussion is framed within the sociocultural perspective that school learning is mediated by participation in culturally and linguistically organised social interaction (Vygotsky, 1978). In examining contexts for children's learning from this framework, we adopt the view that 'context' is the product of participants, actions, and language use rather than a pre-existing set of institutional circumstances that enclose interaction (Heritage, 1997). Similarly, language is seen as bound to the social and cultural contexts within which it is produced and understood, and as such is closely tied to the construction of an individual's personal, social, and cultural identity (Drasgow, 1993; Dyson, 1997). In light of the central tenet of mainstreaming that 'through educational integration, the deaf child will be helped to acquire oral language, come to understand the nuances of everyday social life, and develop a self-concept that he is "normal"' (Lynas, 1984: 129), we focus on how the linguistic interactions in which deaf children participate in class construct their role as participants and define opportunities for cognitive engagement with learning activities. Consideration of educational situations from this perspective potentially deepens our understanding of what is usually referred to in special education parlance as school 'placement' or 'setting'. As Ramsey (1997: 12) points out in relation to deaf learners, close analysis of classroom interaction is necessary 'to distinguish between arrangements of people and activities that are truly contexts for learning and those that are not.'

Methods

The case studies we consider in this article – 'Malia' (Case 1) and 'Hemi' (Case 2) – are drawn from two research projects conducted separately by the present authors during 2000–2001. Biederman examined the role of New Zealand Sign Language (NZSL) in English literacy development in a group of deaf children in a bilingual class at a Deaf Education Centre. McKee investigated the learning context and communication access of deaf children in mainstream classrooms through a set of six case studies. Both studies are concerned with understanding and describing the ways that deaf bilingual children develop and use their two languages to participate in classroom life and to access the curriculum. The studies are complementary in that they examine learning opportunities within types of school settings that are associated with contrasting perspectives on the meaning of 'inclusion' (McCracken, 2001) – i.e. assimilation into the majority group, or separate provision within a minority cultural-linguistic framework.

Data for both case studies were collected using methods of ethnographic field research, as this approach provides a profitable way of coming to know and interpret behaviour and experience (Bogdan & Biklen, 1992). In both studies, the researchers chose to take a more 'passive' than 'participant' observer role (Stake, 1995) while gathering classroom data, although Biederman's year-long bilingual class study entailed more extensive interaction and relationships between the researcher and participants than the McKee study did. Both the researchers are non-deaf but fluent in sign language and have worked previously with deaf children and adults. These identity and language characteristics, coupled with a video camera, made it impossible to blend into the background, particularly since new interlocutors who can converse in sign language are a relatively scarce and interesting commodity for deaf children in New Zealand schools. However, both researchers chose not to actively participate in class activities except as observers, in the hope of minimising the impact of an extra adult on interactions between students and teachers.

Data collection: Bilingual class

In Case 1, the researcher visited the bilingual classroom during literacy activities three times each week throughout the school year. The types of literacy events observed include shared book reading, free reading, group writing and independent writing. A digital video camera was used to record interactions and dialogue, and all relevant materials (including books read and written work produced) were photocopied. The researcher used the videotapes and classroom notes to compose detailed field notes, which included transcription of sign language dialogue using the Berkeley Transcription System (Slobin *et al.*, 2000). Analysis of field notes focused on how students used NZSL and other language resources to participate in classroom culture and more specifically in literacy events.

Data collection: Mainstream class

In Case 2, the researcher spent one week in the mainstream school and observed all class activities, assembly and some playground interaction in order to gain an overview of the child's participation across the range of events at school. Field notes were made on the visual and linguistic accessibility of communication events, on the behavioural and linguistic aspects of the deaf child's interaction with peers, adults and learning materials, and on the responses of others to the deaf child. Samples of key recurring events, including morning news on the mat, story reading, maths instruction, whole-class instruction on topic studies, and reading sessions were recorded on digital video. Selection of video data for transcription and analysis focused on typical episodes in which the teacher aide facilitated communication (such as interpreting teacher-fronted instruction or group work), and situations in which the child had the opportunity for independent interaction with peers and teacher (such as desk work or maths games).

In both studies, classroom teacher, parents, and other school personnel connected with the child were interviewed in order to triangulate information and perspectives about the child's learning situation and to explore beliefs about language use and teaching practices. Documentary evidence of the children's writing samples, recorded achievement levels, and individual educational goals was also collected.

Our interpretation of data is informed by the paradigm of qualitative analysis of classroom interaction and discourse (e.g. Cazden, 1988; Green & Dixon, 1993; Green & Wallat, 1981). Claims surrounding the examples used in this article are also supported by observation of other similar instances occurring in our larger data sets.

Case Descriptions

Bilingual class

The study took place at a Deaf Education Centre that provides services and educational programs to deaf and hard-of-hearing students throughout half of New Zealand. The school's philosophy, as stated in the school brochure, is 'to develop the potential of Deaf and hard-of-hearing students so that they may grow into responsible citizens who respect themselves and others. The school strives to foster in each student a positive self-image and an appreciation of Deaf Culture.' The school is committed to the bilingual–bicultural model of education in which both NZSL and English are regarded as equal in status as languages and are recognised for their important yet distinct roles in the lives of deaf individuals.

One classroom at the school was chosen as the focus of careful observation. The classroom consisted of eight deaf students, one hearing teacher who was fluent in NZSL, one deaf language assistant, and one deaf teaching assistant. All the students had hearing parents, were prelingually deaf, ranged in age from five to nine years, and used sign language as their primary means of communication. One student, Malia, was chosen as the focus for this chapter.

Participant: Malia

Malia was a seven-year-old girl whose family was from the island of Niue. Malia's family moved to New Zealand so that Malia could attend a school for the deaf, an option not available in Niue. Malia was brought to New Zealand around the age of two to have her hearing tested and was found to be profoundly deaf in both ears. She was fitted with two hearing aids, which she wore regularly. Communication at home consisted of a mix of NZSL, spoken English, spoken Niuean and written English. Malia predominantly used NZSL and occasionally used written English[5] to communicate with her family. Malia's mother explained in an interview that the family chose to learn NZSL after discovering Malia's deafness, because they wanted Malia to be able to express herself and because they could see her frustration at not being able to communicate without sign language. Using videotapes, they began learning NZSL.

In the three years following Malia's diagnosis, she moved back and forth between New Zealand and Niue attending the Deaf Education Centre in New Zealand and the primary school in Niue. Since the age of five, Malia has attended the Deaf Education Centre full time, living with her parents and three sisters, who are all hearing. As her family did not have contact either with deaf adults or with other families with deaf children, Malia's primary access to other deaf children and to deaf adults was at school.

Malia was an attentive and well-behaved student and a leader in her classroom community. She regularly sought ways to help the teacher and her classmates. For example, every morning when Malia arrived at school she rushed to the board to write the date and to reorganise the day's schedule. During group reading and writing activities, Malia was eager to respond to the teacher's questions and to display her ability to translate NZSL signs into written English, and vice versa.

Mainstream class

The second study took place in a primary school in a small provincial town that serves a rural area. A significant proportion of children attending the school were Māori, and Māori language was incorporated into signage around the school and into daily communication routines such as greetings and marking the roll. The site of research was a Year 2–3 class consisting of 24 hearing children (aged approximately six to eight years) and one deaf boy, Hemi, who was the focus of this study. Hemi had been with the same group of children since entering school and had known some of them since pre-school. Most of the children knew a small vocabulary of signs, which they used in combination with gesture, speech or mime to communicate with Hemi. The teacher had previously taught Hemi's deaf cousin who is two years older, and the teacher aide working with Hemi had also worked with his cousin. Hemi's teacher had earlier taken a short course in NZSL with a deaf tutor but found it a difficult experience. Beyond greetings and a few signs for giving routine directions, the teacher relied on the teacher aide to interpret any communication with Hemi.

Participant: Hemi

Hemi was a seven-year-old Māori boy who has been profoundly deaf since birth. Hemi's mother is deaf and uses NZSL, which is Hemi's first language. Hemi was learning speech and could say some recognisable words but did not spontaneously use speech alone for conversation. His father and teenage sister are hearing; his sister signs proficiently and can communicate easily with deaf people outside the immediate family, which includes a deaf uncle (the mother's brother) and deaf cousin living locally, and other deaf relatives living elsewhere. Hemi's father signs and understands enough signing for basic communication within the family but could not be described as a proficient signer outside this context. Both of Hemi's parents grew up in the area, and neither achieved school qualifications. They did not have a great deal of contact with Hemi's school and, apart from attending IEP (individualised education plan) meetings, most of their communication was via the teacher aide whom they saw as a key person in Hemi's education.

Hemi's parents chose to enroll him at this school rather than another one closer to his home, because the school had already experienced teaching his older deaf cousin, who could also provide company for Hemi outside of class. The younger sister of this deaf cousin was also in Hemi's class. There was no longer a specialist deaf resource class in the region, and the nearest Deaf Education Centre was in a city two hours drive away. Although his mother felt that Hemi would be better off educationally at the Deaf Education Centre where she herself boarded throughout her schooling, the current policy meant that Hemi was too young to be accepted there as a residential student. His mother hoped that he would transfer there when he was older, while his father believed Hemi was doing well academically with effective support at school and did not want him to leave the family.

Hemi had been assessed as a 'very high needs' student by Specialist Education Services, and had full-time teacher aide support in class from a woman whose main responsibilities were interpreting communication in the classroom and during other school activities, adapting lessons and assisting him with his work, following up speech training, and supervising Hemi's behaviour and use of hearing aids. As is typical of many teacher aides, this woman was largely untrained for these roles (McKee, 2002). She had learned Australasian Signed English locally when Hemi was a pre-schooler, and had known him since that time. She had taken up all available opportunities to learn NZSL at workshops that were offered once or twice a year in the region, and she desired further training.

Two or three times a week Hemi was visited at school by an itinerant teacher of the deaf (a hearing woman) together with a deaf resource tutor (a deaf woman employed as a paraprofessional language/culture model and teaching assistant), and by a speech therapist approximately once a week. The itinerant teacher of the deaf mostly used Australasian Signed English with Hemi, but was trying to learn and use NZSL. She was enthusiastic about working with the deaf resource tutor (a recent innovation), from whom she said she was learning NZSL, and she was also learning about managing teaching interactions with a bilingual deaf child by observing her instinctive teaching strategies. During their visits, Hemi was usually withdrawn from class to work individually on reading and maths, although sometimes the deaf tutor would lead an activity for his class, such as signing a storybook. In his third year of school, Hemi was struggling with new entrant reading books and working on maths concepts at the beginning level of the curriculum. The bulk of Hemi's learning time at school was managed with the support of the teacher aide. On days when this teacher aide was absent, Hemi stayed at home, since the teacher could not manage his participation in class without assistance, and relief staffing was not available.

The following sections will examine data from these two case studies in relation to theoretical claims about interaction and learning.

Mediating Knowledge through a Shared Language

Language is one of the most important symbolic tools for mediating learning through interaction (Vygotsky, 1978). As young deaf children of hearing parents usually do not acquire their family's language naturally, they lack a medium for acquiring world knowledge through situated talk, and most enter school without the same language foundation and store of background knowledge that is expected of hearing children. Deaf children's education therefore must be designed to develop first-language competence and to build a basis of concepts and information about the world. The first question we address in our data is thus: how do communication and instruction in a bilingual class and a mainstream class support the development of first language competence in NZSL and the acquisition of world knowledge?

In addition, learning activities must be organised to facilitate deaf children's acquisition of a second language: the written form of a spoken language (in these cases English). Hearing bilingual students have demonstrated academic and social advantages from native language instruction, showing that skills acquired in a first language can be transferred to a second language (Cummins, 1979, 1981; Greene, 1998; Skutnabb-Kangas & Tuokomaa, 1976; Willig, 1985). Recent studies examining the relationship between deaf students' sign language proficiency and their written language skills also indicate a positive relationship between their abilities in the two languages (Hoffmeister, 2000; Padden & Ramsey, 1998, 2000; Prinz & Strong, 1997; Strong & Prinz, 2000). Such findings have been used in support of a bilingual model in which a natural sign language is used for 'native language' instruction, and written English is learned as a second language, positing that academic skills can be developed in and subsequently transferred from a first to a second language. Theoretical and empirical questions remain about exactly how deaf learners bridge the gap between an internal representation of a signed language and an external (written) representation of a spoken language without direct access to the spoken form (see Akamatsu 1998; Mayer & Akamatsu, 1999; Mayer & Wells, 1996; Padden & Hanson, 2000). However, it is hoped that with appropriate scaffolding (such as developing children's metalinguistic awareness and utilising consistent linguistic strategies for moving between languages) new concepts made comprehensible in sign language can contribute to the development of print literacy (Akamatsu *et al.*, 2002; Bailes 2001; Biederman, 2003; Swanwick, 1998; Wilbur, 2000). Our discussion of data also addresses the question – how do the learning contexts created in bilingual and mainstream classrooms support the linking of first-language communication in NZSL to the development of English literacy?

Example 1: Bilingual class

In the bilingual classroom, the teacher organised learning activities with consideration to students' background knowledge and to their prior language experiences, and she employed specialised strategies for supporting the students' written English development. In the following event, Malia and her classmate, Calvin, were engaged in a small group reading activity with their teacher. The teacher introduced a new book called *Spider's Web* (Eggleton, 1999), and spent several minutes discussing and expanding the students' understanding of spiders and webs. While the dialogue was in NZSL, the teacher explicitly taught Malia and Calvin the English vocabulary associated with the new ideas they were discussing. In the following excerpt from this introductory discussion (and all subsequent examples), signed dialogue is presented in upper-case English glosses that represent sign forms, followed by an English translation in parentheses:

> The teacher shows Malia and Calvin the book, *Spider's Web*. Malia reads the title by signing, 'TITLE SPIDER' and then pausing (*The title is spider... hmm*). Calvin copies Malia signing, 'SPIDER.' The teacher points to the word 'web,' and both students look up at her questioningly, as they do not know the word. The teacher points to the word and shows the students the sign, 'WEB.' She traces the picture of the web on the cover of the book and repeats the sign, 'WEB.' Malia's eyes dart back and forth between the picture and the teacher. Her face lights up with understanding as she makes the connection between the sign and the picture and produces the sign, 'WEB.' The teacher fingerspells and repeats the sign, 'W-E-B WEB' (*It's spelled w-e-b, web*).

In this example, the teacher introduced the new concept of a web by pointing to the written word and the picture and showing the students the word for web in NZSL. When Malia conveyed her understanding of the new concept by producing the sign, the teacher linked this to the corresponding English word through fingerspelling. The techniques of 'chaining' multiple forms of a word through sign and print (Padden & Hanson 2000; Padden & Ramsey, 1998) and 'sandwiching' the signed and fingerspelled forms (Kelly, 1995) supported Malia in building associations between the picture, the sign, the written word, and its orthographic representation in fingerspelling – associations central to her ability to negotiate two forms of language.

Next, the teacher built on the students' understanding of spiders and webs. A selection from that dialogue follows:

> The teacher asks Malia and Calvin, 'WEB, SEE BEFORE WEB (location of the sign indicates the upper corner of the room)?' (*Have you seen a web before, the netting that is in a corner?*) The teacher gets up from her seat and locates spider webs outside the classroom. She calls Malia and Calvin outside, and the two students go excitedly to look at the webs. They return to their seats, and the teacher asks, 'SPIDER MAKE WEB WHY?' (*Do you know why spiders make webs?*) The teacher waits several seconds, but neither Malia nor Calvin answer, so she provides an explanation. She signs, 'SPIDER WEB MAKE WHY? WEB (held on left hand) FLY FLYING (right hand 'flying' sign stops at web hand). STUCK. CANT FLY-OFF. SPIDER COME-ALONG GOBBLE-UP. WHY.' (*Why does a spider make a web? Well if a spider has a web and a fly comes along, the fly will get stuck in the web. It won't be able to fly off. Then the spider can come along*

and eat it up. That's why spiders make webs). Malia responds to this new information by declaring, 'IF HUGE WEB – mimes walking (with arms swinging) then getting stuck in a big web. CAN'T.' (*If there were a really big web and I walked into it, I would get stuck too and I wouldn't be able to get away*).

The teacher recognised that Malia and Calvin were not familiar with webs, so she first showed them real-life webs and then discussed why spiders make webs. Her example made background knowledge explicit and provided conceptual support for the students to understand the story when they read it (Andrews *et al.*, 1994). Malia then likewise re-contextualised the ideas for herself, using the new information in an imaginary story about a giant web expressed in her developing first language.

Following the exchange presented above, the teacher directed the students' attention to the book and its printed text. Together, the students and teacher looked through the pictures and, in NZSL, discussed the story of a spider making a web in the kitchen, the bathroom and the garden. The teacher asked her students to identify each setting pictured and then taught them the English word from the text that corresponded to their signs for each setting. In order to create an additional link between the signed and written forms, students were instructed to fingerspell new vocabulary words, an ability that has been shown to be positively correlated with deaf children's ability to decode printed words (Biederman, 2000; Hirsch-Pasek, 1986; Padden & Hanson, 2000). The teacher continued to extend the students' background knowledge by explaining that, like the book character who was angry about the spider webs in his kitchen and bathroom, she too did not like to have webs in her house. In this instance, she related a new concept through a personal narrative, in keeping with a learning style that is characteristic of other minority language students (Cazden, 1988) and is also typical of explanatory discourse in the deaf community. The students looked through the remainder of the book, learning new vocabulary and discussing the story with their teacher. Subsequently, they read the text integrating the new signs and knowledge they had acquired in the preceding discussion.

This episode illustrates how the teacher used real-world experience and specialised instruction tailored to the students' level of understanding and developing bilingualism in order to expand their world knowledge, increase their communicative competence, and forge associations between their first and second languages. Malia and Calvin were not familiar with spider webs until the teacher showed them actual webs and explained to them in NZSL why spiders create webs. The language and content of the lesson were accessible and comprehensible to the students, thereby providing the opportunity to construct an understanding of the book's content and to acquire vocabulary for the new ideas in both NZSL and English.

Example 2: Mainstream class

In the mainstream classroom, the teacher based instruction and learning tasks on the assumed knowledge and communication experiences of hearing children. The teacher aide tried to adjust instruction to account for the deaf child's different linguistic experience by reducing or expanding information. This adaptation was generally made ad hoc rather than as part of instructional design and was juggled with the responsibility for interpreting ongoing talk in class. The flow of turns in teaching dialogue rarely allowed time for sufficient expansion of concepts or translation of written words that may have been unfamiliar to a deaf student. The characteristics of Hemi's access to new ideas and language during whole class instruction are illustrated in the following description of a session on the topic 'Food for energy'.

The teacher was seated beside a whiteboard easel ruled into three columns headed 'Eat a lot', 'Eat some', 'Eat now and then', while the teacher aide sat at the other end of the whiteboard, also facing the children. The children sat on the mat, facing the board. Hemi sat in front of the aide's feet, so close that when he looked up at her and the board he had to tilt his head backwards. From a deaf perspective, this is an abnormal spatial arrangement for conducting signed communication. The distance between two signers must be sufficient to allow a wide view that takes in the signer's face, body, and any other visual reference points, such as the board and the teacher in a classroom. Hemi was seated in this position in order for the aide to have physical access to 'managing' his behaviour, such as touching him to regain his eyegaze when it wandered. In this case, the teacher aide frequently touched Hemi's head or face to gain his visual attention, apparently unaware that this violated communication norms in deaf culture as well as cultural taboos for Māori. This placement of Hemi also illustrated the teacher's observation that the deaf child and the teacher aide function in a one-to-one learning relationship in the class, in contrast to the one-to-many relationship of the teacher with other students.

The teacher explained that they were going to think of different kinds of food that provide energy and asked for suggestions of 'foods that we should eat a lot of'. As children named particular foods, she prompted them to classify these foods, for example, as vegetable or cereal. This task required students to contrast, categorise and evaluate known food items.

The lesson presupposed awareness that food has an impact on the body's health, an understanding that foods can be grouped into types, and the knowledge that foods have different nutritional value and should be eaten in differing proportions. Hemi was not as familiar with the information underlying this task as most of his classmates to whom the activity was targeted. During this session, the teacher aide signed a very limited portion of what was said, and Hemi's gaze wandered away from her for much of the time, as usual.

In the following extract of transcript, the teacher aide's utterances and Hemi's actions are placed where they occurred parallel to the dialogue.

Spoken dialogue:	**Signed dialogue:**
Note: Unclear utterances are transcribed as (xxx). (T is the teacher)	Signs are represented in CAPITAL LETTERS followed by translation in *lower case italic*. Video time codes appear at intervals to give an indication of the relation between speech and signs. Hemi has his back partially to the camera; unclear signs are transcribed as (XXX). (TA is the teacher aide)
Lee: sandwiches (00:07)	
T: [*writes 'sandwiches' on board*] Anna	
Anna: (xxx)	
T: pardon?	(00:09)
Anna: fruit **T**: Fred? **Fred:** (xxx) **T:** Was that your idea or was that (xxx) – were you going to say that one? Or was that one that you actually– 'cos I heard it whispered just about the time you were going to say it. Do you have another idea or was that yours?	**TA:** SANDWICH *(Sandwich)*. [Hemi is looking at the floor. TA taps him]. SANDWICH *(Hey – sandwich)* FRUIT *(Fruit)*. [TA moves Hemi's head to look up]. HEMI, FRUIT SHE, CORRECT SHE, FRUIT *(Hemi – hey look at me – she said fruit and she's right.)* [Children raise their hands while teacher speaks. TA looks over at T. Hemi follows her gaze and also puts his hand up. TA looks at him.]
Fred: carrots	**TA**: [to Hemi] WHAT? *(What?)*
T: do you think we should eat a lot of that or do you think we should eat some of it? (00:33)	**Hemi:** [lowers his hand] (XXX XXX) (00:33)

Fred: (xxx)	
T: well we'll leave it to come back to that one. This is things that we should eat a lot of. Robert?	**TA:** CARROT, CARROT (*Carrot, carrot)*
	Hemi: (XXX XXX)
Robert: dinner?	**TA:** [nods. Hemi looks down to floor. TA looks away and moves some loose papers off the whiteboard easel. Hemi looks up at TA briefly and then down again].
T: A lot of dinner? Oh yes, now what can you tell me what's something you should eat a lot of when you have dinner?	
Lisa: (xxx)	
T: That comes under vegetables. Vegetables can include any sort of vegetables. They could all come into this part. Tom.	
Tom: Nut**r**igrain	
T: say that again	
Tom: Nut**r**igrain	
T: is that a breakfast cereal?	
Tom: yeah	
T: right so we'll put it under cereal. Any more for 'a lot of'? Kahu?	
Kahu: apples	
T: comes under fruit. Robert?	
Robert: (xxx)	**TA:** [reaches for a marker]
T: Is that – what is that –' cos when you say the name of some of these things – I don't know what they are so you need to tell me where they come under – is it cereal?	**Hemi:** [watches TA while she draws an apple, then looks down at the floor].
Diane: (xxx)	
T: it's a cereal,	**TA:** [draws something that could be a carrot. Hemi looks up to board, then at TA, then looks down].

Children: (xxx) **T:** Right. I'm going to jump to the other end now. Leave this [points to left column on the board] for a little while and I want you to tell me some of the foods that we should just eat now and then. That means we're not going to have them all the time. Sharon?	**TA:** [draws another object, Hemi looks up at board]
Sharon: umm like lollies. (01:53) **T:** lollies [writes on board] Sarah?	(01:53)
Sharon: (xxx) **T:** Now and then food **Sharon:** (xxx) **T:** [writes on board] umm, Kate? (02:18) **Kate:** Chocolate **T:** [writes on board; points to child	**TA:** [pointing to apple on board] EAT LOTS LOTS *(Eat lots of apples)*. [Hemi shakes his head. TA points to all objects just drawn on board]. CAN [points to pictures] CAN *(Those ones you can, those ones you can)*. [Hemi looks down. TA draws a line under the objects. Above the objects she writes 'lots' then underneath them writes 'little'. Hemi looks up at board as TA writes 'little'.] (02:19)
Child: (xxx)	**TA:** LITTLE , EAT LITTLE *(Eat a little bit)* [Hemi nods. TA draws an icecream in a cone]
T: It would come under here won't it. Tina?	**Hemi:** ME ICECREAM 'small-scoop', 'two-scoops' NEG *(I have small icecreams, not big double ones)*

Following this session, the teacher aide commented that the topic was conceptually so far beyond Hemi that she considered it futile to try to interpret fully. As evidenced in the transcript, the few lexical items that were signed were not linked to the preceding talk or to the concepts framing the lesson.

Characteristically of teacher talk (Cazden, 1988), the teacher often restated children's specific or context-embedded examples as more general or abstract categories. For instance, she responded to the answer 'Nutri-grain' by saying 'when you say the name of some of these things I don't know what they are, so you need to tell me where they come under – is it cereal?' The teacher aide interpreted information in the opposite direction, omitting mention of larger categories and re-framing some examples in relation to Hemi's personal experience. For instance, when the teacher later listed chocolate under 'eat now and then', the teacher aide said (in translation) 'If you eat a lot [of chocolate] it will make you sick – have you (done that)?' Hemi apparently expected classroom talk to be personalised, as indicated when the aide signed 'EAT LOTS LOTS' (*Eat lots of apples*), and he responded by shaking his head in disagreement, interpreting this as the aides' wrong description of his own eating habits or perhaps as an imperative, rather than as the teacher's generalised statement about healthy foods. Although the teacher aide's intent in personalising the information was to elicit recognition, this kind of departure from the spoken text points to Hemi's inequivalent exposure to ways of talking and thinking about information that are designed to initiate students into academic discourse.

Hemi's limited access to the dialogue also hampered his comprehension of the written English vocabulary since the teacher's talk, which was not interpreted or was interpreted after a delay, related written words to the discussion (e.g. 'Nutrigrain' – spoken, and 'cereal' – written on the board), or contained deictic reference to information written on the board (e.g. 'this part', or 'Leave this"). During this session, the aide did not use fingerspelling to systematically link meanings, signs and print, as occurred in Malia's class. The aide's decision to draw pictures instead of using signs for basic food vocabulary suggests that she considered Hemi unable to mediate concepts by language alone (in the form of sign or print), even though items drawn (apple, carrot, chocolate) were easily within his productive vocabulary. The aide commented later that she wished she had prepared by bringing pictures of food, reinforcing the impression that her focus was on conveying meaning at a lexical level. Her judgement about Hemi's comprehension was partly conditioned by Hemi's non-attending behaviour, such as fiddling with her skirt and shoelaces and looking at the floor (which she described as a chronic problem). This, in turn, clearly reflected his lack of comprehensible access to the talk of his classmates and teacher, which precluded him from meaningful participation in the activity.

Unlike instruction in the bilingual classroom, which was framed with consideration to Malia's linguistic and world knowledge, this teaching interaction could be described as outside Hemi's 'zone of proximal development' (Vygotsky, 1978). The pedagogical practices employed did not engage him in an activity that could scaffold his knowledge or support meaningful links between NZSL and English.

The teacher was partially aware that Hemi did not understand everything but, since she could not teach in Hemi's language nor fully monitor the extent of his engagement with the activity, she was reliant on the facilitation of the teacher aide. Her perspective was expressed in the following response to an interview question: 'When you're presenting something to the class, how much do you expect the teacher aide to interpret?' (Italics have been added to highlight points arising in the discussion.)

> Probably the basic idea not everything word-for-word, but *the general idea* ... what it is we're looking at – 'food gives you energy'. Not all the little intricate bits, *but just so that he's got the overall understanding*. And [the aide] has got more of an idea of where his level of understanding is because she's working closely with him. So if it's just too difficult for him, then she'll just leave that part of it (...) Sometimes I feel that he loses concentration very quickly and ... *maybe the teacher aide gets to a certain point and then leaves it, whereas I feel the input needs to keep going*. And he needs to be brought back onto task a lot more. *I think, with any child, and he's no different*, if they're not paying attention or they're not focusing ... then you're going to keep saying: 'I'd like you to listen to me now. Can you follow this please'. *If you know it's geared at their level, and to me Hemi is no different from all the other children in here as far as that goes* – I think *he can concentrate if he's made to* for as long as they can – then *it's just a matter of bringing him back on task, all the time* – which is something that I don't have time to do, to keep stopping for him.

The teacher saw the aide as responsible for bridging the language gap, providing modified instruction, and managing Hemi's attention and participation. With regard to content, she hoped that Hemi was getting at least the main ideas, if not the detail, when in fact the reverse was happening: fragments of detail were conveyed that did not amount to 'the general idea'. In viewing Hemi as 'no different from all the other children,' the teacher was articulating her intent to treat him as an 'equal' to his peers. But in doing so, she did not acknowledge his very different exposure to English (such as knowledge of food names in English), his access to prior conceptual knowledge, his experience with question–answer discourse in a group, or the difficulty of maintaining visual attention and displaying relevant responses to a delayed rendition of dialogue.

The teacher observed Hemi to be 'off-task' much of the time in class, and correctly identified that this was partly related to the way the aide functioned (which was quite typical of teacher aides observed working in such situations). In emphasising the need to 'bring him back on task' and 'being made to concentrate', she located the problem in his behaviour rather than in the nature of the interaction he experienced. A more accurate description of Hemi is 'outside of' rather than 'off' task, since he was unable to access the language and the conceptual framework that constructed the content and form of the activity and as such, could only play the role of a marginal participant.

Mediation of Learning and Membership through Social Interaction

An educational context where students have opportunities to interact in learning tasks without adult intervention supports linguistic, academic and social development (Cazden, 1988; Green & Dixon, 1993). Hudelson (1994: 141) notes that, when teachers encourage students to use talk and to use one another as resources in learning, 'children experience a sense of belonging and well-being in the classroom setting and a sense of responsibility for each other.' The importance of a classroom community and the central role of children's talk in supporting their literacy development have been revealed through classroom ethnographies. Work such as Dyson's (1989, 1993, 1997) in urban schools shows African-American students using talk to share imaginary stories that become the focus of written compositions, to provide assistance with spelling and correcting mistakes, and to accomplish social work. In a parallel study of deaf students in a self-contained classroom,[6] Ramsey (1997) observed them using American Sign Language to talk about written English tasks and to support one another's developing competence in reading and writing. Ramsey also observed the same students during regular sessions in mainstream classes, and concluded that this setting gave deaf students physical proximity to their hearing peers but did not provide a context in which deaf and hearing students could interact, communicate and support each other's learning.

Access to interlocutors who share a language and similar experiences allows for learning that is naturally embedded in social interaction and dialogue and enables students to establish their identities as members of a community of learners. Examples 3 and 4 illustrate the extent to which this occurs in each of the two settings.

Example 3: Bilingual class

In the bilingual classroom, Malia and her peers communicated easily with each other and their teacher in NZSL. The teacher created an active language environment[7] in which students had ample opportunity to talk and practice using their developing sign language. Students regularly engaged in tasks that were student-directed and in which they were encouraged to use one another as resources for learning. One such activity was independent writing in which students were seated together at circular tables to write in their journals. They were instructed to use available resources including word lists and environmental print and to talk to their peers about story ideas and to ask for help. In the following example, Malia and Bethany were able to support one another's developing writing skills as they wrote about a forthcoming field trip on a train.

> Malia is drawing a train in her notebook. When she is finished, she begins to compose her story, first writing the word 'Tomorrow.' Bethany spends a great deal of time on her drawing using various colours and details to depict the train. When she is ready to begin writing, she is unsure what to do, so she looks over at Malia for guidance. Bethany asks Malia, 'WHY? DON'T-KNOW?' *(What should I write? I don't know what to do.)* Malia is focused on her own writing, so she just shrugs and does not offer assistance. Bethany repeats her pleas to Malia explaining that she is struggling and does not know what to write. Malia decides to help Bethany and tells her how to begin her story. She signs, 'TOMORROW' and points to the word 'tomorrow' on the word list telling Bethany she should copy the word. While Bethany is copying the word 'tomorrow', Malia turns back to her own writing. Malia wants to write the word 'train,' but she cannot remember how to spell it. She looks to Bethany for help and asks, 'KNOW TRAIN? DON'T-KNOW ME.' (*Do you know the word train? I don't know how to write it.*) Malia looks down at Bethany's paper and notices that Bethany has already written the word 'train' next to her drawing, so she studies the word and then begins to copy it on her own paper.

When Bethany was unsure what to write, she turned to her classmate Malia for assistance. Although Malia was initially reluctant to help, she eventually decided to help Bethany begin her story by telling her what word to write and directing her to the word list from which she could copy the spelling. The girls' roles were then reversed when Malia did not remember how to spell the word 'train.' Hoping Bethany could help her, Malia asked for assistance and was fortunate to find it in Bethany's composition. The exchange continued with both girls continuing to provide support to one another as follows:

> Bethany watches as Malia writes the word 'train'. She reads Malia's sentence, which reads, 'Tomorrow we go tr' and realises that a word is missing. Bethany quickly notifies Malia signing, 'WILL!' (*Hey, you forgot the word 'will'.*) Malia realises that Bethany is right and gestures, 'oops!' She crosses out the beginning of the word 'train' and writes, 'will'. Bethany watches as Malia corrects her sentence and smiles, proud that she was able to help Malia avoid a mistake. Bethany turns back to her

own work and continues copying the word 'tomorrow' from the list. For the remainder of the writing period, Bethany uses Malia's story as a model for her own composition.

Bethany was able to help Malia with the English construction of future tense, a grammatical form the girls were learning to use. Temporality is marked differently in NZSL and English: NZSL uses a time word to establish a time frame in the discourse rather than marking verbs for grammatical tense. Malia's written sentence initially followed NZSL grammar until Bethany reminded her of the need to include the word 'will' to indicate future tense appropriately in English. With Bethany's support, Malia realised her mistake and was able to modify her sentence.

Through their shared first language, the two girls requested and provided assistance to each other as they grappled with expressing ideas in their second language, English. By serving as learning resources for one another, the deaf peers were also constructing their identities as competent learners and partners in the classroom community.

Example 4: Mainstream class

An important argument advanced for mainstreaming deaf children is enriched opportunities for social and academic learning from a range of 'normal' peers. In reality, signing deaf children have restricted access to hearing peers in both sign and spoken language, which impoverishes rather than enriches the social resources available for learning (Cawthon, 2001; Cocks, 1988; Hopwood & Galloway, 1999; Ramsey, 1997). The lack of shared language between Hemi and his peers in class limited his relationship with them as learning partners. This is shown in the following scenario in which Hemi and his classmates sat together while making individual title pages on the theme 'Food for Energy.' They were instructed to write a heading and illustrate the page based on ideas from the preceding discussion on the mat:

Hemi sits at his usual table with two other boys, a girl, and the teacher aide next to him. There is a busy, controlled hum of talk around the room as the children work. Hemi's group works quietly, with little interaction – possibly constrained by the presence of the adult teacher aide at their table. Children at other tables converse about what they are writing or drawing, ask to borrow each other's stationery, and compare their work. Hemi initially spends five minutes laboriously covering his paper with glue and sticking it into his book, while the others at his table work on their headings. The aide looks on and reminds him to ask his mother to buy a new glue stick. When the page is stuck down, the aide tells Hemi to write the heading, pointing to the words on the whiteboard. After scanning a word list on the table with furrowed brow, Hemi looks over at the work of the boy sitting nearest to him. He attracts his attention by waving his pencil near his book and grinning when he looks up. The boys exchange a couple of gestures. Hemi starts to copy the other boy's heading, one letter at a time, then he switches to copying the words from the whiteboard. He looks up between writing each letter suggesting that the words 'food' and 'for' are not familiar enough to write independently. During the session the teacher walks around the room, giving children feedback and direction on their work. Twice she stops at Hemi's table, speaking to two of the children about their work. She glances at Hemi's work, but he is not addressed.

In this 15-minute period, Hemi and his peers did not converse verbally. Instead, Hemi initiated non-verbal exchanges of an eraser and ruler, looked at and copied another child's work, and occasionally pointed to a drawing on a peer's page and laughed or gestured by way of comment. Other children did not initiate interaction with him. Unlike his classmates who were actively conversing and unlike Malia with her peers in the bilingual classroom, Hemi was not able to maintain dialogue with other children about the task (or anything else). Gumperz (1981: 11) claims that '(t)o the extent that learning is a function of the ability to sustain interaction, the child's ability to control and utilise these conventions is an important determinant of educational success.' Without control of discourse skills and shared expectations as to where a conversational exchange is going, 'interactants are likely to lose interest, interactions tend to be brief or perfunctory, and productive exchanges are unlikely to result' (Gumperz, 1981: 12). This precisely appeared to characterise most of Hemi's observed interactions with hearing peers at school. Most of his dialogue in group activities in class occurred within the dyad of the teacher aide and himself; whether the talk was task-related, disciplinary or conversational, she was his essential social and instructional resource.

In fact, Hemi did not seem to be aware that many of the teacher aide's utterances relayed the speech of others. This was partly because the distinction between other people's voices and the aide's own was not consistently framed, and partly because the roles the teacher aide assumed at various times were not made explicit to him. His expectation of communication with the aide appeared to be more in the nature of a personal dialogue running parallel to what others were doing, rather than communication with peers and teacher through an intermediary. This is an understandable assumption for a child of seven, given the unnaturalness of mediated communication even for adults. The aide speculated that Hemi did not fully understand her role as his interpreter, nor his own identity and role in the classroom. She commented: 'He knows that I'm there to *help* him in whatever way I do that, but I don't think he realises that I am actually interpreting. I'm not convinced that he even understands that *he's deaf and everybody else isn't*'. Her comment encapsulates two key aspects of Hemi's learning context. Firstly, his participation was always contingent upon adult help, which cast him as disabled or infantile, rather than bilingual. Secondly, Hemi's social environment did not hold up a mirror to his developing identity as a deaf person, which could help him to define himself in relation to others and to demystify some of his unsatisfactory communication experiences. In the bilingual classroom, Malia's identity as a deaf bilingual learner was developed jointly through interaction with her classmates who shared common experiences and challenges with her, and it was acknowledged explicitly as a feature of membership in the classroom and school community.

Competence in Classroom Discourse as a Marker of Membership

Social competence in the classroom, as Mehan (1974) defines it, requires the child to integrate interactional form with academic content, and to synchronise their behaviour with the changing demands of the context from moment to moment. Our data echo Ramsey's (2001) observation that many deaf students enter school without the specific communicative competencies and knowledge underlying performance of the 'student role' in a classroom, and that this competence cannot be developed by young children through interpreted interaction. Our data also indicate that classroom interaction mediated across languages by an adult (ineptly, in this case) tends to marginalise deaf students, despite best intentions to include them. For Hemi, it was nearly impossible to access the communicative processes and norms that construct membership of a hearing class.

One such norm that rendered Hemi's participation as less than competent in this learning context was the constraint of 'relevant contributions' that operates in classrooms (Cazden, 1988). When the teacher addressed questions to the class, Hemi would often display what he perceived to be expected behaviour by raising his hand enthusiastically when other children did so, usually before the question had been completely signed to him. Before the teacher could call on him, the teacher aide often looked at him and signed, 'WHAT?' or looked away from him, with the effect that Hemi tended to address his comment to the aide or lower his hand. These were apparently the aide's strategies for intercepting responses that might be off-track (as a result of incomprehension or different background knowledge) or untimely, and thus potentially disruptive to the teacher's management of discussion. The teacher aide described Hemi as an imaginative and 'divergent' thinker in explaining his tendency to express ideas that were apparently unrelated to what he was supposed to be working on or unrelated to a topic of talk that had been introduced by an adult. A desire to help deaf children meet the implicit academic goal of generating relevant answers at the right time (Bloome & Thoreau, 1988) – or rather, a wish to avoid demonstrating to the group that they cannot – may explain why a large proportion of deaf children's dialogue in mainstream classes stops at the teacher aide rather than connecting with the teacher or other children.

Hemi's contributions, when called upon, sometimes demonstrated inexperience with hearing audience considerations: the unstated expectations about what to say, when, to whom, and how (Cazden, 1988). This was apparent during a session with a visiting 'Bible in Schools' volunteer, who invited children to share personal news. Hemi raised his hand and was chosen to come to the front and talk. Obviously pleased at getting the floor, he reported (in NZSL) that one night at his house there was a lot of drinking, and Dad and other people got drunk while he was in bed. The teacher aide voiced uncertainty (directed to the adults present) as to whether she had understood his reference to 'drunk' and 'Dad' correctly. Instead of translating the story to the class, the aide tried to divert him to a 'better' topic, signing, 'Tell them about the calves', knowing that he had recently seen some new calves on the farm where his father worked. Hemi obliged by telling that he saw a calf come out the back end of a cow and it was bloody and dead! This story was translated by the aide, with just a slight overlay of amusement at his graphic description. The Bible teacher smiled, thanked him, and called on the next child who talked demurely about going to her friend's house to play.

While Hemi's classmates appeared attentive to his animated signing, it was not evident from their response how much they understood of what he signed in class. The filtering of Hemi's contributions through the reaction and footing of an adult voice was typical of his participation in discussions. Whereas his peers were beginning to discriminate audiences and situations for different content and styles, Hemi could not really test ideas on his peers outside of class because they did not share enough language to communicate beyond the immediate context. Without this experience of informal talk with peers and without accessible feedback from his audiences in class, he could not develop a sense of where he stood in relation to communication norms. Although accepted with apparent respect by his teachers and peers, the delivery and content of Hemi's contributions tended to mark him as a cultural and linguistic outsider. Hemi's exclusion from the subtle conventions of interaction in class means that his chance of educational success in this context will differ significantly from that of his classmates and that of deaf students such as Malia in a learning context where interaction is controlled by norms that are shaped by visual communication and deaf experience (see Erting, 1988 for an account of deaf classroom interaction norms).

Conclusions

For Malia and her classmates in a bilingual class, the sensory and cultural experience of being deaf informed the design and facilitation of learning activities. English language and curriculum content were approached through the lens of how the children, as NZSL users, experienced the world and what they knew about the languages being learned in their school environment. Having direct linguistic access to their teacher and peers allowed for learning that was naturally mediated by meaningful social interaction and dialogue. Participating in a language-sharing classroom community also enabled children to see reflections of themselves in the language and ways of other people around them, and thereby to establish personal identity as competent learners and group members who could look to each other for support and extension in their learning.

For deaf children like Hemi in the mainstream, NZSL may be viewed as a pedagogical tool or conduit for providing the child with 'communication access' to learning activities conducted in English. The use of NZSL by a student in a mainstream school is officially framed as a response to an 'individualised special need', and is less likely to be perceived as central to personal identity (except that signing marks the child as different from others) and potential cultural membership of an adult deaf community. In Hemi's case, his school acknowledged NZSL as his main channel to learning and as part of his social identity, since – unlike most deaf children – he had deaf family members. Nevertheless, Hemi's observed interaction inside and outside the classroom revealed that there was little authentic social context for his acquisition of NZSL at school and minimal shared cultural or pedagogical understanding about how to accomplish academic and social tasks in this language.

Exposure to sign language and personal encounters with disability are valued by mainstream schools as an enriching experience for the hearing students, adding, in the words of Hemi's principal, a 'wonderful dimension to the school'. But when the main exponent of the deaf child's primary language of communication in class (the teacher aide) and the child's peers are less proficient in this language than the child is, it is difficult to show that he benefits equally from the experience. Although Hemi had several hours per week of individual instruction with a visiting teacher who is also a deaf NZSL user, his day-to-day school experience did not nourish his basic communicative competence in NZSL through natural conversations with children and adults for multiple purposes. Nor did this context – that is, the participants and their particular interactions – enable NZSL to be skilfully utilised as a platform for developing second-language skills in the academic domain.

These observations were somewhat apparent to those involved. Hemi's principal, teacher, and teacher aide all independently expressed the view that the only justification for mainstream placement of a deaf child such as Hemi was social/ideological (or, more pragmatically, economic) rather than educational. The principal explained the social rationale as follows: 'When he's a man, he'll be able to go up to the local bar and have a beer and communicate with the person next to him – with his mates.' The individual members of staff involved acknowledged realistic doubts about the capacity of the mainstream situation to provide a context in which Hemi could learn successfully. However, they attributed the difficulty less to the nature of classroom interaction and more to external sources such as lack of special technology (which they imagined deaf schools to use), insufficient time for adapted teaching, Hemi's behaviour, inadequate funding for staff training, and a need for special teaching and assessment techniques. In contrast, Malia's teacher articulated and conveyed through her teaching practice the goal that Malia and her classmates should become capable, literate bilinguals – they should develop their NZSL abilities 'to have an everyday conversation about something that happened at home' and 'to be able to understand each other,' and to learn written English in order to 'enjoy reading and writing.' Malia was expected and encouraged to achieve academically, and her teacher expressed a commitment to finding culturally and linguistically effective pedagogical practices to support her in doing so.

We acknowledge that teaching staff in mainstreaming situations often make significant efforts to adapt their teaching programme to accommodate a deaf student. While these adaptations may appear to enhance deaf students' inclusion, the data presented above suggest that in reality these may not provide a sign language user with adequate linguistic, academic, and social participation in a learning context configured for hearing students. Practices in a bilingual class where instruction and expectations about interaction are specially designed for deaf students developing competence in NZSL and English can indeed foster such participation.

Hemi's principal summed up the mainstream school's quandary, saying:

> Schools don't say 'no' to people – we like to say 'yes' and to include everybody ... and not to be critical of anything ... Teachers, as a breed, try to find ways of making things work. Whereas if we were engineers, we might just say, 'Nah, can't be done!' And find another way of doing it.

His comparison with engineers alludes to the need to clearly identify components and their interrelationship in designing an educational setting that functions for its intended purpose. This article has highlighted some of the components of interaction in classrooms that are engineered – or not – for learning through NZSL and English together. Hearing parents today are more likely to understand that a deaf child will develop a bilingual/bicultural adult identity, and some therefore make the decision to incorporate NZSL in their child's schooling and social experience.

The glimpses of interaction in contrasting school settings presented in this chapter suggest that the choice of communication mode and school placement needs to be guided by consideration of actual, rather than presumed, access to communication, to curriculum learning, and to social interaction. The combination of language choice and social grouping with other language users by dint of school placement results in a particular type of learning context shaped by patterns of interaction that are complex and largely unconscious. While the context created for the bilingual deaf child in the bilingual/bicultural setting included the cultural and linguistic tools needed to mediate the social and academic curriculum of schooling, the mainstream context did not. Further examination of discourse in the contexts in which deaf children are learners can contribute to making more explicit the educational implications of professional advice and parental choices about language use and school placement.

Postscript

Hemi was recently re-observed by a research associate in the same school at the age of nine, two years after the data presented in this article were collected. He is exponentially further behind his hearing peers, and still learning to read new-entrant books. His behaviour is reported to be attention-seeking, and often difficult to manage. Even with his visiting itinerant teacher who is deaf and a fluent NZSL signer, he is generally reluctant or unable to engage in structured learning tasks, either one-to-one or in a group. It appears likely that when he has completed primary school, he will transfer to a residential Deaf Education Centre where the remainder of his education is destined to be remedial.

Acknowledgements

We thank the mainstream school and Deaf Education Centre and all participants in our respective case studies. Rachel McKee's research was funded by a Strategic Development Fund grant from Victoria University of Wellington. Thanks to Wenda Walton, Alan Wendt and Eileen Smith for research assistance on the McKee project. Yael Biederman's research was made possible by a Fulbright Fellowship and supported by Rachel McKee, David McKee and Graeme Kennedy of the Deaf Studies Research Unit at Victoria University of Wellington.

Notes

1. By 'deaf' here we mean individuals with congenital or early onset of deafness and who are profoundly or severely deaf to the extent that spoken language is not easily comprehensible; this group is often referred to as 'prelingually deaf'. People in this category tend to identify socially and linguistically with other deaf people, and call themselves 'deaf' as opposed to 'hearing impaired' or 'hard of hearing,' which are labels perceived as originating in the hearing world. In this article we have chosen not to observe a convention of using upper case 'D' to denote deaf cultural identity, since in the case of deaf children particularly, attribution of cultural identity can be ambiguous.
2. In New Zealand, 24% of children with a hearing impairment are reported to have a familial history of deafness (National Audiology Centre, 2000). This does not always imply having deaf parents: in general, approximately 90% of deaf people have hearing parents, while only about 10% have deaf parents.
3. Kelston Deaf Education Centre (KDEC), in Auckland and van Asch Deaf Education Centre (VADEC) in Christchurch.
4. In some other countries (notably, the USA) this role would be fulfilled by a trained interpreter, but in New Zealand trained interpreters are generally not available to schools for reasons of inadequate supply, funding and lack of recognition of the nature of the task of teacher aides.
5. Malia's mother told us that Malia uses print to communicate with her family. For example, when she wants to eat Weetbix, she'll write 'weetbix' on a piece of paper and show it to her mother.
6. A self-contained classroom is a special class for deaf students within a regular school, equivalent to the New Zealand terms 'unit' or 'resource class'.
7. The terminology 'active language environment' is used in contrast to what Garcia (1999: 191) describes as a 'passive language environment' in which minority-language students rarely have opportunities to talk and to produce original statements. In such settings, students typically simply answer teacher's questions or respond with non-verbal gestures or actions (Ramirez *et al.*, 1991).

References

AC Nielsen (2000) Establishing deaf children's educational needs. Unpublished report for Specialist Education Services, New Zealand.

Akamatsu, T.C. (1998) Thinking with and without language: What is necessary and sufficient for school-based learning? In A. Weisel (ed.) *Issues Unresolved: New Perspectives on Language and Deaf Education* (pp. 27–40). Washington DC: Gallaudet University Press.

Akamatsu, C.T., Stewart, D.A. and Mayer, C. (2002) Is it time to look beyond teacher's signing behavior? *Sign Language Studies* 2 (3), 230 –254.

Allen, T. (1986) Patterns of academic achievement among hearing impaired students: 1974–1983. In A. Schildroth (ed.) *Deaf Children in America* (pp. 161–206). San Diego, CA: College-Hill Press.

Andrews, J., Winograd, P. and DeVille, G. (1994) Deaf children reading fables: Using ASL summaries to improve reading comprehension. *American Annals of the Deaf* 139 (3), 378–386.

Antia, S. (1982) Social interaction of partially mainstreamed hearing impaired children. *American Annals of the Deaf* 127, 18–25.

Bailes, C.N. (2001) Integrative ASL-English language arts: Bridging paths to literacy. *Sign Language Studies* 1 (2), 147–174.

Baker, C. and Battison, R. (1980) *Sign Language and the Deaf Community: Essays in Honor of William C. Stokoe*. Maryland: National Association of the Deaf.

Biederman, Y. (2000) Teaching deaf students to read English using American Sign Language. Unpublished MA thesis, University of California, Berkeley.

Biederman, Y. (2003) Literacy learning in a bilingual classroom for deaf students: Negotiating between New Zealand Sign Language and English. Unpublished doctoral dissertation, University of California, Berkeley.

Bloome, D. and E. Thoreau (1988) Analyzing teacher–student and student–student discourse. In J. Green and J. Harker (eds) *Multiple Perspective Analyses of Classroom Discourse* (pp. 217–248) New Jersey: Ablex.

Bogdan, R.C. and Biklen, S.K. (1992) *Qualitative Research for Education: An Introduction to Theory and Methods*. Boston: Allyn & Bacon.

Cawthon, S.W. (2001) Teaching strategies in inclusive classrooms with deaf students. *Journal of Deaf Education and Deaf Studies* 6 (3), 212–225.

Cazden, C.B. (1988) *Classroom Discourse: The Language of Teaching and Learning*. Portsmouth, NH: Heinemann.

Cocks, I. (1988) The effects of hearing peers signed exact English skills on the social interaction of deaf children in a partially integrated primary school setting. Unpublished master's research paper, University of Canterbury.

Collins-Ahlgren, M. (1989) Aspects of New Zealand Sign Language. Unpublished doctoral dissertation, Victoria University of Wellington.

Cummins, J. (1979) Linguistic interdependence and the educational development of bilingual children. *Review of Educational Research* 49 (2).

Cummins, J. (1981) The role of primary language development in promoting educational success for language minority students. In *Schooling and Language Minority Students: A Theoretical Framework* (pp. 16–62). Sacramento, CA: California Department of Education.

Drasgow, E. (1993) Bilingual/bicultural deaf education: An overview. *Sign Language Studies* 80, 243–266.

Dugdale, P. (2000) Being deaf in New Zealand: A case study of the Wellington deaf community. Unpublished doctoral dissertation. Victoria University of Wellington.
Dyson, A.H. (1989) *Multiple Worlds of Child Writers: Friends Learning to Write*. New York, NY: Teachers College Press.
Dyson, A.H. (1993) *Social Worlds of Children Learning to Write in an Urban Primary School*. New York, NY: Teachers College Press.
Dyson, A.H. (1997) *Writing Superheroes: Contemporary Childhood, Popular Culture, and Classroom Literacy*. New York: Teachers College Press.
Eggleton, J. (1999) *Spider's Web*. Illinois: Rigby.
Erting, C. (1988) Acquiring linguistic and social identity: Interactions of deaf children with a hearing teacher and a deaf adult. In M. Strong (ed.) *Language Learning and Deafness* (pp. 192–219). Cambridge: Cambridge University Press.
Forman, W. (2000) Toward a critique of the exclusive use of oral methods in education of the deaf. *New Zealand Journal of Disability* 7, 40–56.
Garcia, E.E. (1999) *Student Cultural Diversity: Understanding and Meeting the Challenge*. Boston: Houghton Mifflin.
Green, J. and Dixon, C. (1993) Talking knowledge into being: Discursive and social practices in classrooms. *Linguistics and Education* 5 (3/4: Special Issue: Santa Barbara Classroom Discourse Group), 231–239.
Green, J. and Wallat, C. (eds) (1981) *Ethnography and Language in Educational Settings*. New Jersey: Ablex.
Gumperz, J. (1981) Conversational inference and classroom learning. In J. Green and C. Wallat (eds) *Ethnography and Language in Educational Settings* (pp. 3–24). New Jersey: Ablex.
Heritage, J. (1997) Conversational analysis and institutional talk: Analysing data. In D. Silverman (ed.) *Qualitative Research: Theory, Method and Practice* (pp. 161–182). London, Thousand Oaks: Sage Publications.
Higgins, S.P. (1980) *Outsiders in a Hearing World: A Sociology of Deafness*. Beverly Hills, CA: Sage.
Higgins, S.P. (1990) *The Challenge of Educating Together Deaf and Hearing Youth: Making Mainstreaming Work*. Springfield, IL: Charles C. Thomas.
Hirsh-Pasek, K. (1986) Beyond the great debate: Fingerspelling as an alternative route to word identification for deaf or dyslexic readers. *Reading Teacher* 40 (3).
Hoffmeister, R.J. (2000) A piece of the puzzle: American Sign Language and reading comprehension. In C. Chamberlain, J.P. Morford and R.I. Mayberry (eds) *Language Acquisition by Eye*. Mahwah, NJ: Erlbaum.
Hopwood, V. and Gallaway, C. (1999) Evaluating the linguistic experience of a deaf child in a mainstream class: A case study. *Deafness and Education International* 1 (3), 172 –187.
Hudelson, S. (1994) Literacy development of second language children. In F. Genesee (ed.) *Educating Second Language Children: The Whole Child, The Whole Curriculum, The Whole Community* (pp. 129–158). New York, NY: Cambridge University Press.
Johnson, R.E., Liddell, S.K. and Erting, C.J. (1989) Unlocking the curriculum: Principles for achieving access in deaf education. *Gallaudet Research Institute Working Paper 89–3*. Washington, DC: Gallaudet University.
Kelly, A. (1995) Fingerspelling interaction: A set of deaf parents and their deaf daughter. In C. Lucas (ed.) *Sociolinguistics in Deaf Communities* (pp. 62–73). Washington DC: Gallaudet University Press.

Kluwin, T.N. and Stinson, M.S. (1993) *Deaf Students in Local Public Highschools: Backgrounds, Experiences, and Outcomes*. Springfield, IL: Charles C. Thomas

Krashen. S.D. (1996) *Under Attack: The Case against Bilingual Education*. Culver City: Language Education Associates

Lane, H., Hoffmeister, R. and Bahan, B. (1996) *A Journey into the Deaf-World*. San Diego, CA: DawnSign Press

Lynas, W. (1984) The education of hearing-impaired pupils in ordinary schools: Integration or pseudo-assimilation? *Journal of the British Association of Teachers of the Deaf* 8 (5), 129–135.

Mayer, C. and Wells, G. (1996) Can the linguistic interdependence theory support a bilingual-bicultural model of literacy education for deaf students? *Journal of Deaf Education and Deaf Studies* 1 (2), 93–107.

Mayer, C. and Akamatsu, C.T. (1999) Bilingual-bicultural models of literacy education for deaf students: Considering the claims. *Journal of Deaf Studies and Deaf Education* 4, 1–8.

McCracken, W. (2001) Educational placement. In R. Beattie (ed.) *Ethics in Deaf Education: The First Six Years* (pp. 119 –142). San Diego, CA: Academic Press.

McKee, R. (2001) *People of the Eye: Stories from the Deaf World*. Wellington: Bridget Williams Books.

McKee, R. (2002) Teacher aides of high and very high needs deaf students: A summary of findings from the project 'communication access and learning outcomes for deaf learners in the mainstream'. Unpublished paper, Deaf Studies Research Unit, Victoria University of Wellington.

Mehan, H. (1974) Accomplishing classroom lessons. In A.V. Cicourel (ed.) *Language and School Performance* (pp. 76–142). New York: Academic Press.

Monaghan, L.F. (1996) Signing, oralism, and the development of the New Zealand deaf community: An ethnography and history of language ideologies. Unpublished doctoral dissertation, University of California, Los Angeles.

National Audiology Centre (2000) *New Zealand Deafness Notification Data, January to December 2000*. Auckland: National Audiology Centre.

Padden, C. and Humphries, T. (1988) *Deaf in America: Voices from a Culture*. Cambridge, MA: Harvard University Press.

Padden, C. and Hanson, V.L. (2000) Search for the missing link: The development of skilled reading in deaf children. In K. Emmorey and H. Lane (eds) *The Signs of Language Revisited: An Anthology to Honor Ursula Bellugi and Edward Klima*. Hillsdale, NJ: Lawrence Erlbaum.

Padden, C. and Ramsey, C. (1998) Reading ability in signing deaf children. *Topics in Language Disorders* 18 (4).

Padden, C. and Ramsey, C. (2000) American Sign Language and reading ability in deaf children. In C. Chamberlain, J.P. Morford and R.I. Mayberry (eds) *Language Acquisition by Eye*. Mahwah, NJ: Erlbaum.

Paul, P.V. (1998) A perspective on the special issue on literacy. *Journal of Deaf Studies and Deaf Education* 3, 258–264.

Penman, P. (1999) Deaf way, deaf view: A study of deaf culture from a deaf perspective. Unpublished master's thesis, Victoria University of Wellington.

Prinz, P. and Strong, M. (1997) A study of the relationship between American Sign Language and early literacy. *Journal of Deaf Studies and Deaf Education* 2 (1), 37–46.

Pritchett, P. (1998) A survey of the reading comprehension of a sample of New Zealand children with prelingual severe/profound hearing loss. Unpublished MA thesis, University of Melbourne.

Ramirez, J.D., Yuen, S.D., Ramey, D.R. and Pasta, D.J. (1991) *Final Report: Longitudinal Study of Structured English Immersion Strategy, Early-Exit, and Late-Exit Transitional Bilingual Education Programs for Language-Minority Children*. 1–2 (300-87-0156). San Mateo, CA: Aguirre International.

Ramsey, C.L. (1997) *Deaf Children in Public School: Placement, Context and Consequences*. Washington DC: Gallaudet University Press.

Ramsey, C. (2001) Beneath the surface: Theoretical frameworks shed light on educational interpreting. *Odyssey: New Directions in Deaf Education* 2 (2), 19–24.

Schein, J., Mallory, B. and Greaves, S. (1991) Communication for deaf students in mainstream classrooms. *Research Monograph No. 2*, Western Canadian Centre of Studies in Deafness, University of Alberta, Edmonton.

Skutnabb-Kangas, T. and Tuokomaa, P. (1976) *Teaching Migrant Children's Mother Tongue and Learning the Language of the Host Country in the Context of the Socio-Cultural Situation of the Migrant Family*. Helsinki: The Finnish National Commission for UNESCO.

Slobin, D., Hoiting, N., Anthony, M., Biederman, Y., Kuntze, M., Lindert, R., Pyers, J., Thumann, H. and Weinberg, A. (2000) The Berkeley Transcription System. In B. MacWhinney (ed.) *The CHILDES Project: Tools for Analyzing Talk: Transcription Format and Programs*. Hillsdale, NJ: Erlbaum.

Stake, R. (1995) *The Art of Case Study Research*. San Diego, CA: Sage.

Stinson, M. and Antia, S. (1999) Considerations in educating deaf and hard-of-hearing students in inclusive settings. *Journal of Deaf Studies and Deaf Education* 4, 163–175.

Stinson, M. and Lang, H. (1994) Full inclusion: A path for integration or isolation? *American Annals of the Deaf* 139, 156 –158.

Strong, M. and Prinz, P. (2000) Is American Sign Language skill related to English literacy? In C. Chamberlain, J.P. Morford and R.I. Mayberry (eds) *Language Acquisition by Eye*. Mahwah, NJ: Erlbaum.

Swanwick, R. (1998) The teaching and learning of literacy within a sign bilingual approach. In S. Gregory, P. Knight, W. McCracken, S. Powers and L. Watson *Issues in Deaf Education* (pp. 111–118). London: David Fulton Publishers

Townshend, S. (1993) 'The hands just have to move': Deaf education in New Zealand; A perspective from the deaf community. Unpublished master's thesis, Massey University.

VandenBerg, M. (1971) *The Written Language of Deaf Children*. Wellington: New Zealand Council for Educational Research.

Vygotsky, L. (1978) *Mind in Society: The Development of Higher Psychological Processes* (M. Cole, V. John-Steiner, S. Scribner and E. Souberman, eds). Cambridge, MA: Harvard University Press.

Wilbur, R.B. (2000) The use of ASL to support the development of English and literacy. *Journal of Deaf Studies and Deaf Education* 5, 81–104.

Willig, A. C. (1985) A meta-analysis of selected studies on the effectiveness of bilingual education. *Review of Educational Research* 55 (3), 269–317.

Winston, E. (2001) Visual inaccessibility: The elephant (blocking the view) in interpreted education. *Odyssey: New Directions in Deaf Education*, Winter/Spring, 5–7.

Chapter 9

Community Language Teacher Education Needs in New Zealand

NIKHAT SHAMEEM

Introduction

The role that immigrants play in a nation and the degree of support they receive from government agencies are most clearly seen in the specific provisions made for new immigrants to learn about and adapt to the host culture while maintaining and strengthening their own culture and languages. The trend in New Zealand, as in the West, tends to be for the medium of instruction to be the majority language. While this promotes the learning of dominant languages such as English, it also encourages the shift away from the mother tongues of immigrants by the third generation (Holmes & Harlow, 1991; Shameem, 1997, 2000). The teaching and learning of minority languages is generally considered the responsibility of the parents and community. This is despite any awareness there might be in the wider society of the benefits of mother-tongue maintenance. In New Zealand, the revival and development of *te reo Māori* (the Māori language), has raised awareness of the issues of language death and the repercussions of this for Māori culture, identity and self-esteem. Despite this awareness, classes for other community languages continue to be provided in an ad hoc way by parents and other volunteers in the community. Members of most minority communities may have only sketchy knowledge of the - existence of these classes, and this knowledge is mainly disseminated through networking and personal contacts. There is no national language policy in New Zealand to safeguard the linguistic interests of minority communities, or to ensure the continuity of the language and culture of the 40 or so minority speech communities now living in the country (Holt, 1999).

This chapter reports on the nature of community language teaching in New Zealand, specifically identifies the training needs of teachers in Auckland, and presents the outline of a possible professional development programme for them. The participants in this survey, conducted in 2000, were community leaders, teachers, language students (both adults and children) and the parents of children under sixteen. However, data from the community leaders and teachers are the main focus of this chapter.

Community Languages in New Zealand

The term 'community language' has been used in Britain and Australia since the mid-1970s to represent a language other than English or the indigenous languages. In New Zealand, Waite offers the following meaning:

> community languages are associated with communities, which have a primarily ethnic basis. The classical forms of some community languages, in addition to being ethnically based, are strongly associated with particular religions. (Waite, 1992: 56)

The diverse meanings contained in the term 'community language' in New Zealand can be illustrated by the example of Muslim children from a number of minority groups attending Arabic and Urdu language classes. Their mother tongues could be Oromo, Hindustani, Fiji Hindi, Cantonese, Amharic, Pushto, Somali or English. They learn Arabic and Urdu in order to access religious literature, to understand oral sermons, or to show religious affiliation and loyalty towards fellow Muslims. They may also attend community language classes to maintain and learn their mother tongues. Many users of community languages, especially new immigrants, are in reality multilinguals who speak several languages.

A community language can be revered by a minority community as its mother tongue even if members do not speak this language as their first language. This distinction is particularly important among second and third generation immigrants who would have acquired the host language from the environment, but have varying degrees of proficiency in their mother tongue.

The continuing and increasing demand for self-determination by New Zealand Māori has led to increased concern for the maintenance and the revival of te reo Māori, particularly during the latter half of the last century. This concern for Māori bilingualism and biculturalism has encouraged some interest in language and culture maintenance among other minority groups. However, interest has been community-based and often sporadic; little institutional support has been made available for learning programmes designed to encourage multilingualism and multiculturalism (see Abbott, 1989; Kasanji, 1994; Shameem, 2000; Smith, 1994).

Holmes (1996) and Chrisp (1997) both claim that the extent of the support that a community language can expect from the host government depends on how important economically or politically the government perceives such support to be. According to Holmes (1996), the New Zealand government gives greater support to certain Pacific Island language groups such as those from the Cook Islands, Tokelau, Niue and Samoa. This is because the New Zealand government regards itself as having greater responsibilities towards these groups since they form part of its administrative responsibilities in the Pacific. At the interface, the Ethnic Affairs Service in the Department of Internal Affairs has operated an ethnic desk in Wellington since 1992 (Waite, 1992) and has recently opened an office in Auckland. Among other things, the Service prints a regular newsletter with information on educational, linguistic and cultural matters. Its current focus is the development of a strategic plan for the department, which would include specific statements about community languages (Hoffman, 2001).

For adequate language planning, it is imperative that specific knowledge of each speech community is gathered, over and above that available from census data and community language studies carried out to date. Only then will decisions on the nature of necessary support for minority language education be made in a fair and equitable way.

In the last fifteen years sociolinguistic research in New Zealand (e.g. Shameem *et al.*, 2002; Starks, 1997; White *et al.*, 2001) shows that some communities demonstrate a greater degree of language shift than others. Some have shifted in their use of the mother tongue over three generations, while others have shifted much more rapidly. For example, Tongan, Samoan, Cantonese, Greek and Gujarati are reasonably well maintained, while many European languages such as Dutch, Polish and Serbo-Croatian, and the Pacific Island languages (Tokelauan, Cook Island Māori, Niuean and Fiji Hindi) are shifting or have shifted very rapidly, even in the last bastion of mother-tongue use – the home (Bell *et al.*, 2000; Davis, 1998; Holmes, 1996; Meanger, 1989; Neazor, 1991; Roberts, 1999; Shameem, 1995).

However, even those communities that have experienced an almost total shift in language use report a persisting ethnic and cultural consciousness. This suggests that in some communities culture is a strong bond, promoting retention of ethnic identity and pride. Individuals and communities may make a greater effort to retain their culture than their language. This is particularly so in communities such as the Indo-Fijian where the mother tongue has low status and is used only for informal communication (Shameem, 1995).

Community Language Teaching in New Zealand

The need for a national languages policy is perhaps the most important factor influencing the teaching of community languages in New Zealand (see

Hoffman, 1995, 2001; Kaplan, 1993; Peddie, this volume; Shackleford, 1997; Shameem, 2001). Moreover, Hamel (1997) and Corson (1999) claim that policy efforts by the government to support community language maintenance must be specific, and any language teacher education programme should take into consideration the differing needs of each community language. Reflecting the absence of such a policy in New Zealand, little progress has been made by successive governments to identify, locate and support community language schools. Most of these are community-funded or self-funded and are held in a range of formal and informal venues: school rooms, religious and community halls, sitting rooms and garages. Data on the number of schools operating, languages taught, nature of teaching and availability of materials continue to be held at community level only and – as this current research shows – even community leaders were unaware of schools and classes operating within their own communities.

Roberts' (1999) work with three New Zealand language communities showed that they had differing priorities. For example, the Gujaratis preferred to have funding for their own language school rather than have their language taught in a state school; the Samoans wanted support for both; and the Dutch did not give language maintenance classes such a high priority. Bell *et al.* (2000: 27) identify the greatest need in community language education to be for human, rather than material, resources. There is a very limited availability of qualified teachers who are well versed in the theory and practice of language teaching. In fact, teacher education programmes in New Zealand have a history of neglect in their training of bilingual teachers – even for Māori and English (Benton, 1996; Corson, 1999). Kasanji (1994) and Waite (1992) voice their concerns about the lack of teacher education provisions for teachers of community languages, and list a number of points suggested by the speech communities themselves. These include: recognising teaching qualifications acquired overseas by first-language speakers of community languages; offering short-term and mid-term courses for overseas qualified teachers to familiarise them with the local and national education environment in order to allow them to work in a range of language-maintenance settings; recruiting first language speakers of community languages into regular teacher education programmes, in order that primary and secondary schools have access to bilingual teachers; and extending international teacher exchange programmes to include teachers capable of teaching in community languages.

Efforts to revive and maintain community languages need to be regular and on-going. Many community language schools fold up because of problems with funding, insufficient materials and resources, sporadic community support, erratic student attendance, and shortage of suitable teachers (see Kasanji, 1994). Chrisp (1997: 15) suggests four ways of encouraging motivation to learn a community language:

(1) offering incentives so that there is an economic benefit in knowing a community language;
(2) promoting information on the long-term benefits of bilingualism;
(3) installing community information and advisory services to target ordinary people and provide information to parents at the right time – before language shift sets in. Chrisp gives examples on how this is already being done in education and health in New Zealand;
(4) providing language-awareness programmes for secondary and tertiary students, who form a captive audience. Such programmes can be readily managed and influenced by language planners.

Following her interviews with members of five New Zealand speech communities, Kasanji (1994: 14) identified the areas in which support was needed: affordable, suitable and generic training of teachers of any language; a multi-faceted, multi-level curriculum that allows for the teaching of culture; the use of up-to-date, authentic resources. Resources would include the appointment of a person in a Government agency who would support teachers and help with the development of teaching materials. Kasanji believes that the payment of community language teachers is also important.

Kasanji (1994) writes that two levels of support are crucial for the way forward for community language teaching: the formation of an Ethnic Schools Association whose work is similar to Australia's National Languages Institute (see Clyne, 1991: 241); and the provision by a recognised teacher education institution of teacher education programmes for teachers of community languages. She argues that a comprehensive and institutionalised teacher education programme would produce better-trained teachers of community languages, who are well versed in teaching in the local context and who understand the principles of language teaching and learning. She further suggests that such a training programme be part of the New Zealand Qualifications Authority's Unit Standards, which would mean that those taking the course could be cross-credited for a teacher education course and possibly other related training.

Despite the absence of a comprehensive list of New Zealand community language schools and student enrolment numbers, several inferences can be drawn from research studies to date. Community schools are mainly held at weekends, and have varied functions. Most importantly they provide an additional domain for language use. Some schools teach the mother tongue of community members, while others teach a religious language to students who may not all share the same mother tongue. The programmes vary in their emphases on oral and literacy skills; for example, among the Wellington Gujaratis, although conversational Gujarati is most important, literacy skills are also in demand for possible visits 'home'.

The success rates of maintenance classes vary. In her study, Roberts (1999) found that attendance at language school related positively to literacy skills, and less strongly to greater oral proficiency among Samoans and Gujaratis. Zheng (1998) found that students who attended language-maintenance classes in Mandarin Chinese were able to maintain and use their mother tongue at home more readily and with greater fluency. She found, however, that home tutoring of children was also effective. Shameem (1995), on the other hand, found that Indo-Fijian children, if they were Muslim, were attending either Koran schools (where Arabic and Urdu were taught) or, if they were Hindu, Ramayan schools (Standard Hindi and Sanskrit were taught). Any exposure to Fiji Hindi, their mother tongue, was incidental and often did not occur at all because of the ethnic mix of students.

The degree to which a language school is important in the community can be demonstrated by the strength of enrolments and retention power of students. Samoan, Greek, Gujarati, Arabic and Cantonese schools have been operating for several decades in Wellington and Auckland. As Roberts (1999: 143) points out, other schools are in a state of flux. In the more recently immigrant Korean community in Auckland, language schools perform a crucial unifying function, with the whole community being involved and a high level of social and linguistic participation (Starks & Youn, 1998). In Meanger's (1989) Wellington study, 79% of his second-generation interviewees, and in Roberts' study, 85% of all respondents, had attended the Gujarati language school. Some 60% of Meanger's respondents felt the classes were of some benefit, although several of them complained about the non-bilingual (non-English speaking) teacher, the boring teaching methods and some felt resentful at being forced to attend by parents.

Summary

This review of published research has addressed the issues surrounding the teaching and learning of community languages. So long as New Zealand does not have a national languages policy, including a specific goal of community language maintenance, a comprehensive teacher education programme for community language teachers is not likely to be an educational priority.

Although research indicates the importance of home language use for maintenance purposes, attending a language-maintenance school is also helpful in allowing a broadening of domains and uses for a community language and for the development of literacy skills. This in turn will support home and community language use and increase the chances of a community language being maintained beyond the third generation.

Case Study: Community Language Teaching Needs in Auckland

Research questions

A survey was undertaken to determine whether teacher education for community languages is desired and needed in Auckland, and to identify the possible content for such a programme. The following were the primary research questions:

(1) Are current community language teachers trained and qualified? In what areas?
(2) Is further teacher education needed and wanted?
(3) What current needs in language schools would a teacher education programme address?
(4) How would a teacher education programme be delivered?
(5) What would a teacher education programme include?

Participants and networking

Contact with community language schools and teachers was made principally through networking. Social networking has been used internationally and in New Zealand for differing purposes (Boyce, 1992; Milroy & Milroy, 1992; Roberts, 1990; 1999; Shameem, 1995; Smith, 1994; Walker, 1996). It is most useful when there are no comprehensive community lists, or 'sampling frames', such as lists of regular church or mosque attendees. For example, because of the difficulty of differentiating Indo-Fijians from other Indians in lists such as phone books and the ethnic communities directory, Shameem (1995) used personal, social and religious contacts from the first-order zone to contact people in the second-order zone. Zones can be extended to further orders, depending on the depth of penetration needed in the group to be studied. Each person is viewed as a focus with links to other people in the community with whom he or she is in contact. This type of sampling is known as 'non-probability' sampling, where 'there is no way to estimate the probability each element has of being included in the sample and no assurance that every element has *some* chance of being included' (Kidder & Judd, 1986: 149). The benefits of using this technique are economy and convenience – both were important considerations in the current study. Moreover, such samples also yield excellent descriptive data.

It was hoped that the community leaders contacted would be able to provide further addresses of community language teachers, and that these teachers in turn would be able to provide contact with two students in their class and, if these students were under 16, that the teachers would provide contact with their parents as well. Networking proved to be more difficult than anticipated, mainly because in many cases the community leaders did not have contact with language schools and teachers even within their community. Moreover, without face-to-face or telephone contact, the response rate of postal questionnaire returns is substantially reduced. Subsequently, the highest number of returns came from community leaders, with a smaller rate of return from teachers, students and parents.

Questionnaires

A questionnaire was chosen as the most suitable research instrument as it could be sent to as many community leaders as possible within a short time span. Postal questionnaires also allow respondents to take their time to respond, and to retain their anonymity. These are important considerations in immigrant and refugee populations. However, a drawback of the postal questionnaire, compared with interviews, is the inability to control responses and to probe incomplete answers or any misunderstanding of the questions. For example, three of the community leaders who responded gave addresses of teachers of ESOL (English for speakers of other languages) rather than community language teachers, in their community.

Kidder and Judd (1986) and Oppenheim (1992) suggest that a postal questionnaire needs to be reasonably short and easy to answer although Roberts, in her 1999 study, did not find a difference in response rate with a trial run of long and short questionnaires. A short questionnaire limits the researcher's ability to check on the accuracy of response, particularly with attitudinal and sensitive questions, by re-asking the question in another way and co-relating the results. Short questionnaires are, however, easy and less time consuming to code and analyse.

The postal questionnaires in this current survey were short, would have taken no longer than 20 minutes to complete, and were written in simple English. In designing the questionnaire, it was understood that not all respondents would be fluent English users. Hence the questions were simple and had easy answering methods – circling, ticking boxes, and writing one-word responses. Translating the questionnaire into various languages was not an option because of budgetary and time constraints.

The design of the questionnaire was influenced by the main aim of the study, the available time span, the respondents' backgrounds, and the research questions. The four questionnaires used in the survey asked similar questions but from the different perspectives of the various respondents: the community leaders, the teachers, the students and their parents. Survey participants were provided with an addressed, pre-paid envelope for return of the completed questionnaires.

Some 95 eligible questionnaires were returned, which is quite a large number of responses from ethnic minorities, who tend to be reticent about coming forward with their concerns. Of those who responded, 41 responses were community leaders, who may not have been directly involved in community language teaching, 15 were language teachers, 17 were students and 22 were parents. All participants were involved in some way with a minority community and they included people from both refugee and immigrant backgrounds. (The response rates in the four categories were: community leaders 26.9%, teachers 31.9%, students 15.4% and parents 12.1%. The last two categories are estimates only, as the teachers were responsible for giving the questionnaires out to students and parents, and there was no way of knowing how many were actually distributed.)

Analysis of the data was quite straightforward, with descriptive statistics and frequency tables providing sufficient information on key research questions.

Presentation and Discussion of Findings

This section looks first at background factors pertinent to this study, including the languages covered by the study and the reasons why the study of the community language is regarded as important. This is followed by a presentation of the backgrounds of the teachers who responded to this survey in terms of their educational levels, qualifications, fields of expertise and language-teaching qualifications. Teachers, community leaders and parents then gave their opinions on why they thought community language teachers needed to participate in a teacher education programme. All three groups were also asked what qualifications might be most appropriate for these teachers. The final section examines the nature and logistics of the programme required: time for classes, instructional type, and possible content of a course on community language teaching.

First languages

In the current survey (see Table 9.1), community leaders, parents and students reported having 29 different first languages, which represents 90.6% of the 32 languages reported in the 1996 census of languages spoken

Table 9.1 Reported first languages: Community leaders, teachers, parents

First language	*Frequency*
Amharic	5
Assyrian	1
Cambodian	1
Cantonese	2
Chinese	1
Congolese	1
Croatian	2
Dutch	3
English	15
Fiji Hindi/Urdu	1
Fijian	1
Greek	2
Gujarati	2
Hindi	3
Lao	1
Korean	1
Niuean	1
Oromifa	1
Oromo	4
Polish	1
Punjabi	1
Samoan	12
Singhalese	6
Spanish	1
Taiwanese	1
Tamil	1
Thai	4
Tongan	3
Urdu	1
Total (29 languages)	*79*

in Auckland (Holt, 1999). The first languages reported were not the same as the languages taught, which included mother tongues, religious languages and smaller ethnic or regional group lingua franca. Fifteen respondents identified English as their first language although their mother tongue, with which their identity was linked, might have been different.

Most of the 95 respondents had very clear reasons why they or their children/students were learning or should be learning the community language. Respondents were provided with a list of possible reasons for learning the community language, and asked to indicate whether this was very important, important or unimportant for them. Table 9.2 ranks these responses in order of the reasons felt to be of particular importance. More than three-quarters of all respondents said that the language was very important, as it was integrally related to their culture and identity. Two-thirds of them said it was very important that they or the children in their community were able to use the language in order to communicate with their grandparents and other family members. A similar number also

Table 9.2 Most important reasons for community language learning

Reason	*Respondents classifying as most important*	*Total no. of respondents*
Identity and cultural maintenance	77.5%	95
Communication with grandparents and family	63.2%	95
Literacy	62.1%	95
Religion	35.8%	95
Return home	32.6%	95
Parental pressure	53.1%	32

said literacy in the community language was very important. Only a third thought it was most important to learn the language for religious purposes or for visits home.

Teachers and students (32 respondents) were asked how important they felt parental pressure to be in the rate of attendance at community language classes, and of 8 of the 17 students and 9 of the 15 teachers believed it to be a very important factor. Only half the respondents felt that parental pressure was the most important reason for attendance at community language school.

Teacher education and language teaching needs

Contacts that community leaders provided were carefully followed up in order to locate any language teachers, particularly to canvas their attitude towards teacher education. Fifteen of the 47 community language teachers to whom questionnaires were sent returned them.

Teacher profiles

Of the 15 teachers who responded, 80% were women, and half of these were in the 40–50 year age group. The others were almost equally spread in the other 10-year age groups between 20 and 70 years specified in the questionnaires. Those over 50 years were generally retired teachers. All the teachers were well-qualified and held certificates, diplomas and degrees (see Table 9.3). Eight of them – just over half – had more than one qualification. Only one teacher said she had an 'informal' qualification, and this was in addition to a certificate in teacher education.

When asked specifically about their field of teaching expertise, teachers said they were qualified in a wide range of areas with a leaning towards a

Table 9.3 Current teacher qualifications

Qualifications of language teachers	*Frequency*
Informal qualification & certificate	1
Certificate	1
Certificate & diploma	1
Certificate, diploma & degree	1
Certificate & degree	3
Diploma	1
Diploma & degree	2
Degree	5
Total	*15*

background of arts and education. Two-thirds (10) of the responding teachers reported backgrounds in either teaching or education (see Table 9.4). Besides their advanced level of education and qualifications, 11 teachers also indicated that they already had some form of training in language teaching.

Several teachers indicated their wish that, rather than concentrating solely on community languages or first-language teaching, further training

Table 9.4 Teacher expertise

Area of expertise	*Frequency*
Arts, Business	1
Arts	1
Education	3
Education, Business	1
Engineering	1
History	1
Languages	1
Teaching	3
Teaching, Anthropology	1
Teaching, Arts	1
Tutor, Geography	1
Total	*15*

courses might include bilingual education and ESOL teaching. Were this to be done, they believed their employment prospects would be enhanced.

Interest in teacher education

Despite most of the 15 responding teachers saying they had already undergone some language teaching training, 12 of them indicated strongly that they would like to study further in this area. Nearly two-thirds of the 41 community leaders and all 22 parents in the survey were also in favour of teachers participating in a language-teaching education programme.

The responses to an open-ended question about the reasons for participation in such a programme were broadly coded into the categories shown in Figure 9.1. On-going professional development was clearly the most important reason for both community leaders and parents. Six teachers and two parents felt that community language teachers needed to know more about New Zealand systems and methods. The teachers also felt that their current qualifications and experience need to be recognised, valued and factored into the equation in some way. Other issues, such as the possibility of getting paid and to learn more about how to motivate students, did not seem as important to these respondents.

There seemed to be general satisfaction with teachers and teaching in community language programmes. It appeared that any suggestions for further professional development of language teachers were genuinely

Figure 9.1 Reasons for participation in language teacher education: Parents, community leaders

concerned with helping them become *better* rather than helping them become *good*. Several teachers in fact indicated their wish to have training in bilingual and ESOL teaching, rather than a programme that concentrated solely on community language, mother-tongue or first-language teaching. With such training, they would have greater prospects for employment.

Responses strongly indicated a general appreciation by the community of the task that language teachers were performing in their spare time often, with very little remuneration. An in-service programme, which enhanced and expanded their existing skill repertoire, would benefit the whole community.

Education Needs of Community Language Teachers

Qualifications and timing

Research participants indicated that qualifications in community language teaching should span the full range included in the question options (see Figure 9.2). Two thirds of the respondents indicated the desirability of formal qualifications – a certificate, diploma or degree in language teaching – while the others felt that an informal qualification or a certificate was adequate. Teachers seemed to favour the award of a certificate or diploma in language teaching following the completion of training.

When asked to nominate the best time of the week for possible attendance at classes, seven of the teachers said they preferred evening classes, with the second preference (four) being weekend classes. As

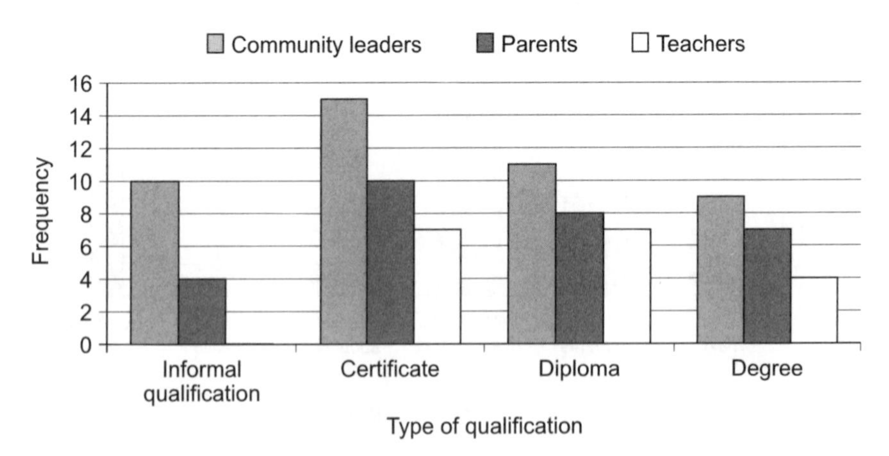

Figure 9.2 Appropriate qualifications in language teaching: Community leaders, parents, and teachers

teachers pointed out, most of them were teaching the community language at the weekends and wished to continue with this pattern – hence their first preference for evening classes. Daytime classes were preferred by only two teachers, confirming current occupational data that teachers worked elsewhere and taught the community language part-time. One teacher was happy to attend classes at anytime.

Instructional styles

Teachers expressed a preference for learning through a range of interactive and informal teaching styles (see Figure 9.3). Assignments were the least popular, and there may be a perception among these teachers that assignments are long, theoretically-based academic essays that would not be suitable in community language teaching. Teachers seem to want useful and practical assessment methods and tasks that are directly related to their language-teaching demands and needs. A majority clearly preferred workshops and group discussions. Four teachers said they would prefer seminars, and three would prefer lectures; of these, six also said these could be combined with other instructional methods. Interestingly, those who preferred seminars did not favour tutorials or lectures in their preferred style. Three teachers preferred an on-line course and only two said they wanted tutorials.

The results indicated a clear shift away from the more 'traditional' methods of learning to more challenging, demanding, practical and functional methods, which multilingual teachers could adapt to suit their particular purposes, needs and contexts. The results also demonstrated

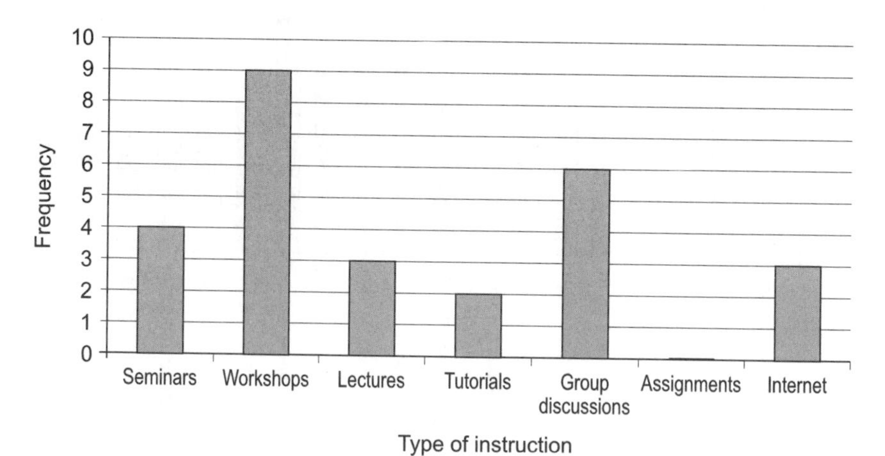

Figure 9.3 Nature of instruction: Teachers

that teachers want greater autonomy in selecting the learning styles: even if they had trained originally using more traditional methods, they were clear in their minds as to what suited them best now. It may therefore be more appropriate to use alternative assessment procedures such as group projects, portfolio presentations, student-led seminars and workshops, and observation of teaching practice in a teacher education programme for community language teachers.

Activities in a language curriculum

In order to identify those classroom activities that are thought helpful to include in a language curriculum, teachers and community leaders were given a list of activities to be placed on a scale of very important, important and unimportant for language learning. Teacher preferences may indicate activities they currently offer in their language programmes. Figure 9.4 demonstrates the activities that teachers and community leaders felt were very important and shows a definite preference for more traditional activities.

Some 80% of the teachers and community leaders gave a very important rating to word study and pronunciation. More than 80% (32) of community leaders and three-quarters of the teachers also felt that conversational practice

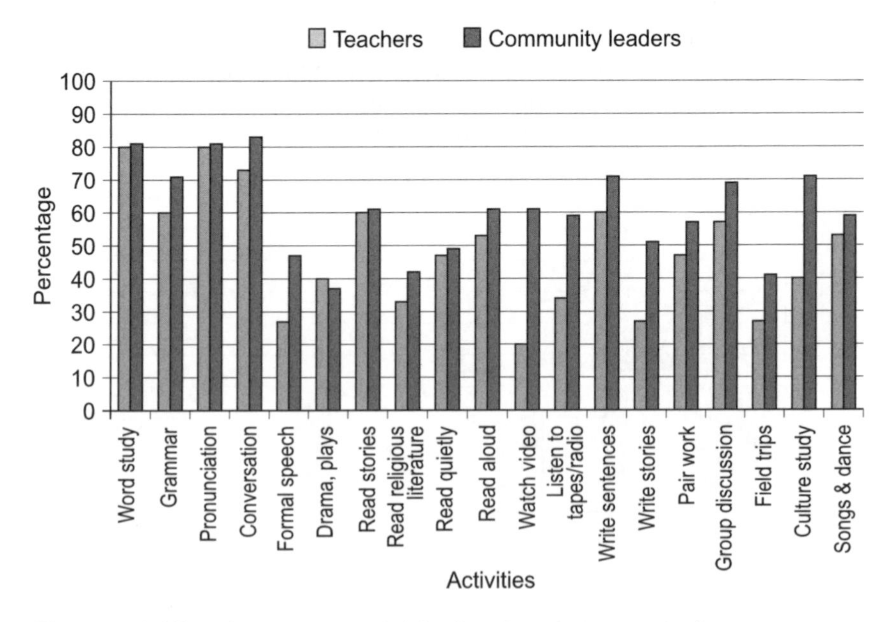

Figure 9.4 Very important activities in a language curriculum

was very important. Generally the community leaders' responses showed a desire for a greater range of activities than the teachers' responses did. While teachers felt that traditional productive oral activities should continue to be targeted in the language classroom, community leaders clearly felt that more communicative methods of learning (group discussion, field trips, watching videos) should be included. Community leaders also showed greater support for more listening activities and the teaching of a wider range of literacy functions. Interestingly, despite the presence of strong Pacific Island rhetorical cultures in the survey, formal speech making and drama were not favoured types of activity. There was clearly more support (almost double) for culture study from community leaders than there was from teachers. Less than half the teachers and community leaders supported the study of religious literature in the language classes. (None of the teacher participants in this study was teaching a religious language.) Generally, the results to this question on activities to be included in a language class indicates a desire for a diversity of activity types covering a wide range of language functions and cognitively demanding uses of language.

Subjects of study in teacher education programmes

Respondents indicated their desire for a programme that would include instruction in dealing with several language-teaching scenarios such as teaching bilingually, teaching ESOL, teaching two languages for different purposes (for example, a religious language and a group lingua franca) and teaching in mixed needs classes.

The data also showed some sharing of teacher and community attitudes towards the possible subject composition of a language-teaching programme, and priorities for both groups are shown in Table 9.5. As in the earlier question on activities to be included in a language-teaching curriculum, teachers and community leaders were asked to rank by level of importance possible subjects for study that would contribute to greater effectiveness in teaching. This would help in devising a programme that teachers saw as useful and practicable.

Teacher rankings differed only slightly from community rankings, and both would need to be taken into consideration in the design and delivery of a language-teaching course. Teaching methodology was identified by 80% (12) of the teachers and 70% (27) of community leaders as possibly the most important part of a programme (see Figure 9.5). Nearly three-quarters (42) of both teachers and community leaders also recognised the importance of a communicative approach to language teaching and learning, and wanted this included in the curriculum. Two-thirds (27) of community

Table 9.5 Ranking of subjects requested in teacher education

Ranking	*Teachers*	*Community leaders*
1	Teaching methods	Communicative approach
2	Communicative approach	Teaching methods
3	Assessment	Literacy teaching
4	Curriculum, Literacy teaching, Motivation	Motivation
5	Management	Curriculum, Management
6	Make and use materials	Make and use materials
7		Assessment

Note: 1 = Most important

leaders and half (8) the teachers felt that techniques in teaching literacy and encouraging student motivation should also be included. Teachers seemed more interested in learning about assessment than community leaders felt was necessary. Classroom management, curriculum design and using materials were supported by approximately half the teachers and community leaders. In a response to an earlier question, a third (6) of the students had felt the teaching curriculum needed revision.

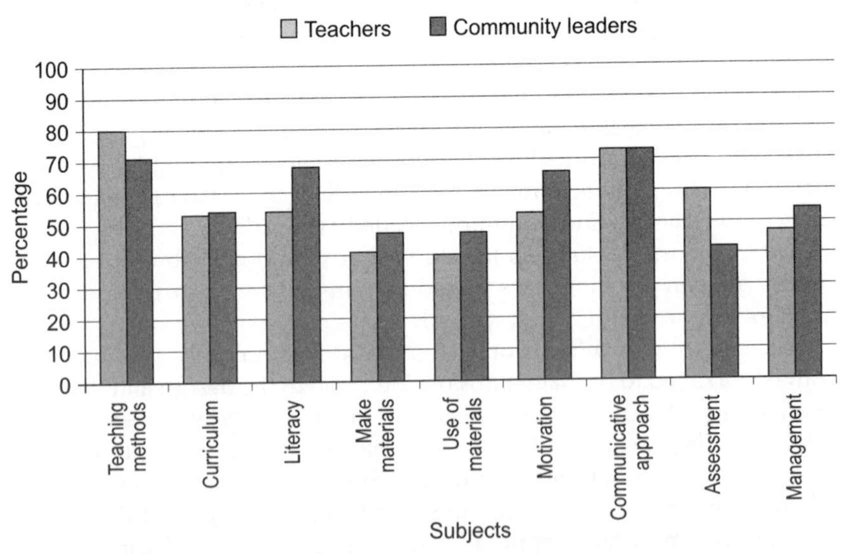

Figure 9.5 Possible subjects of study in community language teaching

The results show the difficulty in designing a programme for community language teachers because of their varying and sometimes contradictory needs. The following points can be established by the course leader at the start of the programme: the ages of the students, their time of immigration, the generation they tend to belong to, their length of residence, their reasons for learning the language, whether they want to learn both language and culture, the skills they wish to learn (passive or active), and practical demands and consideration (such as the availability of human and material resources). For this reason it is important that trainees should be autonomous learners so that they are able to apply the methodologies and content to their own contexts (see Shameem, 2000 and Shameem *et al.*, 2002 for possible needs-analysis questionnaires used in minority language contexts).

Conclusion

This chapter began by surveying the need for urgent action to maintain and develop community languages and avoid an irreversible shift towards exclusive use of the dominant language by second- and third-generation immigrants. Given the lack of official provision for, and even interest in, this matter, whether in New Zealand or elsewhere, the impetus must come from the language communities themselves and their representatives in educational organisations. The case study of survey research discussed above has illustrated some of the issues that arise when seeking to identify community language teaching needs and ways of meeting them. Above all, the study has pointed to the need to involve as many of the members of the community as possible – leaders, teachers, parents and students – and to have on-going consultations with communities. The present study has indicated some of the difficulties involved in the identification of potential respondents and the limitations of the chosen means of data collection. It has also pointed to the diversity of needs that emerge from solicited views. These difficulties and diversities reflect the confusion that emerges from the lack of a coherent national languages policy.

The data in this study indicate strong teacher and community support for the development of a language teacher education programme. However, the specifics of content (methodologies and theories, as well as practical emphases) await further development work by teaching teams within the institution that will deliver the programme. The development of the programme will also require another round of community consultation, in which interested community members are shown possible pedagogical approaches, and their rationales. Community members and teaching staff can then make informed decisions about the details of course content.

Despite the evident need for further development, enough useful information was provided by this study to form the basis of a programme specifically aimed at community language teachers. For example, the best times for delivery of the programme would be in the evenings or at weekends, and the method of delivery would be a practical one, through interactive workshops and seminars. It is important that programme participants also observe the delivery of a number of community language classes so that self-reflection, observation and peer review contribute positively to professional development.

While it is envisaged that trainee teachers will study towards a certificate, it is also possible that these courses will be cross-creditable towards a higher qualification. Although still in its draft stages, following the path where communities have their own input in the development of courses that comprise the certificate programme is a challenging but worthwhile task. Such a process can have only positive ramifications for community language teaching and the maintenance of community languages beyond the third generation in New Zealand.

References

Abbott, M. (1989) *Refugee Resettlement and Well-being.* (Based on the National Conference on Refugee Mental Health in NZ, Wellington, 12–15 May, 1988.) Wellington: Mental Health Foundation.

Bell, A., Starks, D. and Davis, K. (2000) Languages of the Manukau region: A pilot study of use, maintenance and educational dimensions of languages in South Auckland. A report to the Woolf Fisher Research Centre, University of Auckland.

Benton, R.A. (1996) The Māori language in New Zealand education and society. In F. Mugler and J. Lynch (eds) *Pacific Languages in Education* (pp. 209–227). Suva: Institute of Pacific Studies, University of the South Pacific.

Boyce, M. (1992) Māori language in Porirua: A study of reported proficiency, patterns of use, and attitudes. MA thesis, Victoria University of Wellington.

Chrisp, S. (1997) Home and community language re-vitalisation. *New Zealand Studies in Applied Linguistics* 3, 1–20.

Clyne, M. (1991) *Community Languages: The Australian Experience.* Cambridge University Press.

Corson, D. (1999) *Language Policy in Schools.* Mahwah, NJ: Lawrence Erlbaum Associates.

Davis, K. (1998) Cook Islands Māori language in Auckland and the Cook Islands: A study of reported proficiency, patterns of use and attitudes. MA thesis, University of Auckland.

Hamel, R.E. (1997) Language conflict and language shift: A sociolinguistic framework for linguistic human rights. *International Journal of the Sociology of Language* 127, 105–134.

Hoffman, A. (1995) Reflections on a national languages policy. *New Zealand Language Teacher* (Journal of the Association of Language Teachers) 21, 45–50.
Hoffman, A. (2001) A rationale for a languages policy for New Zealand. Online document: http://www.vuw.ac.nz/lals/lang_policy_nz.
Holmes, J. (1996) Community language research in New Zealand: Reflections on methodology. *New Zealand Studies in Applied Linguistics* 2, 1–32.
Holmes, J. and Harlow, R. (eds) (1991) *Threads in the New Zealand Tapestry of Language*. Auckland: New Zealand Linguistic Society.
Holt, R.F. (1999) *The Geographical Distribution of Language Use in the Auckland Region*. Auckland: School of Languages, Auckland University of Technology.
Kasanji, L. (1994) Community language schools and their future. Paper delivered at the Fourth Community Languages and ESOL Conference, Christchurch.
Kaplan, R.B. (1993) New Zealand national languages policy: Making the patient more comfortable. *Working Papers in Language Education* 1, 3–14.
Kidder, L.H. and Judd, C.M. (1986) *Research Methods in Social Relations*. New York: Holt, Rinehart and Winston.
Meanger, S. (1989) Adolescent Gujarati Indians in NZ: Their socialisation and education. MA thesis, Victoria University of Wellington.
Milroy, L. and Milroy, J. (1992) Social network and social class: Toward an integrated sociolinguistic model. *Language in Society* 21 (1), 1–26.
Neazor, C. (1991) Language maintenance and shift in the Wellington Polish community. *Wellington Working Papers in Linguistics* 3, 36–55.
Oppenheim, A.N. (1992) *Questionnaire Design, Interviewing and Attitude Measurement*. London: Heinemann.
Roberts, M.L. (1990) Language maintenance and shift and issues of language maintenance education in a section of the Chinese community in Wellington, New Zealand. MA thesis, Victoria University of Wellington.
Roberts, M.L. (1999) Immigrant language maintenance and shift in the Gujarati, Dutch and Samoan communities of Wellington. PhD thesis, Victoria University of Wellington.
Shackleford, N. (1997) The case of the disappearing languages policy. *The TESOLANZ Journal* 5, 1–14.
Shameem, N. (1995) Hamai log ke boli. Language shift in an immigrant community: The Wellington Indo-Fijians. PhD thesis, Victoria University of Wellington.
Shameem, N. (1997) ESOL and first language maintenance: Language loss or language gain? A case study. *The TESOLANZ Journal* 5, 15–25.
Shameem, N. (2000) Factors affecting language gain and loss in young immigrants and the case of the Wellington Indo-Fijians. *Prospect* 15 (2), 48–64.
Shameem, N. (2001) Many languages, diverse peoples, one nation, Aotearoa. A report on education needs of community language teachers in Auckland, Aotearoa/New Zealand. Auckland: School of English and Applied Linguistics, UNITEC.
Shameem, N. (2002) Autonomy and community language teaching. In M.Hobbs (ed.) *Autonomous Learning: Here and There, Here and Now*. Proceedings from the UNITEC Autonomous Learning Symposium, 2–3 May, UNITEC Institute of Technology.

Shameem, N., McDermott, K., Martin-Blaker J. and Carryer, J. (2002) Through language to literacy. A report on the literacy gains of low-level and pre-literate Adult ESOL learners in literacy classes. A collaborative project by National Association of Home Tutors, UNITEC Institute of Technology, Auckland University of Technology submitted to the Ministry of Education, Wellington.

Smith, H.A. (1994) English language acquisition in the Lao refugee community of Wellington, New Zealand. MA thesis, Victoria University of Wellington.

Starks, D. (1997) Community languages and research methodology in New Zealand: The issue of social networks. *New Zealand Studies in Applied Linguistics* 3, 46–61.

Starks, D. and Youn, S.H. (1998) Language maintenance in the Auckland Korean community. *Many Voices* 12, 8–11.

Waite J. (1992) *Aoteareo: Speaking for Ourselves. Part A: The Overview* and *Part B: The Issues.* Wellington: Ministry of Education.

Walker, U. (1996) Social networks as code determinants in individual bilingualism: A case study of four German-background immigrant children. *New Zealand Studies in Applied Linguistics* 2, 33–48.

White, C., Watts, N. and Trlin, A. (2001) Immigrant and refugee experience of ESOL provision in New Zealand: Realities and responsibilities. *Occasional Publication No. 5.* Palmerston North: Massey University New Settlers Programme.

Zheng, Bihui (1998) Language shift in a group of young Chinese immigrants in Auckland New Zealand. MA thesis, University of Auckland.

Chapter 10

Students as Fact Gatherers in Language-in-Education Planning

DONNA STARKS AND GARY BARKHUIZEN

Introduction

Takala and Sajavaara (2000) point out that language planning can take many forms and can take place in a variety of settings. It can also have a variety of goals: political, economic, educational, or sociocultural. In South Africa, for example, the language-related clauses in the constitution of the country (Republic of South Africa, 1996) not only list the official languages of the country, they also call for the promotion of multilingualism and the development of African languages in order to redress undemocratic language practices characteristic of the previous ruling government. These clauses, together with their associated political ideologies and aims, are translated into statements in a national language policy. This policy, in turn, determines the nature of both regional language policies (in the various provinces, each with their own combination of languages) and policies for domains such as education. Although not always efficiently implemented or accurately interpreted (Barkhuizen & Gough, 1996), the policies provide a useful set of guidelines for the preparation, implementation and evaluation of language-planning activities. A similar planning structure exists in Australia where the country's first national language policy in 1987 has been used 'as a model by most states for complementary policies' (Lo Bianco, 1997: 111).

New Zealand does not have a *national* languages policy. The reasons for this, both historical and current, have been pointed out by a number of commentators and researchers, including Benton (1994; 1996), Kaplan (1994) and Peddie (1997, and this volume). They include lack of government support (in terms of both financial and human resources), changing governments, uncoordinated language planning initiatives, apathy, and priority given to more pressing socio-economic concerns. This means that the various sectors requiring language policies of their own (e.g. tourism, the media and education) have no official guidance in the form of national policy statements to steer their own language-planning activities.

This situation has not prevented language-planning activities from taking place in New Zealand. A number of very significant initiatives over the past decade or so have contributed to our thinking about languages in the country. Although this thinking has not always been translated into action, New Zealand society has become more aware of its increasingly multilingual nature, of the shifts in language use of various sections of the population, and of the necessity for appropriate language planning in order to accommodate these changes. One such initiative was the Māori Language Act of 1987, which recognised Māori as an official language and established the Māori Language Commission, the core focus of its work being the maintenance of *te reo Māori* (the Māori language). The Commission also produced its own blueprint for a languages policy (Māori Language Commission, 1994), which included commentary and recommendations concerning the role and status of community languages, foreign languages and, of course, English and Māori (see Benton, 1996, for a summary of the work of the Māori Language Commission).

A second major initiative was the Ministry of Education's discussion document on a possible national languages policy for New Zealand. The report, *Aoteareo: Speaking for Ourselves* (Waite, 1992), identified six priority areas: revitalisation of the Māori language, second-chance adult literacy, children's English as a second language (ESL) and first-language maintenance, adult ESL, national capabilities in international languages, and provision of services in languages other than English and Māori. The report received mixed reviews, and Peddie (1997; and this volume), who provides a useful background to the report, remarks that it is unclear what planning moves relating to the report have been made since its release.

Further Ministry of Education guidance for language planning and policy comes in the form of curriculum documents such as *The New Zealand Curriculum Framework* (Ministry of Education, 1993) which, in showing 'an openness to linguistic diversity' (Benton, 1996: 75), makes statements about, *inter alia*, choice of medium of instruction, second-language learning, and gender and cultural inclusiveness in language and resources. The framework, which allows for a good deal of flexibility in its interpretation, openly promotes its adaptation to suit the various local conditions and the needs of schools. This is precisely what has happened. McCaffery and Tuafuti (1998), for example, provide an overview of bilingual programmes that have been implemented in schools. Bell *et al.* (2000) report on a study that revealed numerous language-maintenance activities for Māori and Pasifika languages in the Manukau region, especially at the Early

Childhood Development levels. Language planning, therefore, does take place in New Zealand, and language policies do exist. The point is, though, that the planning is not always systematic and the policies are not always explicit.

In this chapter we consider the possibility and the potential of proactive language-in-education planning in schools and classrooms. An essential aspect of language planning is the data-gathering process, a part of which is to understand the language situation that prevails in schools, including the needs of the students, the languages they speak, the language awareness of all school members, and their attitudes towards these languages and towards their use in various domains (Corson, 1999). This chapter reports on a research project that attempted to gather some of these facts from intermediate (i.e. upper primary) and secondary school students in Auckland. The participants are not only members of particular school communities, they are obviously also members of the wider Auckland community: they have lives outside of school, within their families, circles of friends, and church and recreational groups. They are observers, therefore, of language practices in a number of different contexts. The study contributes to language-in-education planning by gathering data that should be useful to those making decisions for effective language provision in schools. Since the data has been collected from a number of schools within one region, the implications of the study will be most relevant to those involved in language planning within and across schools in this region. We argue that researchers could play a very useful role in data-gathering for language planning by working closely with schools and the Ministry of Education, possibly in a linking, mediating role. And we stress the importance of including students in the fact-gathering process.

Figure 10.1 represents a simple model of language-in-education planning for schools that we found useful for framing our discussion of the study and its implications. It starts off with the identification of a language problem. Information is then gathered to help schools understand the problem more clearly and to enable them to make decisions about how to address the problem. These decisions are written up in the form of policy statements in a language-policy document. Next, the policy statements are put into action. The model could be implemented within any one school or across schools. The latter method is appropriate where there are a number of schools within the same region that experience similar sociolinguistic conditions. Participants in the various schools would need to collaborate to coordinate their planning activities at each stage. However, although schools may be similar in some respects, they also have unique characteristics. Policy implementation would, therefore, be adapted to suit the local

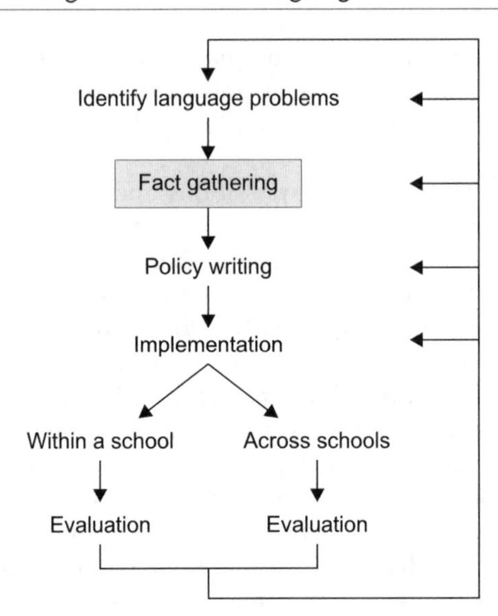

Figure 10.1 Basic model of language planning

conditions of each school. It would be necessary also to 'fit the context' at the other stages of planning, for example, when collecting data. During the implementation phase the results of the action are carefully monitored and evaluated. In a cyclical manner, the evaluation may identify further problems, or require:

(1) further information to be collected;

(2) refining of the policy document; and/or

(3) changing strategies for implementation.

Although students could actively participate in a number of stages in this model (e.g. feedback during evaluation of a policy), their particular role in data-gathering interests us here.

Language-in-Education Planning in Schools and Classrooms

Language-in-education planning is part of the implementation stage of a wider policymaking process, including language-planning initiatives of more powerful groups, such as regional or national governments. Kaplan and Baldauf (1997: 113) warn, however, that 'it is unwise (though it is frequently the case) to assign the entire implementation activity to the schools'. Language-in-education planning operates within a different set of constraints, and has a different set of objectives. Decisions concerning these objectives are seldom written in policy documents. Corson (1999: 1) defines this format of policy statement as a 'document complied by the staff of a school, often assisted by other members of the school community, to which the staff members give their consent and commitment'. Implicit policies for language and learning, on the other hand, already exist in schools, 'in the tacit practices of its teachers and administrators, and it can be inferred from their interactions with students' (Corson, 1999: 3). Members of the school community often participate in these practices on a subconscious level, so their monitoring, evaluation and revision are either neglected or somewhat haphazard.

Language planning, therefore, takes place at various levels, from government departments to individual teachers. The former could be considered macro language planning. Typically, this would include decisions about which languages should be promoted and developed in the educational system (Eastman, 1990). But, as Corson (1999) points out, macro planning could mean that higher bureaucratic authorities devolve language planning activities to lower level structures such as the educational institutions themselves. Although this creates a number of problems for those working in schools (such as whether or not they have the appropriate expertise, motivation and resources to institute language planning as part of their workloads), it allows them the opportunity to make a contribution to solving language problems in their schools. Further, by reporting on their own successes and failures, they are able to feed back information to those making language planning decisions at higher levels outside the school. School-based language planning activities, relative to the broader picture, are at the micro level. Schools could, for example, make decisions about the following (see Corson, 1999; Kaplan & Baldauf, 1997; Paulston & McLaughlin, 1994):

- the language(s) to be taught;
- the medium(s) of instruction;
- the need for a bilingual programme;
- the writing of a language policy document;
- financial, human and physical resources required for any changes or innovations.

Even more micro planning could be any one teacher's policymaking decisions within his or her classroom. For example, in the New Zealand context: Do teachers have an English-only policy in their classrooms? Are international students in ESOL classes given the opportunity to talk about and express their own ethnolinguistic backgrounds?

Figure 10.2 illustrates the relationship between macro and micro language-in-education planning. The diagonal line shows a continuum between the two. The macro is at the higher end of the continuum, and represents larger, bureaucratic structures (such as language boards and government ministries of education) whereas the micro or lower end of the continuum represents schools, departments and classrooms within schools, and individual teachers and students making decisions about practice in their own classrooms. The continuum also represents differing positions of power with regard to making significant policy decisions. Individual school policies, for instance, are by necessity local policies, whereas government-level policies are designed to be implemented in a number of schools within any one jurisdiction.

Figure 10.2 also illustrates opposing forces that determine the language planning process. At both macro and micro levels, language planning can take place from the top down or from the bottom up. Top-down language planning would entail decisions being made by those with more power: governments over the education sector, ministries of education over schools, schools over teachers, and teachers over students. In other words, policies designed by those in power are imposed on those with less power. On the other hand, bottom-up language planning starts 'on the ground': language problems *within* communities are identified, data are collected – Corson (1999) calls this 'fact gathering' – to assess the extent of the problems, the level of language awareness of members of the community,

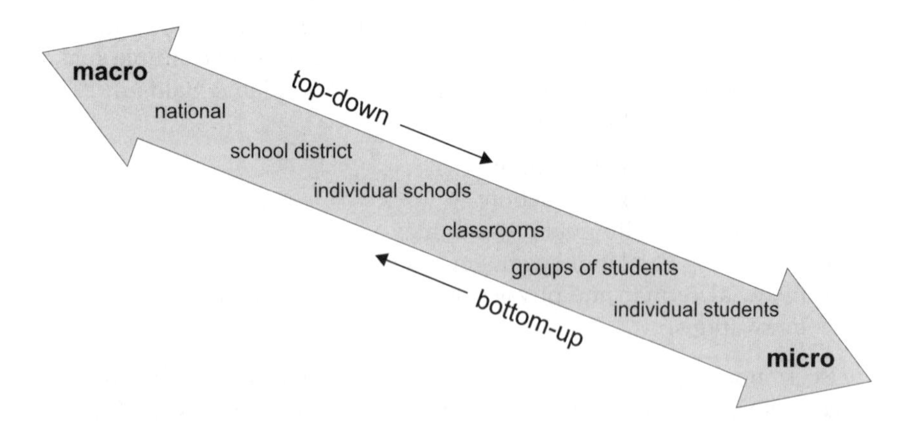

Figure 10.2 A framework for language-in-education planning

their language attitudes, and their language needs. The essence of bottom-up language planning is the identification and understanding of language problems through research, consultation and observation; that is, 'both empirical and conceptual analyses' (Takala & Sajavaara, 2000: 133).

The present research project, then, forms one component of bottom-up language planning: its main purpose is to gather data for use in systematic language-in-education planning in classrooms and schools. In his discussion of school language policies, Corson (1999) distinguishes between large-scale and small-scale data gathering. Large-scale data gathering involves investigating which languages are used by all those in the school, the attitudes of the community and staff towards those languages and their attitudes towards changing the situation. Small-scale data gathering involves more specific focus on teacher attitudes to languages and language varieties within the school and classroom, teachers' views about staff development, and their current practice relating to language use in the classroom. It also involves investigating students' language behaviour, awareness and attitudes. Corson (1999: 45) warns, however, that this is not always easy since 'schools are in competition with all the other demands made on students' time. For many students the serious work of schools lies at the distant margins of their lives'. Involving students, in other words, either as the participants in their teachers' research or as researchers of their own language practices, is difficult and time-consuming, and this is perhaps the reason that students are often left out of fact-gathering activities. Our study is large-scale in that the sample is relatively large and is spread across a number of schools in one region – the city of Auckland. It is located therefore about mid-way on the macro–micro continuum. It is bottom-up in that it focuses on the language awareness and language attitudes of school students.

School Students' Beliefs and Attitudes

Students in schools are an integral part of the learning/teaching process: they are the ones who sit in classes day after day, typically on the receiving end of decisions made about what is to be taught, how it is to be taught and why it should be taught in the first place. Although they have an insider's view of what is going on, their perceptions of what they observe and experience are seldom taken into account. Studies on student perceptions (Barkhuizen, 1998), their beliefs (Cotterall, 1999), their learning strategies (Chamot, 2001) and their attitudes (Gardner & MacIntyre, 1993) make it clear that language learners do have valid beliefs about their experiences in classrooms and schools, and that, given the opportunity, they will articulate them. Kumaravadivelu (1991: 107) says that 'the more we know about the learner's personal approaches and personal concepts, the better and more productive our intervention will be'. By this he means that, if teachers, language planners and administrators are aware of where students are coming from (how they approach language learning, their attitudes to the languages they learn, what they feel about their language learning experiences, and how they act upon these feelings), they will be better able to make decisions that facilitate desired learning outcomes. School students, however, do not live their lives only in schools. They live in the wider community too, and thus their lives intersect with language conditions that may or may not be typical of their school experiences.

In Figure 10.3 the micro–macro continuum illustrated in Figure 10.2 is shown from another dimension: the student is a member of the school community as well as the community outside school, and both communities are located within the broader sociopolitical context of New Zealand society.

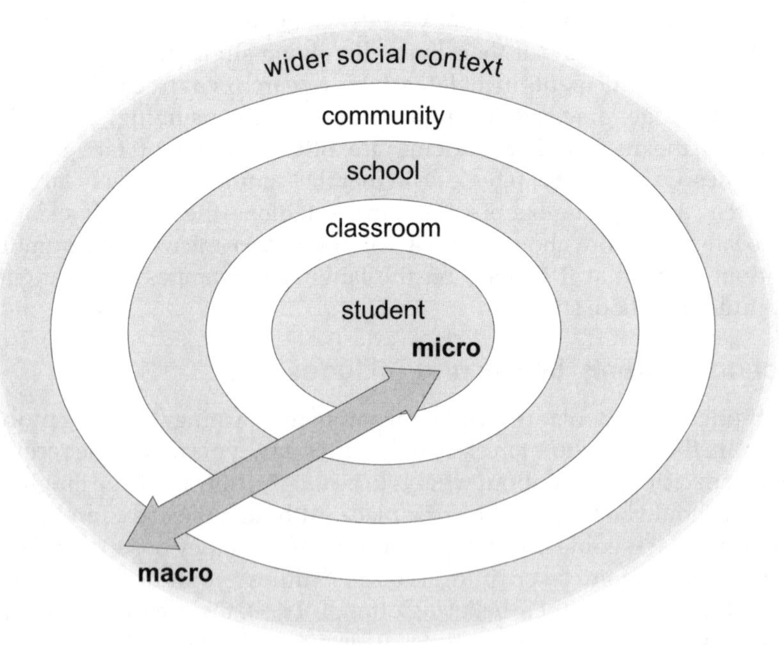

Figure 10.3 The student as a member of the school and the community

The Study

This study is an initial investigation into the suitability of intermediate and secondary students as fact data-gatherers on issues relating to language policy. It uses a short self-report questionnaire to focus on language awareness and language attitudes of students in and out of the classroom. This method was selected in order to canvas a relatively large number of students from a wide range of social, ethnic and regional backgrounds within the greater Auckland area. The questionnaire contained four sections consisting of closed (e.g. yes/no) and short-answer questions (e.g. which languages? father's occupation?). These types of questions were selected to simplify participation by younger adolescents, and to facilitate the administration of the questionnaire. This was particularly important as teachers were given the choice as to who should administer the questionnaire.

The first section of the questionnaire concentrates on language awareness, and includes questions concerning Māori, Pacific Island, and other languages. It considers the students' own basic awareness (e.g. knowledge of greetings, communities and dialects) as well as their awareness of others' language use (e.g. occasions and frequency of exposure to languages other than English). The latter was an attempt to evaluate the place of schools in students' overall language awareness. The section on language attitudes consists of a series of five yes/no questions on attitudes towards diverse linguistic issues: the use of English, bilingualism, comprehension skills in Māori, and community language use. It also includes one open question concerning personal language-learning preferences ('What languages would you like to be able to speak well?'). The third section introduces questions of language policy. It consists of six questions, five yes/no and one open-ended. The five yes/no questions consider Māori and Pacific Island language education, and ESL and community language use. The open-ended question focuses on languages for official purposes. The final section covers basic demographic information (sex, age, education, residence history, parents' education/occupation, ethnicity), students' social networks (their friends, frequency of visits to homes of different ethnic groups), language proficiency, and language use. The language proficiency question, identical to the language question in the 2001 national census (Statistics New Zealand, 2002) focuses on the languages in which one could have a conversation about a lot of everyday things. The question on language use, identical to the language question in the Australian national census, considers language use in the home. The Australian question proved to be less problematic for these adolescents.

The questionnaire was trialled with 13 students aged between 13–18 years. Students filled out the questionnaire, recorded the length of time it took them to complete it, and commented on any difficulties they encountered. All students who trialled preliminary versions of the questionnaire attended West Auckland schools.[1]

Between October 2000 and April 2001, 29 school principals were contacted in South Auckland, in Central/Eastern Auckland and on the North Shore and asked if they would allow their students to participate in a research project on language awareness. These schools were selected on the basis of region, decile ranking, school type (private, Catholic, public), and ethnic composition. Selection was based on Education Review Office (ERO) reports (Ministry of Education, 2001) and on information gathered from school principals with first-hand experience of the diverse nature of their local schools. The research aim was explained, and the principal was given a copy of the questionnaire. The principal (or his/her delegate) was asked one week later if the school would be willing to participate. Thirteen principals agreed, and signed the necessary consent forms. Schools reported back on the potential number of students who could complete the questionnaire, and copies were delivered to the schools.[2] Although the target was one or two classes per school, teachers were given the option as to how many and which classes they wished to survey. Most schools opted for all classes in a particular age group so as not to exclude any particular class. Teachers were given one month to complete the questionnaires, and a telephone number to call when the research was complete. Teachers in all but one of the schools selected to self-administer the questionnaires and to report back any difficulties with the research. The data from each participating school was coded and analysed using a Microsoft *Excel* package.

Participating schools received a summary of their school's responses and were offered a copy of the final report, once completed. On request, schools were given a copy of the *Excel* spreadsheet containing their own data. This feedback aimed to raise awareness of the language situation in individual schools, and to show the value of students as fact-gatherers on language policy issues.

The questionnaires were completed by 979 students from 13 schools. The research was conducted in six full primary schools (Years 1 to 8), two intermediate schools (Years 7 and 8), two mixed intermediate/secondary schools and two secondary schools. Twelve of the schools were public, one was Catholic. The Catholic school was a single-sex boys' school; all the other schools were co-educational. Four schools were located in South Auckland/Manukau, two were on the North Shore, and seven were in Central/Eastern Auckland. Decile rankings ranged from 1 to 9 (these

Table 10.1 Percentage of ethnic groups across schools

European	0–67%
Māori	5–45%
Pacific Languages	2–63%
Asian	0–30%
Other	0–17%

Source: Latest Education Review Office reports, as on 15 February, 2001 (Ministry of Education, 2001)

numbers broadly correlate with the socioeconomic status of the student population). The ethnic composition of the schools varied considerably, often in direct proportion with the school's decile ranking. For example, schools with low decile rankings had a higher proportion of Māori and Pacific Island students.

Table 10.1 shows the range of variability in the ethnic composition of the schools. The European student population across the schools ranged from 0– 67%. The Asian student population varied from 0–30%. One school roll did not have any New Zealand European students; four did not have any Asian students. These were all decile 1 schools. Māori and Pacific Island students also varied in their numbers, but all school rolls listed some Māori and Pacific Island students. Many of the schools had a residual 'Other' category in their ERO reports (see Table 10.1). In three schools, this was further specified as Middle Eastern, European and Filipino. In most instances, it was left undefined.

In Table 10.1 the students are classified into pan-ethnic categories. Pan-ethnic labels for New Zealand Europeans are listed in all ERO reports, and they are also common for Asian groups. Only four of the nine schools with Asian students provided details on their specific ethnic group, and these tend to be, but are not exclusive to, schools with higher percentages of Asian students. Ethnic group membership, if divided, tends to be general (e.g. Asian, Indian, Chinese) rather than specific (e.g. Taiwanese, Japanese), with one exception. Nine schools indicated the cultural background of their Pacific Island students (e.g. Samoan, Tongan). This reporting is not directly related to the overall percentage of Pacific Island students in the schools, as some schools with small percentages of students divide their roll on the basis of ethnic group membership. The number of Samoan, Tongan, Cook Islands and Niuean students correlate approximately with community

Table 10.2 Background of students in the language awareness survey

New Zealand European	320	32%
New Zealand-born Pacific Island	227	23%
New Zealand immigrant	182	18%
Māori	124	12%
New Zealand-Asian	28	3%
Other stated New Zealand ethnicities	43	4%
Did not answer/Did not know	74	7%

size. In 11 of the schools, Samoan students are the most represented, followed by either Tongan or Cook Islands students.

There was a high degree of consistency between the figures reported by the school, included in ERO reports, and those reported in the current research project. The ethnic composition of the student responses corresponds to the ethnic composition of the school as a whole, with one exception. In this case, the overall rank ordering of the Māori and *Pakeha* (New Zealanders of European descent) students in the school is reversed. Our research focused on specific classrooms rather than the school as a whole, and this may have been responsible for some of the discrepancy. Another possible reason is that the pan-ethnic categories in the present study differed from those in the ERO reports. Students in the present study were divided into New Zealand-born and New Zealand immigrants. This had an effect on our percentages of Pacific Island and Asian students because students were divided into two categories in the present study but presented as one category in the ERO reports. Other differences could have arisen because of the way in which the figures are calculated. In this survey, students could elect more than one ethnicity. These students were counted more than once for ethnic identification purposes. The degree of agreement, although unexpected, shows the participants in the study to be typical of their schools as reflected in their school rolls.

Table 10.2 presents an analysis of the ethnic background of the students who participated in this research project. The totals in Table 10.2 exceed the actual number of students because some students chose to self-identify with more than one ethnic group. However, the total number of responses (998) is only slightly greater than the total number of students surveyed. Most of the participants are Pakeha and New Zealand-born Pacific Island students. Another large group, perhaps peculiar to the Auckland area, are those who identify as New Zealand immigrants (18%). Māori are slightly less represented (12%). The gender balance of the students is slightly skewed: 43% of the respondents are female, 54% male.[3] This is due to the inclusion of one all-boys school. Students were aged between 11–19 years. However, the higher rate of participation amongst primary/intermediate schools meant that the majority of the students were aged between 11 and 12 years.

Preliminary comparisons of region, decile ranking and ethnic composition of the schools revealed few systematic differences on the basis of any of these factors. The major differences were between individual schools; suggesting that, for young adolescents, factors within schools may be more important than many other factors. The following section presents a summary of findings based on overall student responses. Where regional differences exist, they are noted.

Results

Three questions served to provide a benchmark for evaluating the importance of the school in the study of language attitudes:

- Are students aware of the languages spoken around them?
- Where do they hear languages spoken?
- How often do they hear them?

These are important issues as most language attitude studies, including those conducted by Te Puni Kokiri (the Ministry of Māori Affairs), focus on groups older than the students in the present study. Students under the age of 16 are seldom considered as participants because of concerns about their ability to reflect on their language use (Te Puni Kokiri, 1998). When younger students are included in studies, details about them are often sought from teachers or parents (Nakanishi, 2000; Roberts, 1999; Verivaki, 1991).

Most of the students who responded were aware of languages other than English being spoken in their presence; 875 (89.5%) claimed that they heard languages other than English being spoken in Auckland. Only 66 students (6.8 %) said they never heard languages other than English. The remainder (37 students, 3.7%) either did not know, or did not answer. Auckland is, for most of these students, a bilingual/multilingual community. Students reported hearing more than one language; averaging 2.7 languages per student.[4] Of particular interest is the naming of the languages. Students not only referred to multiple languages by name, but in many instances they were very specific (e.g. Mandarin, Cantonese, Niuean). Languages heard by more than 10 students are reported in Table 10.3.

The most common language cited in Table 10.3 is Chinese: more than

Table 10.3 Languages that students hear in Auckland

	N	%
Cantonese/Mandarin/Chinese	361	41.2
Samoan	359	41.0
Tongan	307	35.0
Māori	286	32.6
Cook Island Māori	163	18.6
Indian	135	15.4
Japanese	130	14.8
Korean	116	13.2
German	94	10.7
Niuean	76	8.6
French	63	7.2
Russian	35	4.0
Fijian	34	3.8
Spanish	34	3.8
Thai	16	1.8
Vietnamese	12	1.3

41% of the students cited Cantonese, Mandarin or Chinese as a language currently heard in their midst. This is likely to reflect the recent surge in Asian immigrants. According to the national census (Statistics New Zealand, 2002), Asians now represent the third largest ethnic group in New Zealand. A sudden increase in the population of a minority group often affects others' perception of the ethno-linguistic vitality of the minority group (Giles *et al.*, 1985). In other words, a rapid increase in a population could give the impression that a group is larger than it actually is (or, in the case of languages, that languages are spoken more often than they actually are). This could be part of the reason for the high number of respondents citing Chinese. The appearance of other Asian community languages (Korean, Thai, Vietnamese) and of the lesser-spoken languages of recent immigrant communities (e.g. Russian, Spanish, Indian) might also be due to this factor. These languages are spoken by relatively new communities and their presence impacts on these New Zealand students. The second and third most frequent responses are Samoan and Tongan, respectively. These exceed Māori in Table 10.3, even though the 2001 census reports more speakers of Māori than of Samoan or Tongan. The greater number of Pacific Island students in the study undoubtedly accounts for some of this discrepancy. The relative rankings of the Pacific languages by the students appear to be a close reflection of community language use. Samoan and Tongan are the healthiest of New Zealand's Pasifika languages (Bell *et. al.*, 2000; Holmes & 'Aipolo, 1991). Bell *et al.* report that, in Manukau City, 82.7% of Samoan and 80.3% of Tongan five year olds are proficient in their community language. This contrasts with Māori, where proficiency levels are as low as 27.9%. Low proficiency of Māori may mean that it is spoken less often in non-Māori contexts than either Samoan or Tongan, languages that continue to be spoken both in and outside the home. The National Māori Language Survey claims that only 8% of their Māori respondents 'profess to be highly fluent in the language' (Te Puni Kokiri, 1998: 108), and notes that the main use of Māori is on the *marae* (traditional Māori site). Stubbe and Holmes (2000: 250) also note that 'there are remarkably few contexts in which the Māori language can currently be heard'. Hence the more frequent mention of Samoan and Tongan may be a reflection of actual language use.

Similar reasoning undoubtedly accounts for the position of Cook Islands Māori in Table 10.3. The Cook Islands community is numerically larger in size than its Tongan counterpart in Manukau and throughout the country (Bell *et al.*, 2000), yet fewer students report hearing Cook Islands Māori. Taumoefolau *et al.* (2002) report that Cook Islanders have a lower proficiency in their community language(s) than do Samoans or Tongans. Other smaller Pacific languages, such as Niuean and Fijian, which are undergoing rapid language attrition, are also much further down the table. Student awareness of the Pacific languages appears to be a direct reflection of the relative state of those languages in their community.

There are also regional differences in the ranking of the Pacific Island languages that reflect actual regional differences in language use. Pacific Island languages are mentioned by students in South Auckland more frequently than by students in other parts of the city. A similar situation exists on the North Shore with respect to Korean: there are more Koreans on the North Shore, and the Korean language is more prominent in North Shore student responses.

Another category of languages is those that are taught in the curriculum: namely Japanese, German, and French. These may be more salient than many others owing to their privileged status in the schools. The selection of a language as part of the school curriculum may have a profound effect on

Table 10.4 Places where languages are heard

	N	%
At school	1126	44.8
At home	298	11.8
Shops	228	9.0
In the streets	161	6.4
In the playground	127	5.0
Everywhere	116	4.6
Church	111	4.4
When joking around	45	1.7
Marae	27	1.0
Special occasions	22	0.8
Relatives' homes	14	0.5

student awareness of these languages, and of student interest in the learning of these languages. When the responses of individual schools are examined, they correlate with the languages taught in schools on a range of questions dealing with language awareness and language attitudes.

To examine the effect of the school on language awareness, students were asked to indicate where they heard the languages spoken. If the languages are heard only in homes and other semi-private domains, then New Zealand may be considered a largely monolingual community. The answers to this open-ended question yielded interesting insights into young New Zealand society. Students gave an average of three locations where they heard languages other than English.

Table 10.4 lists the places where students heard each language spoken: 849 students responded to this question, providing 2510 responses with an average of 3 responses per student. The place of the school stands out in their responses. The most frequent place where languages are heard is the school, which represented 44.8% of the student responses. School was mentioned almost four times more frequently than the next most common place – the home. This is a surprising finding, and may be due to the research project having taken place in the school. This may have raised awareness of language use in this domain. As stated earlier, most studies of language use are located in the home. Another factor may be the participants themselves: because students filled in their own questionnaires, they may have placed more emphasis on their school life than parents or teachers would (see Eckert 1997 for the importance of peers on language use). Many parents believe that English should be the language of school activities, and their responses may be conditioned by this belief. In most studies, the school is considered a public domain, one where the community language is less likely to be spoken, and where the dominant language (English) is encouraged. The one exception to this is the Māori language survey (Te Puni Kokiri, 1998: 120) which mentions the school as a frequent domain of language use for younger Māori speakers.

While it is undoubtedly the case that English is the language of instruction (and possibly the classroom), English is not *the* language of the school. School is a social milieu in which students interact, establish friendships, learn to negotiate for goods and services, and develop as individuals in whatever languages they choose to do so. It is also a place where students spend a considerable percentage of their time. In addition to classes, breaks and lunch activities, many students spend time in after-school activities. In these instances, the languages around them often include languages other than English. The relatively frequent reference to the playground as a multilinguistic location (see Table 10.4) may be a reflection of this. Because our questions could not be followed up, it is possible that many students who mentioned 'playground' were in fact referring to time spent in the school playground. Shops and streets rank third and fourth on the list of 'places where languages are heard' – locations that highlight the increasingly multilingual status of the community. This is supported by the sixth most common response: 'everywhere'. Also noteworthy, are the relatively low mention of church (perhaps because fewer younger people attend church), relatives' homes, and the marae. With the exception of the home, private and semi-private domains (where community languages are thought to be spoken) are the places reported least in this research. Community languages are reported as heard in public locations, where English is traditionally considered the dominant language. Perhaps this is an indication of New Zealand's changing sociolinguistic landscape.

As an aside, the eighth most frequent response is 'when joking around'. This context is not normally considered as a typical location. The relatively large number of responses may shed some light on the use of languages other than English in the lives of New Zealand's young people. It is quite common for community languages to take on an informal role. Kuiper (forthcoming) notes that Dutch is used in casual asides in meetings of the Dutch society, but it is not used as the language of business. Community languages are often used as a sign of ethnic identity and in-group solidarity. 'Aipolo and Holmes (1991: 11), for example, found that Tongans 'in their

Table 10.5 How often do students hear languages other than English?

All the time	25%
Most of the time	21%
Some of the time	37%
Only occasionally	17%

teens and early twenties' switch freely between Tongan and English as a signal of in-group identity. Students' responses may signal a general pattern of community language use in informal in-group interactions.

In order to evaluate the responses, we need to know the overall frequency with which languages are heard. We asked the students to indicate the frequency with which they heard languages other than English on a scale from 1 (all the time) to 4 (only occasionally) for each language they noted as being heard in their midst. A total of 2215 responses were provided by 788 students.[5]

Table 10.5 shows that 25% of the students indicate that languages other than English are heard all of the time, while only 17% indicate that the languages are heard only occasionally. This is one of the few questions with a strong regional bias. Students in Manukau were more likely to report that they heard languages all the time (33% of all responses), and this is likely to be a reflection of the greater multilingual status of this community. There are more languages spoken in South Auckland than in any other part of the country (see Bell *et al.*, 2000).

In sum, students are aware of the languages spoken around them, and they are able to articulate this awareness. Their views are similar to information presented in the census on language use. Students are in the heart of a changing society; they are not segregated into traditional groups aligned on the basis of family, neighbourhood or friendship in the same way that older members of the community may be. Perhaps they are the most aware members of our changing society, and they form an integral part of it. By 2051, it is expected that a third of all children will be Pakeha, one third Māori, and Pacific and Asian children will make up the rest (Ministry of Education, 2002). It is vitally important that we tap into students' language awareness and language attitudes. One way to do this is to use students as data-gatherers.

So what are student views and expectations concerning languages? Our research asked students the following yes/no questions on English language use, bilingualism, Māori and community language use. The response rate to these questions was high, indicating the suitability of

Table 10.6 Student attitudes towards language use

All should be able to speak English	79.4%
All should understand some Māori	61.0%
Children of immigrants should be expected to speak their community language	72.6%
Grandchildren of immigrants should be expected to speak their community language	46.6%
All should be able to speak more than one language well	50.3%

yes/no questions (rather than open-ended questions) in school contexts. The non-response rate varied from 2 to 4%. The five questions were:

- Do you think all New Zealanders should be able to speak English?
- Do you think all New Zealanders should be able to understand some Māori?
- Should the children of non-English speaking immigrants be expected to speak the language of their parents well?
- Should the grandchildren of non-English speaking immigrants be expected to speak the language of their grandparents well?
- Do you think all New Zealanders should be able to speak more than one language well?

Our first question addressed the issue of whether students feel all New Zealanders should have English skills. Their views reflected not only classroom performance, but also English language for social interaction. This type of information needs to be collected from students, as teachers are often not aware of student interactions outside the classroom.[6] Table 10.6 shows that 79.4% of the students believe that 'all New Zealanders should be able to speak English'. A further study would be needed to understand why 19.6% did not view English as a necessity for life in New Zealand.

The second question focuses on New Zealand's indigenous language. Here, our question concerned language understanding rather than language proficiency. Recent studies by Te Puni Kokiri (2001: 7) suggest there are still many people who believe that Māori language and culture should be for Māori only. Given the varying opinions on speaking the Māori language, it was thought that an understanding of Māori may be a more useful indicator of language attitudes. The results here were less decisive. Although a majority still responded positively, the percentage for positive responses for understanding some Māori (61.0%) is lower than the positive responses for speaking English (79.4%). This may well be a reflection of the use of the language, perhaps based on the fact that Māori is not as commonly heard in these communities as many of the Asian and Pacific languages (see Table 10.3).

Our third and fourth questions consider the importance of maintaining community languages. The results again show that the students are positive towards the maintenance of community languages by community groups, but see the need for language maintenance as short-term rather than long-term. While 72.6% believe that children of non-English speaking immigrants should be expected to speak the language of their parents well, only 46.6% believe that they should be able to speak the languages of their grandparents well. Whether this is because they believe languages cannot be maintained over time or because they believe that it is a difficult and unnecessary expectation that grandchildren should learn the language of their grandparents is a topic beyond this present study. What is clear, however, is that students generally favour the preservation of community languages.

The final question focuses on attitudes towards bilingualism. It may be acceptable for others to speak languages other than English, but do today's students believe that all New Zealanders should be bilingual? The results were ambiguous. Just over half (50.3%) indicated that they believed all New Zealanders should be bilingual, while others responded (46.7%) that they did not believe bilingualism was necessary.[7] This is not surprising, as the 2001 national census revealed that 77% of the New Zealand population report themselves as monolingual English speakers (Statistics New Zealand, 2002). It is likely that the responses to the question on bilingualism as a desired outcome of all New Zealanders reflected students' views about bilingualism for others, perhaps their parents. When asked elsewhere what languages they would like to speak well, 825 students listed languages other than English. While this study does not provide all the answers, it shows that students see themselves as part of a multilingual New Zealand. We also believe that it adds to the case for students as data-gatherers in the development of a successful bottom-up language policy for future generations in New Zealand – and elsewhere.

Conclusion

This study has shown clearly that school students are aware of the languages that they hear around them in their school lives and within the broader community; 89.5% of the respondents, for instance, indicated that they hear languages other than English spoken in Auckland. This surely raises questions in their minds about the place of these languages in New Zealand society: What role should these languages play? How important are they in relation to English? Who should learn these other languages, and why? Do the speakers of these languages also speak English, and if not, do they need to learn English? Is Māori a growing language? Questions of this nature need to be put to young people who are members of both the Auckland community and the school system in the city. As such, these young people form a vital link between the multilingual world in which languages intersect (and in which students live their non-school lives) and the world of school. It has often been pointed out that schools, and the education system more generally, are the nurseries for language change (Kennedy, 1989; Wiley, 1996). They either nurture the seeds planted by those at macro levels of language planning (i.e. localise and then implement the policies) or they plant the seeds themselves. The latter is referred to as *acquisition planning* by Cooper (1989), and implies a process independent of wider language-planning activities.

In either case, students are part of a multilingual community, and as such they deserve to be participants in the language-planning process. Their input provides valuable data for those responsible for devising language policies for education. The findings generated by this study are evidence of that. The difficult question is: how are the data to be translated into policy? In order to do this appropriately and effectively, planners need to ensure that the data collected matches the language problem. We need to ask how the problems are identified, how they are articulated, and how they are examined. Teachers and students in schools recognise language-related problems all the time. It may be easy to notice the symptoms, but it is often much more difficult to identify the causes. Teachers and students live busy lives in schools, and so language issues are not always on top of their work agendas. Teachers do not have time to dwell constantly on the possible causes of the language problems that they observe in their classrooms. Identifying the symptoms and causes of problems, and then clearly stating what they are, are activities that happen haphazardly, intermittently or not at all. Gathering language data in order to understand problems more thoroughly so that policy statements could be made about them, requires even more consideration.

We suggest, therefore, that the role of problem identifier, and especially of data gatherer, should be shared with *researchers*. Researchers in universities or other research institutions could collaborate with schools and ministries of education to coordinate research projects useful to all parties. To a certain extent, this is already happening in New Zealand. The Ministry of Education is currently funding research projects on, amongst others, literacy provision, the teaching of foreign languages, and the education of international students (Ministry of Education, 2003). Researchers *are* involved in these projects: the Ministry issues requests for proposals, then researchers submit their proposals to the Ministry, conduct the research and report their findings to the Ministry. Schools seem to have a less influential role in proceedings. These projects are fairly large scale, with little immediate relevance to specific language problems in specific schools. In addition, they are aimed at solving particular problems (e.g. literacy provision), and are not specifically focused on language-in-education planning and policy.

In their proposed mediating role, researchers would work both with the Ministry and with schools. When problems are identified by schools (with the support of researchers), the Ministry could post these on its web page or publicise them through some other means such as a newsletter. These topics for research could then be taken up by researchers, possibly with funding from the Ministry. If a concern has been raised by a specific school, contact details of the school could be posted so that researchers could directly contact the school. If different schools identify similar concerns, researchers might be able to work across schools. The Ministry of Education's web page might also be expanded to include details of contracted researchers and participating schools, together with details of research projects in progress. In this way, improved reciprocal communication between researchers, the Ministry and schools could be achieved.

The aim of all this activity, of course, is to improve language-in-education planning and policy writing. Conducting independent research projects on a range of different, unrelated language issues is very much like collecting butterflies: it accumulates lots of interesting bits of information. What is needed for language policy, however, is the coordination of this information. This is where the problem and the challenge lies in New Zealand. Who should be responsible for this coordination? Where should the activity be located? How should it be funded, and by whom? One option is that it be confined to the local, micro level within a particular school or collaboratively between schools. Another option is that the Ministry of Education should be integrally involved in these activities. If this were the case, our proposal regarding a Ministry-researcher-schools partnership would be a reasonable one.

Starting with school-generated language concerns and establishing collaborative working relationships between students, teachers and independent researchers in order to investigate these concerns is true bottom-up language planning at work. Corson's (1999) book on policy in schools describes and endorses a critical approach to language planning whereby planners approach their work with a critical eye, always on the look-out for practices and policies that repress, dominate and disempower diverse groups whose practices differ from the norms that they (the planners) establish. In his book, Corson provides a thorough overview of what might comprise a language policy for schools. A summary of Corson's table is presented in Table 10.7.

Corson recommends that schools 'focus on areas that are most relevant to the needs of students and to the language problems that most affect the school and its social context' (1999: 216). Our study has provided information that could feed into the decision-making process at various points within Corson's policy framework, particularly those concerned with language awareness and attitudes. Our data, of course, were collected from school students. To obtain a fuller, broader picture, data should also be collected from teachers, parents and other community members.

Notes

1. The study was granted Ethics Approval by the University of Auckland Research Committee (UARC Ref#2000/014).
2. Schools that elected not to participate either did not specify their reasons or refused because of concerns about it taking up class time.
3. 3% of the students failed to indicate their gender.
4. This number was calculated by dividing the total number of students who provided responses (881) by the total number of language responses given (2436 responses). In 98 instances, students did not know, or did not list any languages for this question.
5. 185 did not answer, 6 responded that they didn't know. These student responses were not included in the percentage figures.
6. The question was worded to refer to all New Zealanders, not just students, although in hindsight, the latter may have been a more telling question.
7. 3% did not respond to this question.

Table 10.7 What a school language policy might contain

ORGANIZATION AND MANAGEMENT OF THE SCHOOL:

Staffing matters

Staff development
Language Policy Coordinator

Policymaking, records, and evaluation

School-based research
Policy implementation and evaluation

The community

The role of parents
School attitudes towards local cultures
Participation of diverse cultures in school governance

Minority-language students

Teacher and school attitudes towards minority languages
Bilingualism and first-language maintenance

Bilingual and ESL teaching

School planning to support bilingual education
Resources and materials for ESL teaching
Teacher development for ESL education
Supporting minority first-language use and development

TEACHER APPROACHES TO LANGUAGE USE:

Critical awareness

Critical awareness
Teacher attitudes towards language and languages

THE CURRICULUM:

Pedagogy

Marking policy
Reading, writing and oral language
Approaches to teaching ESL

Curriculum Content

Language awareness
Critical language awareness

Source: Adapted from Corson, 1999.

References

'Aipolo, 'A. and Holmes, J. (1991) The Wellington Tongan community: Prospects for language maintenance. *Wellington Working Papers in Linguistics* 1, 1–16.

Barkhuizen, G. (1998) Discovering learners' perceptions of ESL classroom teaching/learning activities in a South African context. *TESOL Quarterly* 32, 85–108.

Barkhuizen, G. and Gough, D. (1996) Language curriculum development in South Africa: What place for English? *TESOL Quarterly* 30 (3), 453–471.

Bell, A., Davis, K. and Starks, D. (2000) Language of the Manukau Region: A pilot study of use, maintenance and educational dimensions of languages in South Auckland. Report to Woolf Fisher Research Centre. University of Auckland.

Benton, R. (1994) Towards a languages policy for New Zealand education. *New Zealand Annual Review of Education* 4, 161–173.

Benton, R. (1996) Language policy in New Zealand: Defining the ineffable. In M. Herriman and B. Burnaby (eds) *Language Policies in English-Dominant Countries* (pp. 62–98). Clevedon: Multilingual Matters.

Chamot, A.U. (2001) The role of learner strategies in second language acquisition. In M.P. Breen (ed.) *Learner Contributions to Language Learning* (pp. 25–43). Harlow: Longman.

Cooper, R.L. (1989) *Language Planning and Social Change*. Cambridge: Cambridge University Press.

Cotterall, S. (1999) Key variables in language learning: What do learners believe about them? *System* 27, 493–513.

Corson, D. (1999) *Language Policy in Schools: A Resource for Teachers and Administrators*. Mahwah, NJ: Lawrence Erlbaum.

Eastman, C. (1990) What is the role of language planning in post-apartheid South Africa? *TESOL Quarterly* 24, 9–21.

Eckert, P. (1997) Age as a sociolinguistic variable. In F. Coulmas (ed.) *Handbook of Sociolinguistics* (pp. 151–167). Blackwell: Oxford.

Gardner, R.C. and MacIntyre, P.D. (1993) A student's contributions to second-language learning. Part II: Affective variables. *Language Teaching* 26, 1–11.

Giles, H., Rosenthal, D. and Young, L. (1985) Perceived ethnolinguistic vitality: The Anglo- and Greek-Australian setting. *Journal of Multilingual and Multicultural Development* 6, 253–269.

Holmes, J. and 'Aipolo, 'A. (1991) The Tongan language in Wellington: Proficiency, use and attitudes. In J. Holmes and R. Harlow (eds) *Threads in the New Zealand Tapestry of Language* (pp. 7–30). Auckland: Linguistic Society of New Zealand.

Kaplan, R.B. (1994) Language policy and planning in New Zealand. *Annual Review of Applied Linguistics* 14, 156–176.

Kaplan, R.A. and Baldauf, R. (1997) *Language Planning: From Practice to Theory*. Clevedon: Multilingual Matters.

Kennedy, C. (ed.) (1989) *Language Planning and English Language Teaching*. New York: Prentice Hall.

Kuiper, K. (forthcoming) Invisible immigrants, inaudible language: Nederlands en Nederlanders in Nieuw Zeeland. In A. Bell, R. Harlow and D. Starks (eds) *Languages of New Zealand*. Wellington: Victoria University Press.

Kumaravadivelu, B. (1991) Language-learning tasks: Teacher intention and learner interpretation. *ELT Journal* 45, 98–107.

Lo Bianco, J. (1997) English and pluralistic policies: The case of Australia. In W. Eggington and H. Wren (eds) *Language Policy: Dominant English, Pluralistic Challenges* (pp. 107–119). Amsterdam: John Benjamins.
Māori Language Commission (1994) *Blueprint for a Languages Policy: New Zealand Public Service*. Wellington: Māori Language Commission.
McCaffery, J. and Tuafuti, P. (1998) The development of Pacific Islands bilingual education in Aotearoa/New Zealand. *Many Voices* 13, 11–16.
Ministry of Education (1993) *The New Zealand Curriculum Framework*. Wellington: Ministry of Education.
Ministry of Education (2001) ERO reports. On WWW at http://www.ero.govt.nz.
Ministry of Education (2002) *Multicultural Schools in New Zealand*. No. 5. Wellington: Educational Review Office. On WWW at http://www.ero.govt.nz.
Ministry of Education (2003) Ministry of Education research. On WWW at http://www.minedu.govt.nz/index
Nakanishi, N. (2000) Language maintenance and shift in the Japanese community of Auckland. A study of the interaction between the sojourners and the immigrants. MA thesis, University of Auckland.
Paulston, C. and McLaughlin, S. (1994) Language-in-education policy and planning. *Annual Review of Applied Linguistics* 14, 53–81.
Peddie, R. (1997) Why are we waiting? Language policy development in New Zealand. In W. Eggington and H. Wren (eds) *Language Policy: Dominant English, Pluralistic Challenges* (pp. 121–146). Amsterdam: John Benjamins.
Republic of South Africa (1996) *Constitution of the Republic of South Africa*. Government Printer: Pretoria.
Roberts, M. (1999) Immigrant language maintenance and shift in the Gujerati, Dutch and Samoan communities of Wellington. PhD thesis, Victoria University of Wellington.
Statistics New Zealand (2002) *2001 NZ Census of Population and Dwellings: National Summary*. Available online at: http://www.census.govt.nz.
Stubbe, M. and Holmes, J. (2000) Talking Māori or Pakeha in English: Signalling identity in discourse. In A. Bell and K. Kuiper (eds) *New Zealand English* (pp. 249–278). Amsterdam: Benjamins.
Takala, S. and Sajavaara, K. (2000) Language policy and planning. *Annual Review of Applied Linguistics* 20, 129–146.
Taumoefolau, M., Starks D., Davis, K. and Bell, A. (2002) Linguists and language maintenance: Pasifika languages in Manukau, New Zealand. *Oceanic Linguistics* 41 (1), 1–3.
Te Puni Kokiri (1998) *The National Māori Language Survey*. Wellington: Te Puni Kokiri.
Te Puni Kokiri (2001) Survey of attitudes towards, and belief and values about the Māori language: Final summary report. Wellington: Te Puni Kokiri.
Verivaki, M. (1991) Greek language maintenance and shift in the Greek community of Wellington. In J. Holmes and R. Harlow (eds) *Threads in the Tapestry of Language* (pp. 71–116). Auckland: Linguistics Society of New Zealand.
Waite, J. (1992) *Aoteareo: Speaking for Ourselves*. Parts 1 and 2. Wellington: Ministry of Education.
Wiley, T. (1996) Language planning and policy. In S. McKay and N. Hornberger (eds) *Sociolinguistics and Language Teaching* (pp. 103–147). Cambridge: Cambridge University Press.

Chapter 11

Responding to Language Diversity: A Way Forward for New Zealand Education

TED GLYNN

The ten chapters in this book present a variety of cultural perspectives, data and commentary on the status of policy and practice for bilingual learners in New Zealand. They include an analysis of the rapidly changing ethnic composition of the country's population, case studies providing intensive observation of the experiences of bilingual students in culturally different educational contexts, and research studies that demonstrate the strength of both Māori and migrant communities to collaborate in researching their own language-learning needs and contribute to effective solutions. Each chapter tells its own distinctive story, from its own unique position within contemporary New Zealand education. However the stories intersect and interweave in ways that provide a *whariki* (mat) in which three important and repeating patterns emerge. These patterns reflect the need to develop more effective school and community partnerships, more responsive and inclusive learning and teaching strategies in mainstream schools, and more focused and integrated policy development, particularly with respect to national language priorities, teacher education and research.

The Need for More Effective School and Community Partnerships

Without doubt, as Peddie demonstrates in Chapter 1, the ethnic composition of New Zealand has been undergoing a process of rapid diversification. In the 1970s there was a major increase in migrants from Pacific Island nations, and from the 1980s to the present there has been a continuing increase in migrants from Asian countries. From the 1970s onwards there has also been vigorous and sustained effort by Māori to demand the revitalisation of their language and culture. This has been addressed through the development of *kohanga reo* (pre-school language nests), and *kura kaupapa Māori* (schools that teach the national curriculum through the medium of Māori language, and in accord with a Māori world view). More recently it is being addressed through attempts to introduce more culturally inclusive teaching strategies in mainstream schooling (Glynn *et al.*, 2001).

However, educational policy makers, providers of pre-service teacher education, and providers of continuing professional development of teachers do not appear to have caught up fully with the implications of this diversification. There is widespread concern about the long-standing underachievement in mainstream schools of students from ethnic communities, such as Māori and some Pacific Island communities. This has often been paralleled by widespread deficit theorising – attributing this underachievement to deficiencies within the students themselves or in their languages and cultures. There is also widespread concern at the paucity of trained and trainee teachers from Māori and from migrant ethnic communities. Yet little effort seems to have been made to draw on the depth of language and cultural expertise that resides within these communities, and to learn how to work in partnership with them to address the problems their children face (McNaughton & Glynn, 1998).

Chapter 2 (Glynn and Berryman), Chapter 3 (Berryman and Glynn) and Chapter 4 (McCaffery and Tuafuti) all demonstrate the power of working partnerships between schools and their ethnic communities for improving literacy outcomes for their students.

The mainstream school reported on in Chapters 2 and 3, Rotorua Primary School, was able to represent and affirm the language and cultural identity of its Māori students through its teaching practices, as well as through its intensive consultation and collaboration with its Māori community. The school's principal and many staff shared common tribal descent with most of the parents in the school community, and so the interconnectedness with and commitment to the school's children and their *whānau* (extended families) was especially strong. This was heightened further by the expertise and standing within the community of the home-and-school liaison teacher, who shared responsibility with the researchers for implementing the home-and-school reading and writing programmes. Through the mediation of this liaison teacher, Māori parents and community were able to participate both in defining the nature of the problem and in negotiating solutions that required changes on the part of the school and its teachers. These parents and whānau were not merely on the receiving end of school-devised plans to improve students' literacy through requiring parents to implement additional activities at home. Not only were the reading and writing programmes particularly successful in improving students' reading and writing in English and Māori at school, they also improved the Māori language use of two parents who participated on the basis of very limited oral Māori. A critical element of success of both Māori and English reading and writing in this school was explaining and understanding the implementation and outcomes of the programme using metaphors and concepts that made sense within a Māori cultural world view. Success was also reflected through the parents and whānau assuming a far greater degree of collective responsibility for programme implementation than seen in other schools in the project.

In Chapter 4, McCaffery and Tuafuti draw on three different studies to monitor the English reading outcomes for Samoan students at one mainstream primary school, Finlayson Park. They compared data from Samoan students attending the school's bilingual unit (*O le Taiala*) with data from similar Samoan students attending mainstream English medium classes at Finlayson Park and at a primary school elsewhere. Data presented in this chapter demonstrate a clear advantage for students in the bilingual unit in terms of English reading achievement. Almost all the students in both settings began schooling with English reading levels well below chronological age, but by Year 6, 71% of O le Taiala bilingual students were reading above their chronological age, compared with 27 % of students in mainstream English-medium classes. McCaffery and Tuafuti (like Berryman and Glynn with respect to Māori) attribute much of this success to the fact that the school and the unit affirm and validate the Samoan language and culture through their curriculum and teaching practices, represented through the employment of Samoan teachers and professional support personnel. Both the school and the bilingual unit receive strong support and guidance from parents and other members of the Samoan community. This enables Samoan students to maintain their standing and full participation in the cultural activities of the Samoan community outside the school, while at the same time making effective progress in reading and writing in English. Samoan parents are able to discuss and observe the O le Taiala bilingual programme option, and most are choosing to enrol their children in it.

Both the schools reported on in Chapters 2, 3 and 4 valued the languages and cultural practices of their student communities, and regarded them as central to their students' progress in English literacy, as well as to the students' well-being and cultural identity. The schools were embedded in their local communities and regarded their language and cultural differences as assets rather than as liabilities. The school and community partnerships were successful because the school acknowledged and activated the language and cultural resources located within their communities, allowing themselves to be advised and guided by these communities. Success at school for these Māori and Samoan students did not come at the cost of leaving their language and culture at home.

The Need for More Inclusive Pedagogies and Bilingual Competence in Mainstream Schools

Elsewhere in this book, Vine (Chapter 5), Haworth (Chapter 6), Barnard (Chapter 7) and McKee and Biederman (Chapter 8) all address the central importance of the day-to-day classroom interaction experienced by individual bilingual students in determining the amount and quality of their learning. These chapters present detailed and intensive data that focus on both the cognitive and the social (interpersonal) elements of teaching and learning interactions, exchanges or conversations in different classroom contexts. These interactions occur between bilingual students and their teachers, their classmates, teacher aides and other classroom support personnel. Considered together, these four chapters sharply illuminate the difficulties that can arise when classroom teachers have insufficient bilingual competence to connect with the bilingual student, both at an interpersonal level and at the level of shared experiences within a shared world view of a particular language and culture.

These chapters also challenge our understanding of what it means to have an 'inclusive' classroom, and challenge us to develop pedagogies that include students whose language and culture differs from that of their mainstream teachers and classmates.

In Chapter 7, Barnard presents data that shock us with the painful and alienating experiences of an eleven-year-old Korean boy placed in a regular mainstream urban classroom. Although provided with four hours per week of ESOL tuition in a withdrawal setting, this boy spent the remaining 30 hours per week in 'a context of largely incomprehensible input'. With the aid of a lapel microphone and a Korean translator, we are privileged to hear the private speech of this boy, sampled over an eight-month period. Samples from transcripts of his largely self-directed speech allow us to experience for ourselves the depths of confusion, anxiety, alienation and fear generated for him in this classroom context, as expressed through his first language. The messages in these transcripts provide compelling evidence of the need for more in-school support for students whose first language is not English. They also underscore the urgent need for more competent home-and-school collaboration and for better pre-service preparation and ongoing professional support for mainstream teachers in working with students whose first language is not English.

In Chapter 5, Vine describes the extraordinary length that one Māori teacher went to in order to connect herself with a five-year-old Samoan new arrival who was not a speaker of English. The teacher was not a speaker of Samoan, but was able to modify particular curriculum tasks so that she and the student were able to create space and construct opportunities for him to engage with the curriculum topic on the basis of his own first language. This facilitated his learning of English. She was able to do this on the basis of her considerable teaching expertise and experience, and her appreciation of the student's position as a competent speaker of his first language. However, even this supportive classroom context seems likely to promote his learning of English at the expense of his first language.

This issue is developed further by Haworth in Chapter 6. Her study includes interviews with two ESOL support teachers, and with two classroom teachers of NESB (non-English speaking background) students, as well as direct observation of NESB students in their classroom contexts. Haworth observed a number of effective strategies used by the two teachers, including modifying curriculum tasks by selecting classroom themes that call on students' home cultures (allowing NESB students to engage on the basis of their expertise and experience). Other strategies included providing key vocabulary items and writing outlines. These strategies were preferred because they could be implemented with a whole class, and were likely to benefit all students. However, while these strategies were likely to succeed in engaging NESB students more effectively in classroom lessons, they may result in the specific language and cultural needs of individual students being overlooked. Haworth's classroom teachers were well aware of this danger.

There is a parallel dilemma facing special educators (Moore *et al.*, 1999). Powerful 'inclusive' teaching strategies that maximise the engagement of students with special needs in regular classroom lessons are readily adopted by mainstream teachers because they clearly benefit all students, and can be applied class-wide. However, for students whose special needs arise from their language and cultural differences, such inclusive teaching may submerse or marginalise first language and cultural practices. Such strategies may promote second language learning at the expense of maintaining students' first language and culture.

McKee and Biederman address this issue in Chapter 8, in their comparison of two different educational contexts provided for two deaf children whose first language is NZSL (New Zealand Sign Language). One student attended a bilingual (NZSL and English) class at a deaf education centre, and the other attended a regular class in a mainstream school. The authors asked two questions of each learning context:

(1) How well does this context support the student's development of the first language (NZSL), and how well does the context connect NZSL with written English, so as to improve the student's writing?
(2) How well does this context enable the deaf student to participate in a community of learners and establish their identify as bilingual learners?

To answer each of these questions, the authors carried out a careful examination of cognitive as well as interpersonal aspects of student–teacher and student–student narratives in each context. The results reported in this chapter help us to appreciate the importance of both shared first language knowledge and shared life experiences for the full inclusion of deaf learners in classroom learning contexts, and for learners' continued cognitive development. This study also points up some real dangers in enlisting third parties, such as teacher aides, to mediate the cognitive and social interaction between teacher and student, even when they are competent in the bilingual student's first language. Without appropriate pedagogical knowledge and expertise, third parties may minimise, or even trivialise, the learning task though providing the learner with inappropriately simplified translations.

Finally, these chapters suggest a range of examples of culturally inclusive pedagogies that support the inclusion of students from different language and cultural backgrounds from their mainstream teachers and classmates. Briefly, these pedagogies are those that successfully address the balance of power within learning interactions (Bishop & Glynn, 1999). They involve generating tasks that the bilingual learner can engage in on the basis of cultural familiarity and first-language strengths. They include generating tasks that call for integration across separate curriculum areas. They involve teaching and learning processes that promote reciprocity and shared control between teacher and learner, such as peer tutoring, cooperative learning, and narrative approaches to problem solving.

The Need for More Focused and Integrated Policy Development

The most pervasive theme emerging across all chapters is the call for a New Zealand languages policy. As Peddie notes in Chapter 1, New Zealand does not have, nor has it ever had, a national policy on languages, despite concerted attempts to develop such a policy in the late 1980s and early 1990s, and despite the passing of the Māori Language Act, 1987. Policies of successive governments in the 1990s devolved governance and management powers to individual schools and their communities, leaving schools to makes decisions on which languages they would offer their students, and leaving ethnic communities to make decisions on whether and how they would strive to maintain their heritage languages.

During this period there was steady growth in the number of Māori-medium education initiatives, from pre-school to tertiary level, as well as rapidly increasing language diversity among the student populations in New Zealand schools and communities. However, during this period there has been surprisingly little comprehensive policy development from the Ministry of Education on languages and language use in New Zealand. There has been a commitment to continue to support the development of Māori-medium education through Māori-medium teacher education and continuing development of assessment and teaching resources. This commitment is a response to Māori insistence that the Crown should honour the principles of the 1840 Treaty of Waitangi . In terms of the Treaty, Māori have long claimed their rights to define and protect all their language and cultural resources, and to have their language and culture restored and equitably represented and affirmed within New Zealand state education (Glynn, 1998).

However, while Māori-medium pre-schools and schools have been regarded as critical sites for Māori language revitalisation and maintenance, there has been a lack of clear policy direction and goal setting for NESB students and students learning Māori as a second language in mainstream schools. It appears that most second-language support and provision within schools has generally amounted to first-language submersion, or subtractive bilingualism. Such initiatives have the general aim of promoting student acquisition of English as soon as possible, at the expense of maintaining first-language competence. Examples of second-language learning initiatives that aim to develop students who are competent bilinguals and who are literate in two languages are rare in New Zealand, outside of *kohanga reo* and *kura kaupapa Māori* (McCaffery and Tuafuti provide one such example in Chapter 4).

Both Shameem (Chapter 9) and Starks and Barkhuizen (Chapter 10) offer a way forward, or a way out of this policy vacuum. Shameem laments the lack of a comprehensive teacher education policy for recruiting and training bilingual teachers who are fluent speakers of English and fluent speakers of their community language. Shameem sees these teachers as establishing and staffing community language classes taught either in schools located in community sites or in mainstream schools out of official school time. Perhaps these are also the kind of professionals who are also needed *within* schools to work alongside largely monolingual support teachers, to promote the achievement of bilingual and biliteracy educational goals? Shameem carried out a survey of a sample of 95 community leaders, language teachers, parents and students from a wide range of ethnic communities. She found strong support for the recruitment and training of community members as bilingual teachers to work to strengthen the heritage language within each community. Survey respondents were able to identify specific components that such a teacher education programme should include.

The chapters by Shameem and Starks and Barkhuizen both argue the importance of the resources of experience and expertise that exist within each migrant community. However, Starks and Barkhuizen point to the existence of another extremely important and untapped resource – the day-to-day experiences of all the students in our large multicultural secondary schools. These schools are authentic sites where different languages and cultures converge. Data in this chapter from 939 students from 13 schools show that schools are indeed multicultural and multilingual sites. Students reported hearing many languages spoken at school, and interacting with others from wide ranging language and cultural groups, even more than they do outside school. It is therefore these students themselves who have much to contribute to the development of a languages policy. Starks and Barkhuizen argue that secondary students are well able to examine and discuss issues of language use, language maintenance and language learning. They are well able to collaborate with researchers in designing and carrying out research on these topics. Their in-school experiences qualify them as data gatherers with a clear role in policy development.

The lack of a comprehensive and coherent languages policy in New Zealand poses major challenges for teacher education. The proportion of students in our schools whose first language is not English is growing steadily. The nation needs to recruit into teacher education people who are bilingual in English and in their community language. Teacher education programmes need to better inform their student teachers about models of effective bilingual education, and provide them with up-to-date research information on additive, rather than subtractive, bilingualism. Teacher education programmes should prepare their trainee teachers to work in schools where they will find increasing numbers of bilingual units and classes, and where English as a second language may not be fully introduced until after six or seven years of learning through the medium of the students' first language. It will become more and more crucial for trainee teachers to be bilingually competent and biculturally aware. Teacher education in New Zealand has a long way to go indeed, if it is to meet these challenges. The data and the stories presented in each of the chapters in this book provide valuable information as to how to respond to these challenges.

References

Bishop, R. and Glynn, T. (1999) *Culture Counts: Changing Power Relations in Education*. Palmerston North: Dunmore Press.

Glynn, T. (1998) Bicultural challenges for educational professionals in Aotearoa: Inaugural lecture, University of Waikato. *Waikato Journal of Education* 4, 3-16.

Glynn, T., Berryman, M., Walker, R., Reweti, M. and O'Brien, K. (2001) Partnerships with indigenous people: Modifying the cultural mainstream. Keynote address. Paper presented at the Partnerships in Educational Psychology Conference, Bardon Conference Centre, Brisbane, 20 July

McNaughton, S. and Glynn, T. (1998) Effective collaboration: What teachers need to know about communities. Paper presented at the Annual conference of the New Zealand Council for Teacher Education, University of Waikato, Hamilton, October.

Moore, D., Anderson, A., Timperley, H., Macfarlane, A., Brown, D., Thomson, C. and Glynn, T. (1999) *Caught Between Stories: Special Education in New Zealand*. New Zealand Council for Educational Research.

Glossary of Terms Used in This Book

ako	(Māori) teaching and learning as a unified whole
awhi	(Māori) support
BICS	Basic Interpersonal Communication Skills
CALP	Communicative Academic Language Proficiency
ERUDITE	Educational Research Underpinning Development in Teacher Education
ESL	English as a second language
ESOL	(teaching) English to speakers of other languages
faasamoa	traditional Samoan knowledge
hapu	Māori sub-tribe
hui	meetings held by Māori following Māori protocol
intermediate school	an upper primary school in New Zealand catering for grades 7 and 8
iwi	Māori tribes
karakia	prayer said before and after Māori meetings
kaumatua	Māori tribal elders
kaupapa	Māori world view representing Māori cultural values and practices
Kohanga Reo	Māori 'language nests' for pre-sechool children
kōrero	(Māori) conversation or speech
Kura Kaupapa Māori	Māori-immersion primary schools
mana	acknowledged authority and standing of a Māori person
manaakitanga	the duty of care that Māori demonstrate towards each other
manuhiri	visitors to a Māori home or marae
marae	traditional land incorporating a Māori meeting house
NESB	student learners from Non English-Speaking Backgrounds
Ngā Kete Kōrero	the assessment framework for Māori language reading texts
NZSL	New Zealand Sign Language

O le Taiala	the name of the Samoan Bilingual unit at Finlayson Park School
Pakeha	(Māori) a term for New Zealanders of European descent
palangi	(Samoan) a term for New Zealanders of European descent
Pasefika	(Samoan) New Zealanders of Pacific Island descent
Pasifika	The Ministry of Education's term for Pacific Island students
patipati	(Māori) encouragement
Poutama Pounamu	figurative name for one of the Māori Education Research Centres
primary school	most New Zealand primary schools take children from their fifth birthday for six years of schooling (*see* **intermediate school**)
rangatiratanga	the way in which Māori are guided by thir own elders
rumaki	total Māori immersion classes
Tatari Tautoko Tauawhi	a Māori tutoring programme for older remedial readers
te reo Māori	the Māori language
te Puni Kokiri	the Ministry of Māori Development
te Tiriti o Waitangi	the Treaty of Waitangi (1840) between the Crown and Māori
teina	(Māori) a younger and less exper ienced relative
tikanga	preferred customary practices of Māoris
tuakana	(Māori) and older; more knowledgeable relative
Ulimasao	the Samoan Bilingual Education Association
vaa	(Samoan) a canoe
waka	(Māori) a canoe
wairua	(Māori) spiritual well being and self-esteem
wānanga	Māori tertiary institutions
whānau	immediate or extended Māori family
whanaungatanga	(Māori) interconnectedness through relationships
whakatau	a form of Māori welcome
whakama	(Māori) self-consciousness
Whare Kura	Māori immersion secondary schools
whaea	(Māori) mother, or respected older woman

Index

Items in *italics* are defined in the Glossary.